WHILE EUROPE SLEPT

ALSO BY BRUCE BAWER

Stealing Jesus:
How Fundamentalism Betrays Christianity

Beyond Queer:
Challenging Gay Left Orthodoxy (editor)

House and Home (with Steve Gunderson and Rob Morris)

Prophets and Professors:
The Lives and Works of Modern Poets

A Place at the Table:
The Gay Individual in American Society

The Aspect of Eternity

Coast to Coast

The Screenplay's the Thing:
Movie Criticism 1986–1990

Diminishing Fictions:
Essays on the Modern American Novel and Its Critics

The Middle Generation

WHILE
EUROPE
SLEPT

HOW RADICAL ISLAM

IS DESTROYING THE WEST

FROM WITHIN

BRUCE BAWER

BROADWAY BOOKS
New York

FOR TOR ANDRÉ

PUBLISHED BY BROADWAY BOOKS

A hardcover edition of this book was originally published in 2006 by Doubleday.
It is here reprinted by arrangement with Doubleday.

Published in the United States by Broadway Books, an imprint of
The Doubleday Broadway Publishing Group,
a division of Random House, Inc., New York.
www.broadwaybooks.com

BROADWAY BOOKS and its logo, a letter B bisected on the diagonal,
are trademarks of Random House, Inc.

The author has received support from the Norwegian Nonfiction Literature Fund.

Book design by Patrice Sheridan

The Library of Congress catalogued the hardcover edition as follows:
Bawer, Bruce, 1956–
While Europe slept : how radical Islam is destroying the West
from within / by Bruce Bawer.—1st ed.
p.   cm.
Includes index.
1. Muslims—Europe. 2. Islamic fundamentalism—Europe. 3. Europe—Emigration
and immigration. 4. Muslims—Public opinion. 5. Public opinion—Europe.
6. United States—Foreign public opinion, European. I. Title.
D1056.2.M87B39 2006
305.6'97'094—dc22
2005051904

ISBN 978-0-7679-2005-6

PRINTED IN THE UNITED STATES OF AMERICA

3   5   7   9   10   8   6   4   2

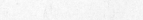

Contents

Acknowledgments

I'M DEEPLY GRATEFUL to my agent, John Talbot, and my editor, Adam Bellow, for their extraordinary commitment to this project and their diligent work on its behalf. Copious thanks to Daniel Feder at Doubleday for his skillful contributions and many kindnesses; to Lars Hedegaard and Helle Merete Brix for sharing their time and thoughts; to the Norwegian Nonfiction Writers and Translators Association for its generous support; to Paula Deitz and the late Frederick Morgan for their steadfast loyalty and encouragement; and to Harry T. Cleven, Hege Storhaug, Rita Karlsen, Janniche Brustad, and Suman Lahiry for helping in various ways. Weblogs by Leif Knutsen, Marten Barck, Gunnar Nyquist and Hans Rustad, Jan Haugland, Michael Moynihan and Billy McCormac, Mikkel Andersson, Lars Hvidberg, Kim Møller, Arjan Dasselaar, Pieter Dorsman, David Kaspar, and Marten Schenk pointed me to materials I might otherwise have missed. Thanks also to my aunt, Ruth Thomas Cook, who not only provided moral support but even came up with the title. My greatest debt is reflected in the dedication.

None of the above persons, needless to say, is responsible for my opinions or errors.

I

◆

Before 9/11: Europe in Denial

ON THE MORNING OF November 2, 2004, I sat at my mother's kitchen table in Queens, New York, drinking instant coffee and thinking about George W. Bush and John Kerry. It was Election Day, and I was irked that since I was flying back home to Oslo that evening, I'd miss the vote count on TV.

The phone rang. "Hello? Oh, yes. Just a moment." My mother held out the phone. "It's Mark." I took it.

"Mark?"

"Hi, Bruce. Have you heard about Theo van Gogh?"

"No, what?"

"He was murdered this morning."

"You're kidding."

Mark, like me, is an American with a Norwegian partner. But though he moved back to New York years ago, he still starts the day by checking the news at the Web site of NRK, Norway's national radio and TV network. Switching into Norwegian, he read me the story. Van Gogh, the Dutch filmmaker and newspaper columnist, had been shot and killed in Amsterdam. Shortly afterward, police had arrested a twenty-six-year-old Dutch-Moroccan man.

Later, I'd learn more. Van Gogh had been bicycling to work along a street called Linnaeusstraat when Mohammed Bouyeri, the Dutch-born son of Moroccan parents and a member of a radical Muslim network, had shot him, knocking him off his bicycle. Bouyeri, wearing a long *jellaba*, pumped up to twenty additional bullets into van Gogh's body, stabbed him several times, and slit his throat. He then pinned to van Gogh's chest with a knife a five-page letter addressed to the filmmaker's collaborator, Parliament member Ayaan Hirsi Ali, quoting the Koran and promising her and several other Dutch leaders (whom he named) a similar end:

> I know definitely that you, O America, will go down. I know defi-
> nitely that you, O Europe, will go down. I know definitely that you,
> O Netherlands, will go down. I know definitely that you, O Hirsi Ali,
> will go down.

According to witnesses, van Gogh had said to his murderer (who at the time was living on welfare payments from the Dutch government): "Don't do it! Don't do it! Mercy! Mercy!" And: "Surely we can talk about this." The blunt, outspoken van Gogh had been an unsparing critic of European passivity in the face of fundamentalist Islam; unlike most Europeans, he'd understood the connection between the war on terror and the European integration crisis, and had called America "the last beacon of hope in a steadily darkening world." Together he and Hirsi Ali had made a short film, *Submission*—he'd directed, she'd written the script— about the mistreatment of women in Islamic cultures. Yet at the end, it seemed, even he had grasped at the Western European elite's most unshakable article of faith—the belief in peace and reconciliation through dialogue.

At first glance, Hirsi Ali might have seemed an unlikely ally for van Gogh: a vivacious Somali-born beauty who'd forsworn her native Islam, she was devoted to the preservation of Dutch democracy and the rescue of her country's Muslims—especially women—from the tyranny of their subculture. I'd read a good deal about her in the Dutch press and hoped to write about her myself; in fact, a friend of mine who worked for an Oslo think tank had arranged to meet her in The Hague the following Monday and had invited me to go along. I'd already booked the flight.

Van Gogh's murder came as a shock, even though I'd seen something like it coming for years. In 1998, I'd lived in a largely Muslim neighborhood of Amsterdam, only a block away from the radical mosque attended by Bouyeri. There I'd seen firsthand the division between the native Dutch and their country's rapidly growing Muslim minority. That division was stark: the Dutch had the world's most tolerant, open-minded society, with full sexual equality, same-sex marriage, and libertarian policies on soft drugs and prostitution. Yet many Dutch Muslims kept that society at arm's length, despising its freedoms and clinging to a range of undemocratic traditions and prejudices.

Did Dutch officials address this problem? No. Like their politically correct counterparts across Western Europe, they responded to it mostly by churning out empty rhetoric about multicultural diversity and mutual respect—and then changing the subject. I knew that by tolerating intolerance in this way, the country was setting itself on a path to cataclysmic social confrontation; yet whenever I tried—delicately—to broach the topic, Dutch acquaintances made clear that it was off limits. They seemed not to grasp that their society, and Western Europe generally, was a house divided against itself, and that eventually things would reach the breaking point.

Then came 9/11. Most Americans were quick to understand that they were at war and recognized the need for a firm response (though there was, and continues to be, much disagreement as to whether the response decided upon was the right one). Yet while most Western European countries participated in the invasion of Afghanistan and several helped topple Saddam, America's forceful approach alienated opinion makers across the continent and opened up a philosophical gulf that sometimes seemed as wide as the Atlantic itself.

Why was there such a striking difference in perspectives between the two halves of the democratic West? One reason was that the Western European establishment—the political, media, and academic elite that articulates what we think of as "European opinion"—tended to regard all international disputes as susceptible to peaceful resolution. It was therefore ill equipped to respond usefully to sustained violence by a fierce, uncompromising adversary. Another reason was Western Europe's large immigrant communities, many of them led by fundamentalist Muslims who looked forward to the establishment in Europe of a caliphate governed according to sharia law—the law of the Koran—and who viewed Islamist terrorists as allies in a global jihad, or holy war, dedicated to that goal. A fear of inflaming minorities who took their lead from such extremists was one more reason to tread gently. Few European politicians had challenged this passivity. The Dutchman Pim Fortuyn had done so, and been murdered for it. Not even the March 2004 bombings in Madrid—"Europe's 9/11"—had fully awakened Europe's sleeping elite.

True, not all European Muslims shared the terrorists' goals and loyalties. Many, one gathered, were grateful to be living in democracies. Yet even they seemed hamstrung by the belief that loyalty to the *umma* (the worldwide Islamic community) overrode any civic obligations to their *kaffir* (infidel) neighbors. Hence most European Muslims responded passively to van Gogh's murder. Few spoke up against the extremists in their midst. The pressure—from without *and* within—to stick by their own was, it appeared, simply too overwhelming. And the potential price for betrayal was an end not unlike that dealt out to Theo van Gogh.

That evening I flew back to Oslo. At one point, over the Atlantic, the pilot got on the loudspeaker with an update on the U.S. presidential race, telling us how many electoral votes each candidate had secured so far. Bush was ahead. But not until I was standing at the baggage carousel in Oslo—barely awake after a sleepless night over the Atlantic—did I learn how the vote had turned out. On an electronic news crawl above the carousel I read the words BUSH GJENVALGT—Bush reelected.

I had mixed feelings about the victory: while the president seemed to have a far greater understanding than his opponent of what we were fighting *against* in the war on terror, some of his domestic actions made me wonder which of the candidates had a stronger sense of what we were fighting *for*. But in New York City and the Western European capitals, I knew, there was little ambiguity. Bush's win was bad news—period.

Two days later I was in Amsterdam, where van Gogh's murder was being called the Netherlands' 9/11. Understandably, Hirsi Ali had canceled all appointments; but since I'd already booked a flight and a hotel room—and was curious to see people's reactions firsthand—I went anyway.

It was easy to be lulled by the illusion that things were as they always had been. At the Amstel Taveerne, one of Amsterdam's trademark "brown cafés," there was tub-thumping music, easy laughter, even a rousing chorus of "*Lang zal je leven*" ("Long may you live") to mark a patron's birthday—in short, that feeling of communal coziness and camaraderie, known as *gezelligheid*, that the Dutch treasure above all. Yet this impression was misleading. The Netherlands, I knew, was undergoing a sea change. By the time I'd arrived in Amsterdam, there'd been several arrests; legislators had been placed under round-the-clock protection; government buildings in The Hague looked like an armed camp. Vice Premier Gerrit Zalm, who'd called Fortuyn dangerous because of his blunt rhetoric about Islam, now declared war on radical Islamism. Politically correct attitudes about immigration and integration, until a week earlier ubiquitous in the Dutch media, were hardly to be found. "Jihad has reached the Netherlands," one commentator wrote. Another asked: "Has the Netherlands become a country in which you can no longer say what you want, or does the taboo apply only to [comments about] Islam?" (This was a nation, after all, to which philosophers and poets from all corners of Europe had fled centuries ago to be able to speak and write freely.)

I found my way to the scene of the crime. I foolishly assumed I'd have trouble locating the exact spot. In fact, an area of about seventy-five by ten feet along one side of Linnaeusstraat had been cordoned off. It was piled high with floral tributes, and about fifty people crowded around it, most of them deep in thought. I circled the site slowly, reading notes that had been left there. "This far and no further," read one. Another read: "Long live the Netherlands; long live freedom of speech!"

From there I took a long tram ride to the Muslim neighborhood called the Oud West, where a policewoman told me flat-out not to venture into such areas. "The mood in all of the Netherlands is very tense right now," she explained in a slow, deliberate, distinctively Dutch way. Earlier that day, a journalist's car had been smashed. Later, I learned that Rotterdam police had destroyed a street mural—featuring the words "Thou shalt not kill," a picture of an angel, and the date of van Gogh's murder—because the head of a nearby mosque had called it racist. Wim Nottroth, a cameraman who tried to protect the mural, had been arrested, and a camerawoman who filmed its destruction had been forced to erase part of her videotape.

I left the Oud West in a cab. Talking with the driver, I mentioned Theo van Gogh. Like many Dutchmen, he seemed reluctant to speak about such things to a foreigner. But then he said simply, "I am leaving the country. And I am not alone."

That Wednesday, police officers and marines carried out a daylong siege on an apartment in an immigrant quarter of The Hague. During the week, there were attacks on mosques and Muslim schools. I'd long been concerned that if liberals didn't address the problem of fundamentalist Muslim intolerance responsibly, it would be answered with the intolerance of the far right. In the 1930s, Europeans had faced a struggle—and, many thought, a need to choose—between two competing totalitarianisms. Was this the Continent's future as well? Was this another Weimar moment?

A great deal of water had flowed over the dike since I'd lived in Amsterdam. There'd been 9/11, then Fortuyn's murder, then Madrid. After each atrocity, I'd expected Western Europe—part of it, anyway—to wake up and smell the coffee. In the Netherlands, to be sure, 9/11 had opened some people's eyes to the truth of Fortuyn's arguments about fundamentalism, and his murder had ushered in a frank public debate about immigration and integration. But in elite circles—in the press clubs, faculty lounges, and offices of government bureaucracies—denial and appeasement had continued to reign supreme, leading to few, if any, meaningful reforms.

That night, walking along the familiar old canals of Amsterdam and watching the warm yellow light from house windows twinkling on the surface of the water, I wondered: would the anger blow over again? Or would the Dutch, this time, act decisively to protect their democracy? Might this, in turn, initiate a wave of reform across Western Europe?

It was impossible to know. For the time being, however, most Dutchmen appeared to agree strongly with Paul Scheffer, who wrote: "We cannot hand over our country. . . . Words such as diversity, respect and dialogue fade against the dark context of this ritual assassination." Diversity, respect, dialogue: this, of course, was the mantra of political correctness, a habit of thought that in America is an annoyance but in Europe is a veritable religion—its tenets instilled by teachers and professors, preached by politicians and journalists, and put into practice by armies of government paper-pushers. It was political correctness that had gotten Europe into its current mess, and only by repudiating political correctness did Europe stand a chance of averting what seemed, increasingly, to be its fate.

I thought back to my first visit to Amsterdam. It seemed a lifetime ago—but it was only 1997.

I'D BEEN A lifelong New Yorker. If you'd asked me in, say, 1996, I'd doubtless have told you that I'd spend the rest of my days there. Then, suddenly, everything changed. A long-term relationship ended, and I found myself wanting to *go*.

At first I considered only American cities. The idea of living abroad didn't occur to me: I was American, through and through. I loved my country—which, then as now, I regarded as the world's greatest, not because of its wealth or power, but because of its culture and values. Americans' patriotism springs not from a common ethnicity but from a shared belief in individual liberty. The United States is not yet a perfect union (I've made a career largely out of lamenting its imperfections), but over

the generations it's gradually become better, fairer, more just—and it's
done so by constantly struggling to be truer to its founding principles.

It was precisely this love of America that made my gaze turn toward
Europe. Like many American writers, I'd lost track of the number of
times I'd made sweeping generalizations about my country. "We Americans are . . ." "Americans believe . . ." "To be an American is to be . . ."
But how do you really know what it means to be an American if you've
never lived anywhere else? Eventually you want to test your generalizations—to find out if you know what you're talking about.

There were other factors. Like every American who'd ever paid at-
tention in school, I felt a sympathetic connection to Europe. Europe was
Mozart and Beethoven, Matisse and Rembrandt, Dante and Cervantes.
Europe was the continent from which my ancestors had migrated—
Englishmen, Scotsmen, and Welshmen in search of economic opportu-
nity in the new colonies and (later) the fledgling Republic; Anglo-Irish
Quakers longing for freedom of worship; French Huguenots escaping
brutal persecution by the House of Bourbon; Polish Catholic subjects of
Austrian emperor Franz Josef fleeing the ravages of World War I.

I was also drawn to Europe's linguistic abundance. For me, trying to
get along in a tongue other than my own was a thrilling challenge. I still
had a vivid memory of my one barroom conversation in fractured German; I remembered every one of the handful of occasions on which my
seven years of Spanish had actually come in handy; and I recalled even
the most inane and trivial exchanges I'd had in my highly inadequate
French during the week I'd spent covering the Cannes Film Festival
in 1990.

So it was that now, ready for a fresh start, I found myself yearning to
pick up a new language. First I bought a Berlitz teach-yourself-Danish
tape; then, changing my mind, I snapped up a set of cassettes for learning Dutch. And in August of 1997 I visited Amsterdam—not yet intend-
ing to move there, but simply wanting to see the sights and try out my
language skills. The trip was so exhilarating that I went back in November and again in January. I felt I was making up for lost time, throwing
myself into the world after years of sitting at my desk.

Between trips, I wrote letters in Dutch to friends I'd made. On my
January visit, my friend Jordy greeted me by exclaiming over my efforts.
"That's real Dutch!" he said, astonished that I'd mastered the syntax. I
could scarcely have been more delighted if I'd won a Pulitzer.

Why did I choose—and keep returning to—Amsterdam? Culturally,
I was awed by the Netherlands: its young people came out of high school

fluent in four languages; it had gay marriage; its book-buying levels were the world's highest. The American novelist Richard Powers had lived in the Netherlands, and described it as "one of the few places on the planet where Western civilization almost works." Another writer, my friend Matthew Stadler, had taught in Groningen and exulted over his students' sophistication. He called the country "magical." It didn't take long for me to see what they meant.

Besides, I felt comfortable there. If New York could sometimes feel like a cauldron of anger and aggression, the Dutch were inherently peaceable. Back in 1990, loitering on the Croisette, Cannes' seaside promenade, I'd realized I could spot American men from afar just by their swagger: they looked ready to defend themselves at a moment's notice. Doubtless this appearance of preparedness had been useful on the frontier, but it looked ridiculous on the Riviera, where nobody carried anything deadlier than a baguette. How often had I stood in a New York subway surrounded by men, many of them far smaller than I, and been unnerved by an air of physical threat that emanated from them like the smell of sweat? Yet in Amsterdam, wedged on trams amid natives who towered over me (in the Netherlands I was, at six feet, below the average height for the first time in my life), I felt only benign energies.

Amsterdam seemed to me the leading edge of a world that had moved beyond bigotry. It was the one place I'd ever been where homophobia really seemed to have disappeared. When groups of straight teenage boys walked by the open door of a gay bar, they didn't yell "faggot"; they didn't elbow one another and point and make nervous jokes; they didn't show any discomfort or anger at all. They just walked by. It was remarkable.

European perspectives appealed to me as well. "In the United States," Simone de Beauvoir once observed, "one is always concerned to find out what an individual does, and not what he is; one takes it for granted that he is nothing but what he has done or may do; his purely inner reality is regarded with indifference, if, indeed, any note is taken of it." This is especially true in certain parts of Manhattan; it wasn't in the Netherlands. Though they were justly famous for their thrift, Dutch people's sense of identity and self-worth didn't depend on jobs or salaries. One evening a Dutchman introduced himself to me at a café. I told him my name, and then, at a loss for something else to say, I asked, "What do you do?" He shook his head and smiled. "We don't ask that so soon," he said. "Not like you Americans." My friend Jordy often mentioned his parents, to whom he was very close; but not until my fourth visit did it emerge that his father was president of one of the Netherlands' half dozen largest corporations. Jordy hadn't been hiding this fact—it just hadn't occurred to him to mention it.

Then there was *gezelligheid*, a cherished value in the Netherlands, as it is, under different names, in much of northern Europe. Ask a Dutchman what *gezellig* means and he'll tell you proudly that it's untranslatable—it describes a concept so essentially Dutch that it can't be rendered into English. The dictionary offers these equivalents: "enjoyable," "pleasant," "companionable," "social." These aren't words your typical American would use to describe a person, place, or experience that's given enjoyment. In America—where our pop culture repeatedly tells us that you're Number One or you're nothing—praise is almost invariably expressed in hyperbolic terms: we use words like "great," "terrific," or "fantastic" very loosely. The Dutch are more appreciative of and satisfied with everyday pleasures; they aren't reaching for the unattainable; nor do they feel compelled to claim more for a person or experience than it merits.

While Americans often focus on future payoffs, preferably bountiful ones—isn't that what the American dream is all about?—the Dutch, like many other Western Europeans, attend to the present moment and its small rewards. Instead of habitually inflating language, indeed, the Dutch *un*-inflate, appending the suffix "*je*," a diminutive, to almost every imaginable noun. Thus a Dutchman invites you out not for a *bier* but for a *biertje*, not for a *praat* (a talk) but for a *praatje*. If you're his friend, he might call you not *vriend* but *vriendje*. The overall effect of all these diminutives is to give you a sense of a people taking special care not to overstate or make excessive claims. American kids learn to be proud of how big, rich, and powerful America is; I was surprised how many times I heard Dutch people say, "We are a little country."

Finally, there was Dutch secularism. I'd spent most of 1996 researching and writing a book called *Stealing Jesus*. The project had obliged me to immerse myself in American fundamentalism, and I hadn't quite gotten over it—the claustrophobic narrowness of its conception of the divine, its adherents' breathtaking combination of historical ignorance and theological certitude, and its dispiriting view of religion as a means not of engaging life's mysteries but of denying and dispelling them through a ludicrously literal-minded reading of scripture. The book had come out in late 1997, and during the ensuing months—between trips to Amsterdam—I'd spent countless hours talking with, or answering letters from, people whose fundamentalist upbringings had been case studies in hypocrisy and psychological abuse.

One night I read from *Stealing Jesus* at Atlanta's gay bookstore, Outright. The reading itself took up less time than the question-and-answer session, during which audience members talked affectingly about their fundamentalist childhoods. Many still couldn't let go of the religion that had scarred them, in most cases quite severely. A powerfully built middle-aged man said quietly, and in a deep, firm bass that suggested rock-solid certainty, "I know God disapproves of my being gay. I just have to hope he'll be merciful with me." And a skinny, sweet-looking boy in his twenties didn't hide the terror that had been stirred in his soul by my denigration of biblical literalism. "I know you mean well," he assured me in a gentle, quavering voice, "but if you don't believe in the Bible, you're just not a Christian." It angered me that in a nation with the world's best schools and universities, a nation responsible for history's greatest scientific and technological breakthroughs, a nation founded not on fundamentalist Christianity or "family values" but on a belief in the individual's inalienable human right to life, liberty, and the pursuit of happiness, so many people had been brought up on, and damaged for life by, life-denying, spirituality-crushing lies.

In the Netherlands, where political discourse had moved beyond "culture war" platitudes, I felt light-years removed from the foolishness of fundamentalism. There, for the first time, I allowed myself to feel the rage that had built up inside me. Yes, I loved my country, but I also realized that I wanted to be away from it—away from the idiocy, the intolerance, the puritanism. More and more, I felt I belonged in Europe.

On my first flight back to New York from Amsterdam, a KLM flight attendant passed down the aisle, handing out customs declaration cards for us to fill out—one color for Americans, another for Dutch citizens. I watched him as he made his way toward me down the length of the economy-class cabin. Pointing at each passenger in turn, he said either "U.S.?" or "Nederland?" depending on what he guessed their national identity to be. Somehow he got it right every time. Then he pointed at me.

"Nederland?" he asked.

Shortly after my second trip—by which time I'd decided to sell my apartment and move—something thoroughly unexpected happened. To make a long story short, I fell in love—and it was mutual. Together we made arrangements to move to Amsterdam.

The weekend before the big relocation, we flew to Georgia to attend a wedding. During the reception at the tony Atlanta Women's Club on fashionable Peachtree Boulevard—in the heart, that is, of "civilized" Atlanta, "the city too busy to hate," that fabled oasis of tolerance in the midst of the Bible Belt—we stepped outside to get some air. While we stood chatting innocuously on the sidewalk in our suits and ties, a pickup truck sped by.

"*Faggots!*" a male voice shouted.

It was, somehow, a fitting sayonara.

ON SEPTEMBER 15, 1998, we left New York with two cats, a laptop, and a couple of suitcases crammed with clothes and books. Everything else I owned—mainly books—had been packed up in boxes and stored in my father's basement in Queens.

My father wasn't happy about the move. His parents had fled Europe during World War I, and the Continent was linked inextricably in his mind with war, poverty, and oppression. In his eyes, you didn't move to Europe—you fled it. Though he was a brilliant, learned man, I thought he was wrong on this one—I thought he was living in the past.

But I gradually came to feel that he had a point. Not that Amsterdam lost its appeal: I continued to love its human scale, its perfect flatness, the fact that the highest points on the skyline were centuries-old steeples. I loved the profusion of bicycles and the near absence of cars. I loved being able to get everywhere on foot or by tram or train. I loved the romance of being enveloped by the sounds of a language that was still a mystery in the process of being revealed to me. I loved the fact that every day I encountered innumerable cultural differences that made life fascinating and that I would never have learned about in any other way. I loved going out in the evening with the person I loved and walking home together along a breathtakingly beautiful canal where we could look through the uncurtained windows of elegant old brick houses into people's tidy, book-lined living rooms. (The Dutch, for centuries, have made a practice of keeping their windows uncurtained, so as to prove to their neighbors that they're not up to anything shameful.)

What more could one ask of life?

Yet as my weeks in the Old World stretched into months, my perceptions shifted. For one thing, I began to appreciate American virtues I'd always taken for granted, or even disdained—among them a lack of self-seriousness, a friendly informality with strangers, an unashamed curiosity, an openness to new experience, an innate optimism, a willingness to think for oneself and question the accepted way of doing things. I found myself toting up words that begin with *i:* individuality, imagination, initiative, inventiveness, independence of mind. Americans, it seemed to me, were more likely to think for themselves and trust their own judgments, and less easily cowed by authorities or bossed around by "experts"; they believed in their own ability to make things better. Reagan-style "morning in America" clichés might make some of us wince, but they reflect something genuine and valuable in the American air. Europeans might or might not have more of a "sense of history" than Americans (in fact, in a recent study comparing students' historical knowledge, the results were pretty much a draw), but America, I saw, had something else that mattered—a belief in the future.

Yes, many Europeans were book lovers—but which foreign country's literature engaged them most? America's. They revered education—but to which country's universities would they most like to send their children if they had the means? Answer: the same country that performs the majority of the world's scientific research, wins most of the Nobel Prizes, and has twice as many university graduates as Europe. Yes, more Europeans were multilingual, but so what? If each of the fifty states had its own language, Americans would be multilingual too. And yes, America was responsible for plenty of mediocre popular culture; but Europeans, I was beginning to learn, consumed this stuff every bit as eagerly as Americans did—only to turn around and mock it as "typically American."

Like many other Americans, I'd identified my country with its most insipid pop-culture products and Europe with the highest of its high culture. But my perspective soon changed. Where would Europe be without American jazz, blues, rock? America's music *is* Europe's music. Ditto film and television. Every Western European alive today has grown up with American popular culture; it's shaped their sensibilities; without it, their day-to-day cultural experience would be inconceivably poorer, their lives, quite simply, less fun. The more time I spent in Amsterdam, the more I was aware of this—aware of the staggering richness of my country's cultural heritage, both "high" *and* "low," and of how much Europeans valued it, whether they were willing to admit it or not.

Other perceptions shifted too. I'd been impressed that the Dutch were less preoccupied than Americans with what people did; they cared more about one's "inner reality." Now I was beginning to see the flip side of this. Americans believe in practicing what you preach, in taking action, in *doing something*—not just meaning well and mouthing pieties. And let's face it: what you do (or don't do) is crucial to an understanding of who you are. It's the very definition of character. Anyone can mean well; but when you're facing a terrorist enemy, what does your exquisite "inner essence" amount to if you don't actually do something?

I'd loved the Dutch devotion to *gezelligheid*—to small daily pleasures—and had looked askance at the American fixation on outsized rewards and successes. But the longer I stayed in Europe, the more I found myself viewing American ambition as a good thing. Life without it, I saw, could be a pretty pallid, hollow affair. Furthermore, I'd begun to see that in much of Western Europe, the appreciation of everyday pleasures was bound up with a stifling conformity, a discomfort with excellence, and an overt disapproval of those who strove too visibly to better their lot. Sometimes it could even seem as if Western Europe's core belief was in mediocrity.

As I sought to ease my way into Dutch society, I felt the Dutch pushing back. I learned that if America was a melting pot, the Dutch had a history of *verzuiling*, or pillarization—the division of society into religious and ethnic groups, each with its own schools, unions, political parties, newspapers, and, in recent times, TV channels. There was tolerance, yes; but it was a tolerance that regarded you not as an individual but as a member of a group; it took for granted not intermarriage and integration, but a persistent, generation-to-generation cleavage. Yes, institutional *verzuiling* was now largely a thing of the past—but the mentality lingered. However long I might stay in the Netherlands, I saw, I would always remain an outsider.

I'd loved the peaceableness of Dutch men as compared to the macho swaggering of Americans. But the flip side of that un-macho behavior was a kind of passivity that, in the aftermath of 9/11, would emerge as something less than a perfect virtue.

Finally, I'd rejoiced in the fact that Western Europeans weren't Bible-thumpers. But I was beginning to recognize that certain elements of the Continent's ever-growing immigrant population represented even more of a threat to democracy than did fundamentalist Christians in the United States. In Western Europe, not to put too fine a point on it, fundamentalist Muslims were on the march. Their numbers—and power—were large and growing rapidly. And the ultimate objective of many of their leaders was far more than a ban on abortion or gay marriage.

———

ONE EVENING ten weeks after our move, we were strolling along the Singel, a canal in the heart of Amsterdam, when suddenly a wiry, dark-skinned boy in his late teens stepped directly into my path. Staring up at me, he demanded money in broken English.

He was trying to come off as tough and dangerous, but his large brown eyes shone with anxiety. Looking beyond him, I saw half a dozen of his friends hovering at the edge of the canal, about twenty feet away. They were bigger than he—older, meaner. Could it be that they were putting him through some kind of test or initiation rite?

Loudly and firmly, I told the boy to hit the road. His eyes widened in astonishment. His friends glanced uncertainly at one another. After a moment's hesitation, they all beat it.

As soon as they were gone, my partner told me something I hadn't realized: the boy had pulled a knife. My partner, standing a couple of feet away from me, had seen it, but the boy had been so close to me, and had held the knife so low, that it had been outside my field of vision.

I'd lived in New York City for forty-one years, and now, after ten weeks in Amsterdam, I'd experienced my first mugging.

During our six months in Amsterdam, we lived in three flats in quick succession. The first was a large, windowless, garagelike ground-floor room in a charming neighborhood; the second, while in a dicier part of town, was elegant and high-windowed, with a postcard view of the Oude Schans canal. These apartments were, respectively, on the *centrum*'s southern and eastern fringes, just inside the boundary that separates it from the city's outskirts.

The third was west of downtown and just outside that boundary, in the largely Muslim Oud West. Our address was Bellamyplein, a claustrophobia-inducing square of Dickensian ugliness. If we looked out the window at any time of day, we were likely to see one or more women pushing baby carriages, with one or more children tagging along behind them. Invariably the women wore *hijab*, the Muslim head covering. In most cases (and I didn't learn these distinctions until later) it took the form of a *chador*, a single long piece of cloth that covers the entire body and leaves only the face visible; less often, it was a *niqab* or *burqa*, which shields everything except the eyes. (Relatively few of the women wore the less severe variety of *hijab* known as *dopatta*.)* A few doors away from

*Defined by Fahrat Taj, a Pakistani student in Norway, as a "length of cloth worn over the shoulders and/or around the shoulders and/or on the head, but such that it is not tightly bound around the head."

us, a huge Turkish flag flew over the entrance to a building labeled "neighborhood center." One day we peered inside. A dozen or so Turkish-looking men, middle-aged and older, scowled back. We didn't go in.

The contrast between central Amsterdam and the Oud West was remarkable. On any given day, the downtown streets teemed with people—but unless you were near the train station or on a low-budget shopping street such as the Nieuwezijds Voorburgwal, you hardly ever saw a woman in *hijab*. Indeed, if you lived in Amsterdam and never left the city center, you could almost forget that Islam existed. Wandering along the broad canals of the Grachtengordel, all of them lined with handsome, picturesquely tilted old houses, you saw plenty of native Dutchmen—and, during the warm months, a profusion of tourists—but few men, and almost no women, who looked North African or Middle Eastern. If you got on a tram or subway, however, and took it a few stops in almost any direction, you'd confront a vastly different reality.

For one thing, Amsterdam's suburbs were as ugly as its *centrum* was beautiful. There were stretches of southwest Amsterdam—an immense, sprawling area that tourists never visit—where you could look in every direction and see nothing but an endless vista of concrete monstrosities that looked like warehouses, separated by forlorn stretches of weedy grass and linked by an elevated train line whose tracks were supported by a structure that was also a concrete monstrosity. The waves of people that flowed among these buildings were predominantly dark-skinned; many, if not most, of the women wore the *burqa*. Signs in Arabic proliferated; so did baby carriages.

I would later encounter this same contrast in other European cities. Across the Continent, Islam was a huge and growing presence. Yet Muslims were segregated to an extraordinary degree. In metropolis after metropolis, the city centers were virtually 100 percent European; the outskirts were increasingly Muslim.

Immigrant ghettos, of course, are nothing new. They've played an enormous role in America's history, and for millions of families they've been a natural stage in the transition from foreigner to hyphenate to native. It's common in ghettos to encounter immigrants who can't speak the language of their new country and who have pretty much the same attitudes, values, and way of life they had in their homeland. In most cases, integration takes place largely in the next generation: the children of immigrants go to school, grow into full-fledged members of society, and leave the ghetto behind.

But that's not the way things work in Europe nowadays. By the time I arrived in Amsterdam, its immigrant community, like those in most major European cities, had existed for decades. Inhabiting it were not only immigrants but the adult children and grandchildren of immigrants. Though born in the Netherlands, many either spoke no Dutch or spoke it very poorly. Their cultural values, to all intents and purposes, were still those of the Islamic world, and the people whom they thought of as their leaders were not the elected members of Parliament but the imams and elders who ruled their communities like tribal chieftains, enforcing traditional practices with uncompromising authority and relentlessly reminding them of the evils of the West.

Many of those leaders preached contempt for European democracy, for the European acceptance of gay relationships, for the equal role of women in European society; they rejected freedom of conscience, denounced the separation of church and state, and insisted that Muslims had no obligation to obey the rules of secular society. "These Germans, these atheists, these Europeans don't shave under their arms," preached one Berlin cleric in 2004, "and their sweat collects under their hair with a revolting smell and they stink. Hell lives for the infidels! Down with all democracies and all democrats!" That same year, a preacher told a Copenhagen audience that "secularism is a disgusting form of oppression. . . . No Muslim can accept secularism, freedom, and democracy. It is for Allah alone to legislate how society shall be regulated! Muslims wish and long for Allah's law to replace the law of man." And in February 2005, Abu Abdullah of London's Finsbury Park Mosque called non-Muslims "filthy" and urged his congregation to take part in jihad, telling them that if they could not fight in Iraq "then this is our front line here." Muslims can hear this kind of rhetoric not only at mosques but also courtesy of Arabic-language satellite TV channels such as al-Jazeera, which celebrates suicide bombers as "martyrs" and (in the words of Middle East expert Fouad Ajami) offers "an aggressive mix of anti-Americanism and anti-Zionism."

Most of my ancestors had moved to America with the intention of becoming Americans—or, at the very least, of having children and grandchildren who'd be Americans. Many Muslim immigrants arrive in Europe with very different ambitions. All want a share in Western prosperity; fewer care to adapt to Western ways. Their connections to their homelands remain very strong. Unlike my Polish grandmother, who died seventy-five years after emigrating to America without ever having left New York State, many European Muslims travel regularly back to their homelands: at this writing there are as many direct flights every week between Oslo and Pakistan as there are between Oslo and the United States.

A Muslim in Europe, after all, is not an island unto himself. He's part of a family—which, in turn, is part of a vast clan, some of whose branches live in the family's homeland, and others, perhaps, in other European countries and/or North America. He's also part of a community whose members keep a very close eye on one another. Clan and community ties are intense, and the power of clan and community leaders is absolute. On the largest scale, moreover, the European Muslim is part of the *umma*—the worldwide brotherhood of Islam. "From my background," Hirsi Ali has told the *Guardian*, "being an individual is not something you take for granted. Here [in the Netherlands] it is all you, me, I. There it is we, we, we."

Flowing out of this *we*-feeling is the obligation of clan members in Europe to send money regularly to clan members back home. Many European Muslim men even own second residences in their ancestral villages, purchased with the money they've earned (or received in government support) in Europe. Some also have additional wives and children there who live off their European income. (Muslim men may have up to four wives at a time; so far, most European governments recognize only one.) Some immigrant families, indeed, are not really immigrants at all: they maintain a European residence, which enables them to collect a variety of benefits, but spend less time there than in the countries from which they've supposedly emigrated. They're less like immigrants than like diplomats—emissaries who return home frequently and have no doubt about where their loyalties lie.

In Pakistan, there's actually a region called "Little Norway" or "Little Scandinavia" because many of the local clans have outposts, as it were, in Norway, Sweden, or Denmark. (In August 2005, Socialist Left Party leader Kristin Halvorsen even included the region on her campaign tour.) Once dirt-poor, European members of these clans now own fine homes in the area, some with servants, swimming pools, and multiple cars. When a Norwegian newspaper profiled one of these successful immigrants—who lived in Drammen, near Oslo, and had bought a lavish home in "Little Scandinavia" with money supposedly earned through decades of hard work as a taxi driver there—Oslo's Human Rights Service added a detail to his curriculum vitae: back in "Little Scandinavia," it turned out, the cabbie owned not only a house but also an entire extended family, whose members worked as slaves in his brick factory.

———

IMMIGRANTS TO EUROPE bring with them many tribal customs that are flagrantly inconsistent with a Western understanding of human rights. These customs represent flash points of latent or potential conflict between Muslim communities and their host societies, though for a long time the European media and political establishment did their best to downplay or ignore them.

Perhaps the most barbaric and least publicized of these customs is female genital mutilation (FGM), a practice well-nigh universal in some Islamic cultures. As Hirsi Ali has explained, Arab countries safeguard female virginity "by keeping women in the house"; in other regions, however, where "you need the labor of women outside," virginity is safeguarded by "cut[ting] off the clitoris of the woman [and sewing] together what is left." The specifics of this procedure vary—and are not pleasant to describe—but it usually involves total or partial removal of the prepuce and/or clitoris. The labia minora and majora may also be excised, and the vagina stitched up to the size of a pinhead. Traditionally, the mutilation is carried out at ages ranging from infancy to late puberty, but in Europe it's frequently performed when the child is very young, because parents know they're doing something that's frowned on and, as they say, "a baby can't tell lies." The mutilation—which rarely involves anesthesia—can cause blood poisoning and excessive bleeding, and often results in lifelong physical pain, chronic infections, and extreme discomfort during urination and sex.

Parents give many reasons for the perpetuation of this brutal custom. At the top of the list is the conviction that women's sexual feelings are sinful and their sexual organs unclean, and that mutilation therefore provides protection from sin. Such thinking comes naturally in patriarchal subcultures that teach men to view women as property, female sexual desire as nothing more than a menace to family honor, and female sexual pleasure as something therefore best obliterated as early as possible.

Then there's the practice known as "dumping"—the shipping of European Muslim children to their parents' homeland to attend Koran school. The purpose is unambiguous: to prevent their integration into Western democracy by "reeducating" them in traditional values and fundamentalist interpretations of the Koran. The bills for this "reeducation" are often paid by European mosques—which, in turn, receive funding from both European and Muslim governments. Some children are sent to these schools as early as age three. Though born in Europe, they have little connection to mainstream European culture; in their ancestral homelands, they live with relatives who share the Koran school's goal of preventing them from *ever* developing such a connection.

In 2004, my friends Hege Storhaug and Rita Karlsen of Human Rights Service came back from a trip to Pakistan with a harrowing eyewitness account of a Koran school in Gujarat: "From the outside, it looked like a prison. It was dark and cold and there was no electricity." The children, all Scandinavian girls, didn't look well; many were undernourished. There were no desks, chairs, or educational materials in sight. The windows were barred, and were so high up that the girls couldn't look out and outsiders couldn't look in. Between the first and second stories, there was no floor but only a grating. "We looked down and saw the children below, looking up at us." At any given time, about 250 Muslim pupils are known to be "missing" from schools in Oslo alone.

To be sure, European Muslim children don't need to be sent abroad to be brainwashed in the ideals of jihad and martyrdom. In Amsterdam, moving among the native Dutch—whose public schools taught children to take for granted the full equality of men and women and to view sexual orientation as a matter of indifference—I felt safe and accepted. Yet many youngsters in the Netherlands attended private Islamic academies. These schools—which, like the mosques, received subsidies from the Dutch state as well as from Islamic governments—taught hatred of Jews, Israel, America, and the West. They taught that women should be subservient to men and that Muslims should keep their distance from infidels. They taught young people to view the democratic societies in which they lived with contempt and to regard them as transitory, destined to be replaced by a Muslim caliphate governed according to sharia law. And they reinforced the sexual morality that the young people learned at home, which allowed polygamy (for men), prescribed severe penalties for female adulterers and rape victims (but not rapists), and demanded that homosexuals be put to death.

Such schools weren't unique to the Netherlands, of course—they existed across Western Europe. Nor did Muslim children in Europe need to attend private academies in order to be inculcated with traditional values. In 2004, it emerged that an outfit called the Islamic Foundation was responsible for "giving court-mandated religious instruction to Muslim children" in German public schools. Many German teachers were less than pleased with the results: one of them complained to *New York Times* reporter Richard Bernstein that some girls, under their Muslim teacher's influence, had dropped gym and swimming (a common problem) and some had begun wearing *hijab*. Bernstein also quoted a TV report on Muslim textbooks used in Germany, which teach that "the Muslim people's existence has been threatened by Jews and Christians since the Crusades, and it is the first duty of every Muslim to prepare to fight against these enemies."

Among the critics of this indoctrination was Marion Berning, a Berlin grade-school principal who, prohibited from sitting in on the religion classes, entered a classroom anyway and pretended to fix a window. While she was there, the teacher explained to a roomful of docile girls and rowdy boys that "women are for the house, for the children." Since these classes had begun, Berning had seen her Muslim and non-Muslim pupils grow apart from one another; fighting and name-calling had increased, and more and more Muslim girls were withdrawing from school trips and athletics. The story was the same across Europe. In Milan, for example, school officials were caving in to Muslim parents' demands that their children be put in Muslim-only classes to insulate them from a "secular atmosphere"—that is, from the democratic West in which they lived.

For a long time, many European officials saw intermarriage as the key to integration. They assumed that when the children of immigrants grew up, they'd marry ethnic Europeans and raise European children. Ghettos would fade away; segregation would be a thing of the past. But that didn't happen. Levels of intermarriage and integration have remained exceedingly low—and ghettos are expanding. Why? The answer, in two words: family reunification. Under the immigration laws of most Western European countries, if you're a citizen or permanent resident, your foreign spouse, children, and (in some cases) other family members may enter the country and live with you. Many immigrant communities, through a pragmatic twist on the tradition of arranged marriage, have exploited this provision brilliantly—and in doing so have changed the face of both Western Europe and Muslim marriage.

Imagine, if you will, a girl whose parents moved from Morocco to Belgium before she was born. She's a Belgian citizen and, as such, theoretically entitled to all the rights of any Belgian citizen. But when she reaches her mid-teens or thereabouts, her father will arrange for her to marry someone in Morocco—or (much less likely) someone in the Moroccan community in Belgium or perhaps in the Netherlands or France. The prospective husband will almost certainly be a member of her extended family—probably a first or second cousin. She may or may not have met him before. She may or may not like him. She probably won't want to marry him. But she'll almost certainly obey. Because she knows what may happen if she does not. (Boys are forced into marriages too, though generally speaking they undergo less of a risk if they refuse.)

Storhaug and Karlsen have called forced marriage "a modern-day commerce in human beings." They've also pointed out a fact most European politicians would prefer to ignore—that a forced marriage will likely involve forced sex, sometimes on a daily basis. Human Rights Service studied ninety cases of forced marriage in Norway and found that only three of the wives were not raped—either because they'd run away in time or because the marriage was pro forma. Girls forced into "marriages" who try to fight off their "husbands" on their "wedding nights" can't expect parents or in-laws to come to the rescue. One girl said that when she screamed out for help, her new in-laws, still celebrating the wedding in an adjoining room, "just turned up the volume on the music." Another girl said, "I'll never forget the day after the wedding night. Everyone must have seen the pain in my face. But even my own mother gave no sign that I could ask for the least amount of support and comfort from her."

Traditionally, in Muslim countries, a new wife moves in with her husband's family—never the opposite. Among European Muslims this custom has been entirely overthrown. Nowadays, when a transnational marriage between Muslim cousins takes place, the spouse that migrates is invariably the non-European spouse, whose first residence after migrating is, as a rule, his or her in-laws' home. These marriages—which in Norway have acquired the name "fetching marriages"—accomplish two things. They enable more and more members of an extended Muslim family to emigrate to Europe and enjoy Western prosperity. And they put the brakes on—or even reverse—whatever progress the European-born spouse might have made toward becoming Westernized. In other words, the disease of integration is prevented by injecting into the European branch of the family a powerful booster shot of "traditional values"—that is, a hostility to pluralism, tolerance, democracy, and sexual equality. These inoculations have proven extraordinarily effective.

For fathers, this anti-integration effort is of particular urgency where their daughters are concerned. In most European Muslim families, the female sex role is severely circumscribed: women and girls alike understand that they're subject to the authority of men and that they must abide by extremely narrow rules of conduct. A female who oversteps her proper role or defies male authority is viewed as having stained her family's honor, and may end up paying the ultimate price. The best way to avoid this eventuality is to ensure that one's distaff offspring not become infected by the West.

Some parents will go to extraordinary lengths to prevent such infection, combining "dumping" and forced marriage in a triumph of complete non-integration. The parents of one Norwegian-born girl sent her back to their homeland at age three to attend Koran school. While they collected child benefits in Norway, she stayed at the school. Graduated at sixteen, she was married off at once. Just before having her first child, she returned to Norway—not knowing a word of Norwegian, and not having been educated in anything but the Koran—and brought her husband over through family reunification. Some months after giving birth, she contacted her Koran school to reserve a place for her child, who, like her, would be enrolled at age three. Far from being unique, this young woman exemplifies the ideal toward which many immigrant families strive in their effort to exploit European munificence while avoiding pollution by European culture.

To be sure, most Muslim children in Europe attend regular public schools, where even the most sheltered girl will be influenced to some degree by Western culture—inevitably picking up ideas about her right to date, have a career, select her own husband, and make her own decisions. This is why importing spouses is so crucial. By compelling his daughter to wed an illiterate villager for whom the very idea of female independence is anathema, who believes it's a husband's God-given right and duty to beat such ideas out of her (or, for that matter, to beat her for any reason whatsoever), and who will restrict her movements outside the home as fully as possible, a father can fight off the influence of the West and ensure that his daughter, though living in Europe, will have a life very much like that of a peasant woman in a Pakistani village.

The typical Muslim girl in Western Europe thus lives with the probability that she'll someday be compelled to marry an imported husband whom she'll be expected to obey without fail. If she refuses to have sex with him, her parents and in-laws will consider it only reasonable for him to force himself on her; if she tries to fight him off, it'll be perfectly within his rights to handle her as brutally as necessary. And if she disobeys him publicly—thereby damaging the family's honor—the whole family may consider it his sacred obligation to dispatch her in an "honor killing."

In January 2002, a young Swedish woman named Fadime Sahindal, who'd become a media star after refusing to submit to a forced marriage—

and whose ethnically Swedish boyfriend later died under mysterious circumstances—was murdered by her father. On his arrest, he readily confessed and called his dead daughter a whore. The story made headlines
across Scandinavia. But this and other high-profile cases are only the tip
of the iceberg; most honor killings in Europe, it's believed, never even
come to the attention of the authorities. In 2004, Britain's public prosecutor began reinvestigating no fewer than 117 suspicious deaths or disap-
pearances to determine if honor killings had taken place. Over a
six-month period in 2004–2005, eleven women were victims of honor
killings in The Hague alone.

Here's a sampling of representative British cases. In south London in
2002, a young woman who'd been raped was murdered by her family to
restore its honor. The next year, in Birmingham, twenty-one-year-old
Sahjda Bibi was stabbed twenty-two times in her wedding dress by a
cousin for marrying a divorced man and not a relative. In the same year,
a Yorkshire teenager was murdered by her father in Pakistan over a relationship the family hadn't known about until her boyfriend dedicated a
love song to her on Pakistani-language radio. In London in 2003, a lively
sixteen-year-old London girl named Heshu Yones—who'd fallen in love
with a Lebanese Christian boy and planned to run away with him—was
stabbed eleven times by her father, who then slit her throat. In a fare-
well note to her father, Heshu referred to the frequent beatings he'd
given her:

> Bye Dad, sorry I was so much trouble.
> Me and you will probably never understand each other, but I'm sorry
> I wasn't what you wanted, but there's some things you can't change.
> Hey, for an older man you have a good strong punch and kick.
> I hope you enjoyed testing your strength on me, it was fun being on
> the receiving end.
> Well done.

At the trial, the prosecutor noted that Heshu's father "didn't approve of
her more Westernized lifestyle—wanting to be with friends and having
a mobile phone." Though the Muslim Council of Britain issued a statement saying that it didn't condone Heshu's murder, Council spokesman
Inayat Bunglawala added that "many Muslims would understand Yones
being upset by his daughter's apparent rejection of her faith" and by her
"growing up not with his value system but someone else's." As journalist
Val MacQueen noted in reporting this story, this was "the value system

of a country that the father, a Kurdish refugee, had begged on his knees to get into." It was revolting, moreover, to see Bunglawala referring sympathetically to the "value system" of a man who'd just hacked his child to death.

What makes these murders different from others that take place every day in the West is that many members of the perpetrators' subculture consider them defensible. According to the *Sun*, Yorkshire police investigating the song-dedication murder "met a wall of silence in the girl's Pakistani community." After the murder of Fadime Sahindal, Norwegian Muslims asked by reporters for their comments declined to condemn it outright. More than one insisted that the father had done what he had to do. "I can't say it was right and I can't say it was wrong," volunteered one Oslo merchant. Did this unwillingness to criticize an unspeakable crime betoken approval of the father's actions or fear of challenging community norms? Either way, it was chilling.

It's impossible to bridge the gap between a Western mind-set and one that makes "honor killing" possible. Imagine that your daughter is raped—and that in response you feel obliged to kill her. Such scenarios are played out in Europe with increasing regularity. Honor killing, to be sure, is not an exclusively Muslim phenomenon—the first one uncovered in Sweden was by a Palestinian Christian who murdered his daughter in 1994 for spurning an arranged marriage—but most such crimes in Europe are, indeed, committed by Muslims and many Muslims do, indeed, have trouble condemning them.

Sometimes girls are taken abroad to be murdered. Such was the case with Pela Atroshi, who, in 1995, at age fifteen, emigrated from Iraq to Sweden with her parents and six siblings. Pela soon looked like an integration success story—she learned Swedish, was a good student, and made non-Muslim friends. This infuriated her father, who accused her of "living a European life." One night when she was nineteen, she made the mistake of staying out all night. Her parents were livid; several men in the family insisted she be murdered. Pela fled to safety, but after being told she was forgiven she returned home and contritely agreed to submit to an arranged marriage. When she traveled with her father to Iraq for the ceremony, however, it turned out that her family had arranged not a marriage but a murder. An Iraqi court sentenced Pela's father and uncle to five months' probation for the crime. The reason for the lenient sentence was that their "motive was honorable."

Often women are gang-raped as punishment for something the men in their family have done—and are then murdered by the men in their family to dispel the shame of the rape. And sometimes European Muslim girls are murdered for "offenses" they've committed during their sojourns abroad. In 2000, a twelve-year-old with a Swedish passport was out shopping with her mother and brother in her family's hometown in northern Iraq. There she met a neighbor boy, who gave her a ride in his car. This breach of honor—riding unchaperoned with a boy to whom she was not related—"made the whole family angry," recalled a relative. About sixty family members held a conference at which they discussed murdering the girl. Eventually they decided not to do so. But not everyone agreed. One day in May 2001 the girl, now thirteen, walked out of her family home to find three of her uncles and four of her cousins waiting. They pumped eighty-six bullets into the girl's body. (Like her, two of the uncles were Swedish citizens.)

Horrible though all this is, it's nothing compared to the sharia-run Europe of fundamentalist imams' dreams. What would sharia law mean to Europe? A partial answer: converts from Islam to other religions would be executed; thieves would have their arms amputated; women would be required on pain of beating (or worse) to conform to a severe dress code; adulterous women would be stoned to death; so would gay people.

It's certainly no secret what most European Muslims think of homosexuality. "After more than twenty-five years in the immigration field," writes Kirsten Damgaard, a Danish cultural psychologist, "the Muslim immigrants I have personally met who find homosexuality acceptable can be counted on one hand." In 1999, a speaker at a student conference on "Islamophobia" at King's College, London, began by announcing politely, "I am a gay Muslim." That effectively ended his presentation. His audience, mostly Muslims, responded by shouting furiously, rushing the stage, and confronting him aggressively. "Security was called," reported the *Guardian*, "and the conference came to a premature end." Then, in October 1999, the Shari'ah Court of the UK declared a fatwa against Terence McNally, who in his play *Corpus Christi* had depicted Jesus Christ as gay. (In Islam, Jesus is counted among the prophets.) Signing the death order, judge Sheikh Omar Bakri Muhammed charged that the Church of England, by failing to take action against McNally, had "neglected the honour of the Virgin Mary and Jesus." According to the sheikh, McNally could escape punishment only by converting to Islam. "If he simply repents," the *Daily Telegraph* helpfully explained, "he would still be executed, but his family would be cared for by the Islamic state carrying out the sentence and he could be buried in a Muslim graveyard."

A few weeks later, British Muslim leaders were busy battling the repeal of Section 28, Great Britain's notorious antigay law. Dr. Hasham El-Essawy, director of the Islamic Society for the Promotion of Religious Tolerance in the UK and (according to the *Telegraph*) an "Islamic moderate," found it appropriate to quote the Koran's punishment for lesbians—"Keep the guilty women in their homes until they die, or till God provides a way out for them"—and for homosexual men: "If two of your men commit the abominable act, bother them. But, if they repent . . . then bother them no more." El-Essawy made clear his "moderation" by contrasting his view with that of some other Muslims, who, he explained, "believe that the punishment for homosexuality is death."

Kheir Sajer, an Oslo Muslim who describes Islamism as a "cancer" in his community, tells of an Oslo imam who has preached that Christians, under sharia law, must pay *jizya*, the protection tax demanded of all infidels living in Muslim lands: "In Norway, they don't do this. Therefore the Muslims have a right to steal from them. If a Muslim walks straight into a store and steals, it is thus a legitimate act." Other Oslo imams, says Sajer, agree.

After Sajer wrote about these matters, local Islamists mobilized a propaganda campaign against him, threatening his friends, claiming he'd "mocked Allah and the Prophet Muhammed," and labeling him a drug user and homosexual ("a serious accusation in the Muslim community"). Since "most refugees and immigrants listen to the congregation's imams and believe what they say," friends and neighbors turned against him. He was persecuted for months: "They use a method we know very well. When one of them sees me walking in the street, he calls an ally and tells him what direction I'm going. After five minutes I notice someone walking behind me." When he heard that fiery discussions about him were taking place at a certain Oslo mosque, he went there, and heard someone say angrily: "Here comes the infidel, who smears Islam and Muslims. Here is the Norwegians' agent who writes for a handful of kroner!" Sajer, who recognized the man as a doctor at a major Oslo hospital, noted wryly that this outcry against "Norwegians" took place in a mosque financed by Norwegian tax money.

When he contemplated going to the police, a fellow Muslim advised him to back off. "You know that some of them have a position in Norway and can wreck things for you with your residency permit. You'll be sent back without even knowing why." It was then that the truth sank in: ·"Those who have the power aren't the police, but these Islamists. And the law that applies in Norway isn't Norwegian law, but sharia. . . . The security Norway has given me is in danger. For these fanatics want to hijack my freedom and my soul. They want to play leaders for the Muslims. They want to exercise power against us. They want to gag us." Why, he asks, should this be so? "Why do these Islamists have so much power over us? Why are they supported by the state, without supervision, without control, and without other Muslims being able to voice their opinions about them? There's a big difference between a Muslim and an Islamist, just as big as the difference between a German and a Nazi."

LIVING IN AMSTERDAM in 1999, I didn't yet know about such things. But I wanted to learn. Information, alas, wasn't easy to come by. (The Internet wasn't yet the comprehensive source it has since become.) Day after day I sat at cafés paging through Dutch, British, French, German, Italian, and Spanish broadsheets (the supply of foreign papers at many Dutch cafés being extremely generous), but saw hardly any reference to European Muslims. I scoured several of Amsterdam's excellent bookstores, plus the large lending library on Prinsengracht, but found almost nothing. (I know now that Pim Fortuyn's first book, *Against the Islamicization of Our Culture*, had been published two years earlier, but I never ran across it. I also know now that the Dutch writer Paul Scheffer warned in *NRC Handelsblad* in 2000 that "the culture of tolerance is reaching its limit," but I missed that at the time, too.)

To be sure, I tracked down plenty of books about Islam itself, or about Islam *and* the West, which I read attentively. But I found only a few about Islam *in* the West. Nearly all took a sanguine view. For example, American scholar John Esposito, in *The Islamic Threat: Myth or Reality?* (1992), exhaustively argued that there *was* no such threat, period. Now, Esposito was supposedly an expert. (In 2005, the American Academy of Religion would present him with the Martin E. Marty Award for the Public Understanding of Religion.) But I found his position puzzling. Even my limited observations told me that fundamentalist Islam was on the march in Europe and wasn't adapting itself to democratic values. It seemed clear that eventually there'd be a confrontation—or capitulation. Yet Esposito wouldn't admit this. *Nobody* admitted it.

On the contrary, most writers on the subject maintained that Islam was precisely what the West needed. Adam LeBor, in *A Heart Turned*

East (1997), contrasted what he saw as the high spiritual and moral values of Islam with what he characterized as Western decadence. LeBor, an Englishman, approvingly quoted a French Muslim leader on the desirability of letting "Muslims in the West introduce [Westerners to] a new approach [to both family life and life in society]—or rather a much older one—founded in spiritual values, rather than material ones." Islam, wrote LeBor, "can bring to Europe [something] immeasurable, intangible, but nonetheless vital"—namely, "God and spirituality. The missing part of the jigsaw puzzle of life in the late twentieth century." LeBor complained at length about the "challenge" the United States offers to Muslims because of the clash between Muslim values and the crassness of American culture. Like many other Western writers, LeBor seemed to view fundamentalist Islam in the West as akin to a spice that enriches an otherwise bland dish. But his own account made clear that the religion doesn't work that way. It doesn't flavor—it transforms, subdues, conquers. Islam means "submission," and in its fundamentalist form, at least, it demands nothing less. A Western society that accepted such a religion as its spiritual component would soon prove itself highly inhospitable to, among much else, any writer who might not share LeBor's unadulterated admiration. Nowhere in his book did LeBor acknowledge this problem; nowhere did he say a single positive word about Western freedoms, individuality, sexual equality, or protection of minority rights. Nor did he address the traditional Islamic division of the world into the *Dar al-islam* (the "House of Islam") and the *Dar al-Harb* (the non-Muslim "House of War," so called because Muslims living in it are commanded to help bring it under Islamic rule through jihad). Instead LeBor insisted unwaveringly upon the virtue and piety of fundamentalist Muslims and the greed and decadence of their Western oppressors.

Hunting down statistics, I discovered that upwards of 7 percent of the Netherlands' population—and nearly half of Amsterdam's—was of non-Dutch origin. (That was in 1998; Amsterdam is now more than half non-Dutch.) Of the largest immigrant groups, the Turkish and Moroccan communities dated back to the 1970s, while immigration from Surinam and the Netherlands Antilles, both former Dutch colonies, had peaked in the 1980s. As many as three out of five Turkish and Moroccan immigrants in the Netherlands were unemployed; two out of three children in Amsterdam schools were non-Dutch.

Every Western European country has its own distinctive mixture of minority groups and its own modern immigration history. (The chief exceptions are Finland and Iceland, which have almost no immigrants;

Portugal and Ireland also have relatively few.) Sweden's largest non-Western groups are Iraqis and Iranians; Norway's are Pakistanis; Denmark's are Turks; Belgium's (like the Netherlands') are Moroccans and Turks; Britain's are Indians, Pakistanis, and Bangladeshis; France's and Italy's are from North Africa; Spain's are from Morocco; Germany's from Turkey, Switzerland's from the Balkans, Austria's from both.

If the first large wave of immigrants to most of these countries came thirty or more years ago and consisted mainly of guest workers, the arrivals in recent decades have tended to come either as "refugees" or "asylum seekers" or through so-called "family reunification." I put these terms in quotation marks because the policies governing all these categories of immigrants have long been seriously flawed and outrageously abused. Most "refugees," for example, are not refugees at all. Migrating, one researcher has observed, is now "a consciously planned act of subversion." Those illegitimately seeking asylum routinely destroy their identity papers on the plane to Europe—a simple ruse that enables them to avoid deportation and secure residency on humanitarian grounds. The scale of this deception is reflected in the fact that 94 percent of the asylum seekers who come to Norway carry no identification. (This trick is also frequently used by terrorists to evade detection by European security services.)

Muslim immigrants in Europe, I learned, tended to come not from cities but from poor, remote villages—which meant they were more likely to be religious conservatives who were both unfamiliar with and hostile to Western values. And many had become even more conservative and religious since migrating to Europe—so that the Muslim you passed on a street in Amsterdam, Paris, or Berlin might well be even more intolerant than his cousins in rural Morocco or Anatolia.

Beyond this I knew little about European Muslims. And I wasn't alone. In 1998, Europeans were clueless. The media hadn't covered the topic, the parliaments hadn't debated it, the professors hadn't taught about it. Only since then has awareness begun to spread—thanks less to the media, parliaments, and professors than to a relative handful of intrepid souls bent on getting the word out.

One thing we know now is that many immigrants have been extremely successful at exploiting the generosity of Western welfare states, where it can be a simple matter to walk into a government office and walk out with cash in your pocket. In Norway, the handouts come in a wide variety of forms—among them public assistance, unemployment benefits, relief payments, child benefits, disability, cash support, and rent allowance. One reason the Scandinavian welfare system has worked as well as it has is that most Scandinavians have been pretty good about not taking excessive advantage of it. Yes, Scandinavians do take more sick days than Americans, but they're generally responsible about getting jobs and supporting themselves and they don't habitually drop into the welfare office or social security office and ask for money they don't really need. To a surprising extent, much of the social security apparatus functions on a sort of honor system: unless you require it, you don't ask for it.

Alas, this is a different kind of honor than many immigrants are familiar with. Most come from poor villages in undeveloped countries with high levels of corruption—a background that tends to breed cynicism, duplicity, and an exceptional skill at manipulating the system. For people with such backgrounds, the goal is to grab everything one can get; only a fool would not take maximum advantage of the kind of bounty that Western Europe offers. Besides, many of them are told by their religious leaders that Muslim law gives them the right to abuse the infidels' system as much as possible—the right, in Kheir Sajer's words, to "cheat and lie to the countries that harbor them." They are told to view the benefits they receive as *jizya*—the tributes that the infidel natives of Muslim-occupied countries are obliged to pay to Muslims in order to preserve their lives. For some immigrants, therefore, the sky's the limit. In Denmark, Muslims make up 5 percent of the population but receive 40 percent of welfare outlays. Statistics for other countries are comparable.*

The ease with which immigrants can rip off the system sometimes boggles the mind. In 2005, it emerged that the Norwegian government was paying disability benefits to many Moroccan immigrants who'd moved back to their homeland and who, to maximize their intake, used multiple names, lied about how many dependents they had, and used false doctors' certificates to attest to their incapacity for work. Despite the immense scale of the welfare-state bureaucracy, it appeared that the veracity of such information or the validity of such documents is rarely if ever checked. About 15 percent of Moroccan immigrants in Norway are on disability, and up to a quarter of them actually live in Morocco, where a Norwegian disability pension is equivalent to a rich man's

---

*In addition to the usual aid categories, there's a cornucopia of miscellaneous outlays: at least one Norwegian county encourages integration by paying immigrant teenagers up to $75 per annum to join a youth club or sports team. While Norwegians must pay a fee of about $2,000 for a driver's license, moreover, an immigrant on the dole can get one free on demand.

income. A man with a family, noted *Aftenposten*, can receive Norwegian disability payments of up to $3,000 a month. A reporter who went to Morocco to seek out people on Norwegian disability was scolded by a man in Casablanca who told him that Norway "needs to be stricter" with his countrymen. Needless to say, there's no reason to believe that immigrants from other nations aren't also riding this first-class gravy train.

"Integration in Denmark," wrote Ina Kjøgx Pedersen in *Weekendavisen*, "begins at the social security office." But those offices, she added, in an article based on a study by Omar Dhahir, are the setting for severe cultural clashes. A trivial remark by a social worker will be perceived by a client as a profound insult; the client will respond with words intended to outrage the social worker's sense of honor ("if you don't do what I say, I'll fuck your sister"); the social worker, in turn, will answer with a joke that in the client's culture would be inconceivable ("my sister will like that"). Some clients lay waste to social security offices and hit social workers—not out of frustration but because they've learned that such bullying gets them what they want. Pedersen quotes Dhahir as saying that "in the Arabic culture . . . the authorities have great power. People behave respectfully toward them." But not in Denmark. The Danish government is not repressive; welfare workers tend to be sympathetic and eager to help. Many immigrants perceive this as weakness, and exploit it, "tyrannizing" the social workers. Dhahir suggested that in the encounter between social worker and immigrant client, translators should be doing more than just translating between languages; they should translate between cultures. But is the problem that immigrants who exploit Danish generosity don't understand, or that they understand all too well?

Nima Sanandaji, who came to Sweden as a refugee when he was a child, has described how the Swedish asylum system encouraged segregation, alienation, and reliance on welfare: "In the refugee camp nobody did anything. Nobody learned how to speak Swedish. Nobody was integrated in the Swedish society and nobody was allowed to get a job. . . . We became used to the idea that social security was responsible for our lives." And the social services folks helped foster this attitude: they "assumed that the people they supported had no sense of responsibility. . . . If you told them that you had spent all your money at the beginning of the month and didn't have any left, they gave you some more."

After the 2005 terrorist attacks on London, it emerged that the four suspects had raked in more than half a million pounds in welfare benefits from the British government. The *Telegraph* reported, too, that Hizb ut-Tahrir founder Omar Bakri Muhammed (who preached that "we will conquer the White House . . . we will be in charge and Muslims will control the earth") was getting "£331.28 a month in incapacity benefit and £183.30 a month in disability living allowance"; in addition, he collected a "housing benefit" and a "council tax benefit," not to mention his wife's welfare intake of "at least £1,300 a month." (Curiously, no mention was made of child benefits for his seven progeny.) Even his car had been acquired free of charge under a government program.

Thanks in some cases to abuse of the welfare system, in other cases to hard work, and in many cases to both, millions of European Muslim parents have been able to give their children comfortable, prosperous lives. Yet many of these children have been raised to despise the societies that have made this comfort and prosperity possible. Polls show that young European Muslims today—even those born in Europe—identify more with their ancestral homelands than with the countries whose passports they carry. No surprise there. After all, their families have never really left the Islamic world—they brought it with them. Their neighborhoods aren't temporary ghettos that will fade away with integration; they're embryonic colonies that will continue to grow as the result of immigration and reproduction.

"Colonies" is no exaggeration. As the British historian Niall Ferguson puts it, "a youthful Muslim society to the south and east of the Mediterranean is poised to colonize a senescent Europe to the north and west." Bassam Tibi, a liberal Muslim who teaches at a German university, has warned that "either Islam gets Europeanized, or Europe gets Islamized." (He prefers the former.) And in July 2004, Bernard Lewis—perhaps the most distinguished Western expert on Islam—predicted that Europe would be Islamic by the end of the century. The historian Bat Ye'or agreed. Indeed, she's introduced a useful term to designate the geographical entity that's taking shape as the result of Europe's Islamicization: "Eurabia."

Anyone who doubts these prognostications need only look at the numbers. Today, in most of Western Europe, the Muslim share of the population is somewhere between 2 and 10 percent. In Sweden, Austria, and the Netherlands, the figure approaches the high end of that range; in France, it's 12 percent. A glance at the relative rates of reproduction suggests that this percentage will rise precipitously over the coming generation. Among native Western Europeans, the fertility rate ranges from 1.2 to 1.8—well below the "replacement rate" of 2.1. This means that the native populations of these countries will decline considerably over the next generation, and the number of retired persons will approach the number of employed persons, causing an economic crisis. Meanwhile, the number of Muslims will increase dramatically, partly through continued immigration and partly through reproduction (the fertility rate of Muslims in Europe being considerably higher than that of non-Muslims). Already, in most of Western Europe, 16 to 20 percent of children are Muslims. Within a few years, every fifth or sixth young adult in Western Europe will be a Muslim; within a couple of generations, many countries will have Muslim majorities. Informed observers predict a coming "explosion" of fetching marriages that will take Europe beyond the point of no return.

The imams know this. "Muslims have a dream of living in an Islamic society," declared a Danish Muslim leader in 2000. "This dream will surely be fulfilled in Denmark . . . We will eventually be a majority." A T-shirt popular among young Muslims in Stockholm reads: "2030— then we take over." In many places in Europe, agitation for the transfer of sovereignty has already begun. In France, a public official met with an imam at the edge of Roubaix's Muslim district out of respect for his declaration of the neighborhood as Islamic territory to which she had no right of access. In Britain, imams have pressed the government to officially designate certain areas of Bradford as being under Muslim, not British, law. In Denmark, Muslim leaders have sought the same kind of control over parts of Copenhagen. And in Belgium, Muslims living in the Brussels neighborhood of Sint-Jans-Molenbeek already view it not as part of Belgium but as an area under Islamic jurisdiction in which Belgians are not welcome.

The main reason I'd been glad to leave America was Protestant fundamentalism. But Europe, I eventually saw, was falling prey to an even more alarming fundamentalism whose leaders made their American Protestant counterparts look like amateurs. Falwell was an unsavory creep, but he didn't issue fatwas. James Dobson's parenting advice was appalling, but he wasn't telling people to murder their daughters. American liberals had been fighting the Religious Right for decades; Western Europeans had yet to even acknowledge that they *had* a Religious Right. How could they ignore it? Certainly as a gay man, I couldn't close my eyes to this grim reality. Pat Robertson just wanted to deny me marriage; the imams wanted to drop a wall on me. I wasn't fond of the hypocritical conservative-Christian line about hating the sin and loving the sinner, but it was preferable to the forthright fundamentalist Muslim view that homosexuals merited death.

Given what I'd seen and heard of evangelical Christianity in America, I hadn't been terribly upset that Christian belief in Western Europe had declined precipitously since World War II and that the churches were now almost empty. But I was beginning to see that when Christian faith had departed, it had taken with it a sense of ultimate meaning and purpose—and left the Continent vulnerable to conquest by people with deeper faith and stronger convictions. What's more, no longer able to take religion seriously themselves, many Europeans were unable to believe that other people might take religion very seriously indeed.

The situation was alarming. The very things I most loved about the Netherlands—and about Europe—were the things most threatened by the rise of fundamentalist Islam. Yet the Dutch did nothing. Why did they refuse to deal with something that obviously endangered their freedom? Didn't they see what I did? Didn't they notice the look of rage in the eyes of many Muslim men at the sight of that ultimate spectacle of dishonor—a Dutch woman bicycling to work? Or did they assume that such men, simply by inhaling the damp Dutch air, would somehow magically become open-minded and secular?

One evening we had dinner with Stephan Sanders, a maverick gay conservative writer who appeared frequently on Dutch TV and was well known for his blunt expression of unorthodox views. In passing, he mentioned that the Netherlands, unlike the United States, had no Religious Right. I knew very well that the Netherlands did have a Religious Right; that it consisted of Muslim, not Christian, fundamentalists; and that sooner or later the Dutch would be forced to deal openly with the challenges it posed. For the time being, however, they were plainly too uncomfortable with the idea. Criticizing any strand of Islam in any way felt too much like voicing racial or ethnic prejudice. Indeed, the Dutch (like Western Europeans generally) viewed Islam less as a religion than as an expression of ethnic identity. While enthusiastically condemning Protestant fundamentalism—which hardly existed anymore in that once severely Calvinist country—the Dutch couldn't bring themselves to breathe a negative word about Islamic fundamentalism.

By the time I left the Netherlands, I knew all this. And I also knew that the Dutch would eventually have to face it too.

On Saturday, March 6, 1999, in pelting rain, a huge crowd of people filled Dam Square in the center of Amsterdam, waving signs and banners. Almost all were dark-skinned; women in *hijab* abounded; tiny children pressed flyers on passersby. On a portable stage, a man delivered a political speech in a voice whose fury and passion would mark him as something other than ethnic Dutch even if his skin color didn't. The cause du jour: allowing "white illegals"—that is, illegal immigrants who hadn't been convicted of anything other than immigrating illegally—to stay in the Netherlands. I scribbled down the slogans from some of the signs, the rain immediately smearing my ink almost into intelligibility. They were all in Dutch, and each contained at least one misspelling: *"Human rights for everyone! Also for 'white illegals'!" "General pardon for 'white illegals'!" "No person is 'illegal'!"*

ON APRIL 1, 1999, we moved from Amsterdam to Oslo; and on May 8, in a simple and beautiful ceremony at the Oslo Courthouse, our partnership became official. In the eyes of the Kingdom of Norway—though not the United States of America—we were now each other's spouses and next of kin. Thanks to "family reunification," I had a right to Norwegian residency.

The differences between Amsterdam and Oslo were considerable. Amsterdam is the crossroads of Western Europe; Oslo is a marginal outpost. The Netherlands is the most densely populated country in Europe (not counting Monaco and Vatican City); Norway is the least (not counting Iceland). These demographic distinctions translate into major cultural contrasts. The Dutch are cosmopolitan; Norwegians can be surprisingly provincial. The Dutch delight in speaking other languages, and will switch into English no matter how stubbornly you try to get them to speak to you in Dutch; Norwegians, though usually good at English, tend to be shy about speaking it until they've had a few drinks, after which point it can be hard to get them to stop.

Yet for an American, the similarities between the two places outweighed the differences. Living in Oslo, I soon saw that many of the conclusions I'd come to about the Netherlands applied equally to Norway. In both, political correctness reigned supreme.

Some months after our move to Oslo, I took advantage of an offer that the government extended to every new immigrant: five hundred free hours of Norwegian classes. The classes were held at the Rosenhof Adult Learning Center, a sprawling old school building that reminded me of my junior high school in Queens. Most of the students there were immigrants; most were also Muslims with little, if any, education. Many couldn't even read or write their own native languages.

My class was the exception. I'd been placed in a room with other relatively well-educated people with backgrounds in languages. There were

eighteen of us, from America, England, France, Germany, the Netherlands, Poland, Ukraine, Serbia, Israel, Pakistan, China, South Korea,
Singapore, and Australia. Several of my classmates were formidably multilingual. The Ukrainian woman knew three or four Slavic languages;
the Dutch guy spoke French, German, and Spanish; and the Pakistani
was fluent in Urdu, Farsi, Bengali, and French. And everybody spoke
English.

As enjoyable as my steadily improving fluency was the feeling of
community in the classroom—a community that extended across barri-
ers of generation, nationality, and economic status. And, not least, religion: several of us were Christians; three (I think) were Muslim; one was
Jewish. The Muslims, none of whom were fundamentalists, were easy-
going and conspicuously Westernized. Yet they were the exceptions at
Rosenhof. In classes down the hall, women in *hijab* sat with male relatives providing the family escort without which they were prohibited
from leaving home. And these were the ones with permissive husbands:
many women who would live in Norway all their lives were married to
men who, viewing Western language as an instrument of corruption,
would never let them learn Norwegian.

Our class was lively, irreverent, fun; as we learned Norwegian, we
also learned about Norwegian folkways, and gained insights into our
own and one another's native languages and cultures. Our discussions
brought into focus previously unexamined attitudes and assumptions
that our native cultures had bred into us; and as we recognized in all this
the common foibles and follies of the human species, we laughed—
laughed in easy self-mockery, and laughed, too, in celebration of the opportunity we'd been given to grow beyond our native cultures.

From the other classes we never heard the sound of laughter.

ONE EVENING not long after our move to Oslo, my partner and I
stood waiting for a tram—as it happened, directly in front of the courthouse where our partnership ceremony had taken place. On the bench a
few feet away sat a young Muslim couple. Standing nearby were two
young women kissing each other. The Muslim wife, in *hijab*, stared at
them, her eyes blazing with rage. She was obviously out to intimidate.

My partner and I exchanged a look. The Muslim woman kept staring. The hate in her eyes was unsettling. Finally my partner couldn't take
it anymore. "Please stop that," he said to her, in a gentle, pleading tone.

"This is Norway. We don't do that to people here." Instantly, her husband leapt to his feet in fury. His wife, he said, had just moved to Norway, and didn't yet understand Norwegian ways. She jumped up, too, visibly alarmed by his anger, and stood in front of him, apparently worried he'd get violent.

"You'd better drop it," one of the lesbians said to my partner. "You're just getting him mad, and when he gets home he'll let off steam by beating *her* up." My partner complied.

One morning two months later, my partner was headed for work on a crowded tram when he noticed the same Muslim couple among his fellow passengers. His eyes met the husband's. *"Soper!"* ("Faggot!") the man shouted, charging at him. "Nazi!" he added, inexplicably. My partner got off at the next stop. So did the man, who leapt on him, kicking and punching. This was in a busy downtown square, crowded with people on their way to work; but although several passersby stopped to watch the assault, no one made a move to intercede. Fortunately, my partner was taller and stronger than his assailant and managed to subdue him, after which a member of the crowd that had formed around them led the man away.

My partner phoned me at once to tell me what had happened. Though he was not badly injured and wanted to let it go, I argued that the crime should be reported. Finally, he agreed. When we got to the police station, the officer on duty told us that the assailant and his wife were there already—and that the wife had accused my partner of attempted murder. This, he explained wearily, was a familiar tactic in the immigrant milieu: rushing to the police station to file charges against your victim before he can report you.

We were outraged. But the cop shrugged it off and urged us to do the same.

Some time later we were walking along a busy street in downtown Oslo when suddenly a wiry youth was in our faces, raving at us in a Middle Eastern language, his eyes ablaze with rage. In front of and behind us were several of his friends, all moving aggressively. I said, "Get lost." He didn't. We tried to ignore him, though when he shoved his finger in my face, I pushed his arm away. At this, he grew more aggressive. One of his friends intervened, saying to me in Norwegian, "Sorry," and then, as the raving continued, "It's fine." "It's *not* fine," I replied sharply. The friend answered with a look that chilled me. I thought: If we had encountered this group in a deserted alley, we'd have been lucky to make it out alive.

Yes, there are bad kids everywhere, in every ethnic and religious group—kids who are rebelling against their parents' authority and values. That's not what's going on in Europe today. These marauding kids don't reject their parents' values—in all too many cases, they embody them. While their sisters, as a rule, were being trained in submission—and to walk an extremely narrow line if they didn't want to be beaten—these boys were being raised to be belligerent. They were taught that God had given them authority over women and made them superior to infidels. They were taught that they owed no deference to any unbeliever—whether teacher, police officer, or government official—because in the eyes of God, no non-Muslim has a legitimate right to occupy a position of power over Muslims. To them, the infidels' "law" is a joke, and values such as pluralism, tolerance, and sexual equality are alien and immoral. They see Western society as the enemy, European men as wimps, European women as sluts. Their supreme shared value is a primitive cult of honor, according to which if your daughter dates a Norwegian boy, she damages the family's honor and merits death, but if your son rapes a Norwegian girl, it's her fault. Given such training, it's little wonder that gang violence and mayhem are a growing problem across the Continent.

To be sure, if some gang members have learned anti-Western attitudes at their parents' knees, others have parents who dearly wish they'd go straight and get a job. A not inconsiderable number of Muslim youths raised by hardworking, honest immigrant parents have learned (generally from some imam or other pious mentor) to view those parents as cowards and traitors to Islam for having worked hard, respected the *kaffir*, and obeyed European laws. If some young Muslim men drink alcohol, have sex, and commit crimes that aren't really motivated by religion at all (although the rhetoric they hear in their communities makes them feel less guilty about robbing non-Muslim homes, raping infidel girls, and beating up gays), others, such as van Gogh's killer and the 7/7 London terrorists, are well-educated, devout, celibate teetotalers who would never commit rape or robbery—and who look forward to performing acts of mass murder in the name of Allah.

Our encounter with that gang in downtown Oslo took place on a Thursday night. The next morning, the newspapers ran updates on the recent brutal murder of an eighty-three-year-old woman. The killers, it turned out, were Libyans who'd been granted asylum in Norway—one of them on the grounds that he'd been condemned to death in Libya (for what crime, the newspapers didn't know). He lived in a refugee center—

and nobody, not even the police, had been told he was a felon, because that's not allowed. The next day, the top news story was a shooting at Oslo Airport—the result of a Pakistani honor feud.

On the following Tuesday, *Dagbladet* front-paged an unusually frank statement by the head of Kripos, Norway's FBI. To stop the appalling crime rate, he argued, changes were needed in immigration policy and in punishments for gang crime. *Dagbladet* noted an earlier suggestion of his: that the police be given access to asylum seekers' fingerprints. Apparently this was perceived as a radical proposal. "You realize you may be seen now as someone who hates foreigners?" *Dagbladet* asked him. "Yes," he replied, "and I have no problem with that. Someone must dare to say it out loud."

That was in 2003. Those willing to "say it out loud" are still few and far between.

Meanwhile the problems simply grow worse. In some urban areas of Europe, all order has broken down. Young men roam the streets in packs and commit crimes in the daylight, in front of scores of witnesses, without fear of being stopped or punished. "In many French cities with a growing radical Islamist population," notes Sorbonne professor Guy Millière, "no teenage girl can go out in the evening, at least not without a full *burqa*"—otherwise she's admitting she's a whore and asking to be raped. Statistics for the Dutch city of Amersfoort are probably representative of much of Europe: the police have files on 21 percent of local Moroccan boys and 27 percent of Somali boys, and suspect that 40 percent of the Moroccans between age fifteen and seventeen are involved in crime. In 2005, one Dutch commentator, drawing on a news story about Moroccan gangs in Den Bosch, did a little arithmetic and determined that 80 percent of Moroccan boys in that city were "involved in street violence."

Gay-bashing is on the upswing.* In May 2002, a German gay couple, Dennis and Aribert Otto, were attending a multicultural street festival in Berlin when someone behind them shouted: "Gay pig! You should all be gassed." They turned to see ten immigrant youths coming toward them. The gang beat them viciously. "Five minutes later," reported *Welt am Sonntag*, the two men "were lying on the ground bleeding while 'One World' was being sung two blocks further down. That day they lost their belief in the ideal of a multicultural society in which minorities act together in solidarity."

*Though it's known that the frequency of gay-bashing incidents has skyrocketed in Europe, no statistics are available, since researchers (whose disinclination to criticize Muslims apparently trumps their concern for abused gays) don't dare touch the subject.

I wasn't familiar with "One World," so I looked it up online. I found the lyrics—where else?—on a UN Web site. Here's an excerpt:

Even if we are different in ages and gender
We make friends in the same way
Even if we live in different continents and countries
We play in the same way
We are the friends of One World
We are the children of one family.

In short, it's multiculturalism set to music. The message: all cultures are equal, and all cultural differences superficial. No matter where people come from, their values are essentially the same: they all cherish peace, they all believe in "live and let live," they all want the best for their children. Where serious differences do exist, moreover, it is invariably the West, with its evil history of colonialism and racism, that is inferior; in case of conflict, it is invariably the West that is at fault. There is, moreover, nothing that the West can teach other cultures, though we can of course learn much from them. This is the line the political and media establishment has sold to the people of Western Europe. To suggest that it's not entirely true—that, indeed, there exist cultural differences that can cast a dark shadow over this sunny "It's a small world" sensibility—is *verboten*.

Typically, despite previous convictions, Dennis and Aribert Otto's assailants were given suspended sentences.

In April 2005, a colleague of mine discovered the reality of European gay-bashing the hard way. Chris Crain, editor of the *Washington Blade*, one of America's leading gay newspapers, was walking hand in hand with his boyfriend in central Amsterdam when a young Moroccan man spat in his face. Crain stopped and asked him why. The man, who was with a friend, muttered: "Fucking fags." Suddenly, wrote Crain, "the two somehow turned into seven—and five of them were ganging up on me. . . . It seemed like every direction I turned, I got another punch to the face, and when they kicked me to the ground, time seemed to stop." Fortunately, when Crain's boyfriend came to his aid, the men fled. Though dozens of people had witnessed the crime—which resulted in serious bruising and a broken nose—"none of them had acted or even yelled anything."

WHY DID OSLO cops back off from dealing with immigrants? Why had people in Amsterdam been so unwilling to discuss seriously anything having to do with immigrants? And why did the papers and TV news hardly ever contain so much as a hint of the truth about any of this? The longer I lived in Europe, the clearer it became that the answer lay in the ironclad multiculturalism that ruled the minds of the political, media, and academic establishment. To be sure, it took me a while to gather that there *was* such an establishment—and that it exercised immense control over the news and opinions to which the public was (and wasn't) exposed.

The ideological accord that characterizes Western Europe's establishment politicians and journalists has no parallel in the United States. American political journalists, though likely to sympathize more with Democrats than Republicans, see politicians of both parties as natural antagonists—people whose lies, inconsistencies, and hypocrisies it's part of their job to point out. Political journalists in Europe are more inclined to view mainstream politicians as fellow members of an educated elite whose joint task is to keep their shared social-democratic ideals alive and well. If American journalists have done a terrific job of painting our politicians as rascals and incompetents, European journalists have done an equally terrific job of painting mainstream European politicians as noble statesmen—or, in Tony Judt's words, "a brilliant elite."

Western Europe's establishment is composed of people most of whom entered its ranks as politicians, professors, journalists, or bureaucrats straight from university. Some future politicians join the elite's junior auxiliary as early as secondary school, serving in the youth divisions of political parties, which are important breeding grounds for aspiring party hacks. In most Western European countries, the political system is essentially a private club: in "Labor Youth" or "Socialist Youth," you learn everything from the right kinds of suits to wear and the right places to eat to the right way to dodge questions about troublesome issues. You learn to be loyal to your fellow club members and to disdain as "populists" those who pay too much heed to the opinions of the rabble. In short, you learn to fit in. You learn not to rock the boat. You learn to be slick and smooth and "sophisticated." And you learn to think of yourself not as a servant of the people but as one of their betters, teachers, and protectors.

If you do all this properly, you can coast through life as a career politician, winning elections when you can and being appointed to posts—including prestigious positions in the UN or EU bureaucracy—when you can't. (One reason why European elites are so high on both the UN and EU, I've come to believe, is that these institutions offer plenty of glamorous positions into which an ambitious European politician can ascend after reaching the top of the ladder in his own country.)

And you'll be applauded as "brilliant" by your fellow elite types in the academy and the press, who subscribe to the same dogma and who understand that it's part of their job to preserve the elite's power and to keep feeding the people the same line about the brilliance and vision of their own leaders and the idiocy of America's. It's all part of the legacy of Europe's long feudal tradition.

American politics is different. An American politician who's spent his whole life in politics is automatically suspect. Why should someone who doesn't have firsthand knowledge of what it's like to hire and fire, create jobs, run a business, and meet a payroll be given the power to make decisions that will affect the way these things are done? In Western Europe, by contrast, most of those who reach high office have been active in party politics since they were very young. Those who are most lavishly rewarded tend to be those who display the strongest loyalty to the party and its platforms. Original thinkers are not welcome. People who might shake things up are closed out. A Ronald Reagan or Arnold Schwarzenegger could never have attained high office in most of the countries of Western Europe.*

America has two major parties, each of which brings together a range of political philosophies that don't necessarily get along well together. At present, the Republican Party includes Christian conservatives and big-business libertarians, pro-war Jacksonians and antiwar Buchananites, while the Democratic Party's cast of characters ranges from classical liberals like Joe Lieberman to radicals like Michael Moore. In America, a political party is supposed to be a big tent. People aren't expelled for disagreeing. The system's far from perfect, but it allows room for dissent, for organic growth, for fresh and even shocking ideas.

The party system in Western Europe is different. Most national legislatures include members of several different parties; most governments are coalitions of two or more parties. Except in Britain, the two sides of the Western European political spectrum correspond not to the Democrats and Republicans in the United States but rather to, say, the mainstream and radical wings of the Democratic Party.

---

*One of the rare exceptions to this rule is Silvio Berlusconi, who in addition to being prime minister of Italy is also a business tycoon. Partly because he's a successful capitalist, and partly because he's a strong ally of America, the European media treat him with unmitigated contempt, accompanying virtually every mention of his name with a reminder of his history of financial scandals; by contrast, you would never know from most European coverage of Jacques Chirac that any hint of financial impropriety had ever clouded his reputation.

It all sounds very politically diverse, and when it comes to certain relatively minor domestic issues, it *is* diverse, with a good deal of vigorous argument about, for example, budgetary questions. (As I write this, the top headline on the Norwegian Labor Party's Web site reads "Must allocate more for psychiatry," while the Norwegian Conservative Party's Web site celebrates the end of artificially high fixed prices on new books.) On major issues of political philosophy, however, party differences shrivel. Though the "left-wing" parties are proudly and openly social-democratic and the "right-wing" parties are not, in practice the mainstream parties rarely if ever challenge the social-democratic belief in a controlled economy and income redistribution—a system that schoolchildren are taught to view as the perfect balance between American-style capitalism and Soviet-style Communism.

In the view of many European governments, there's hardly any limit to the state's proper purview. (Thus Norway's cabinet includes a minister of culture and church affairs; Germany has a minister of family affairs and women; and Denmark has a minister of gender equality.) European governments take for granted the state's power—and obligation—to shape citizens' personal choices through an extraordinarily intrusive array of prohibitions, taxes, and subsidies. For example, the Norwegian government believes cars and alcohol are bad, and hence taxes them punitively; conversely, it believes newspapers and mosques are good, and thus subsidizes them lavishly.

While the mainstream parties may haggle, then, over whether to trim this or that budgetary item or slightly lower this or that tax, on certain questions they all stand shoulder to shoulder—even against a majority of the population. Take the death penalty. The almost universally accepted fiction is that Europeans despise America for having capital punishment; the reality is that many Europeans—some polls suggest a majority—would like to have it too. The problem is that no mainstream party will support it.

The same pattern has long been followed in regard to immigration and integration issues. For years, while ordinary Europeans grew increasingly concerned about these questions, mainstream European parties— in collaboration with the media and academia—effectively prevented public discussion of them. Virtually anyone who tried to initiate debate was pilloried, smeared, and besmirched. The top-down organization of the major parties kept politicians in line; the philosophically lockstep honchos at news organizations (many of them government owned or subsidized) kept unorthodox views off the airwaves and opinion pages.

Yes, there are independent thinkers whose perspectives one can find (if one looks hard enough) in the occasional newspaper piece or, increasingly, on Internet weblogs; by and large, however, unorthodox views are effectively barred from the mainstream media.

That's where the so-called "populist" parties come in. In many European countries, such parties have been the only ones to address with candor the issues of fundamentalist Islam, immigration, and integration. And they've been powerfully stigmatized for doing so. Establishment politicians talk loftily about what's best for "society," for the "community," for "the people," but when other politicians come along who actually speak to the people's concerns on the most urgent issues, those same establishment politicians condemn them as "populists."

In America, populism has taken a variety of forms, from the right-wing racism of George Wallace to the agrarian socialism of Huey Long. In Western Europe today, however, "populism" serves as a code word for "fascism"—or, at the very least, a crude, know-nothing *simplisme*. Some of the Continent's "populist" parties, such as Vlaams Belang (formerly Vlaams Blok) in Belgium, the National Front in France, the Freedom Party in Austria, and the National Party in Germany, are indeed more or less fascistic groups, fixated on racial, ethnic, and cultural identity. Others, such as the Progress Party in Norway, the UK Independence Party in Britain, List Pim Fortuyn in the Netherlands, and the Danish People's Party in Denmark, may attract intolerant and xenophobic elements but appeal mainly to citizens who are concerned about preserving liberty and equality.

Yet however undeserved, the fascist stigma is potent. It's meant to be. It actually keeps many people who sympathize with populists from voting for them. Jonathan Friedman, an American professor at the University of Lund, has suggested that one reason why no populist party has ever earned enough votes to win a seat in the Swedish Parliament is that Swedish elections aren't entirely secret—other people in the polling place can look at your ballot and see which party you support. The sense of embarrassment over voting for populists is just that strong.*

*On the eve of the German elections in September 2005, I was at a bar in the affluent Södermalm neighborhood of Stockholm, where a middle-aged woman shared with me her political views—which turned out to be identical with those of the Swedish establishment. Angela Merkel, head of Germany's Christian Democratic Union Party, was a "fascist." Kjell Magne Bondevik, who'd just been voted out of power as prime minister of Norway, was a "fascist." Norway's Progress Party, which had scored big in the same election, was "fascist," too. And of course the Swedish Democratic Party was also "fascist."

In the view of the European establishment, "populist" ideas are not only fascist; they conflict with the European ideal of solidarity. And solidarity doesn't just mean a spirit of community—it means a spirit of community *mediated through government institutions*. It means an abiding respect for, and deference to, the wisdom and judgment of those who've made careers in mainstream politics. Though Europeans do indeed joke and complain about their politicians in the same way Americans do, underneath the jokes and complaints lies a deeply ingrained tendency to trust their government, to view it as benign, to see it as always and ultimately being on the side of the people (even if one disagrees with this or that specific policy), and to cherish it as a precious counterweight against the dread power of corporations and other private enterprises. (In Europe, big business is always a threat—never big government.)

The pro-liberty "populist" parties tend to see things in a way that's more familiar to Americans. They're suspicious of overly intrusive and bossy government and regard a large private sector as a positive thing, both for the economy and the people's freedom. The increasing success of many of these pro-liberty parties is a measure of the increasing distance between the people and the mainstream parties that purport to speak for them. It's also a measure of the growing intensity of feeling that surrounds certain issues—immigration and integration now being at the top of the list.

The political establishment has routinely acted to keep pro-liberty parties out of power, even if some of them enjoy the support of a large portion of the electorate. Meanwhile, establishment journalists do their part by misrepresenting "populist" ideas, maligning their leaders, and mocking their supporters. A 2005 study of five major Danish papers showed that they referred to right-wingers as "radicals" or "extremists" seven times as often as they did left-wingers. Sometimes the establishment goes further. In 2003, the Danish Supreme Court fined Pia Kjærsgaard of the Danish People's Party fifty thousand kroner for making "racist" statements that were not racist at all. And in Sweden, youth members of socialist parties have disrupted meetings of the Swedish Democratic Party with baseball bats and pepper spray.

When I first moved to Norway, I knew little about this. What I did know was that a staggering percentage of Norwegians bought three or more papers a day. I was awed. How different they were from Americans! How curious about the world! How well informed! In time, however, this enthusiasm was tempered. I saw that although Oslo had several daily papers, there was plenty of important news that somehow seemed never to be reported in any of them, and a wide range of opinion that virtually never made it anywhere near their editorial pages. By American standards, indeed, the papers' cumulative ideological range was quite narrow—from one end of the left to the other. The same went for the TV news operations, the largest being government-owned NRK. On major issues, I saw, the media were all essentially agreed. Jews? The Holocaust had been wrong, but Israel was now using it to justify persecution of Palestinians and perpetuate the "cycle of violence." The American economic system? Cruelly inequitable, period. (Prior to 9/11 and the invasion of Afghanistan—which gave opinion writers meatier fare—it seemed that hardly a week went by without a full-page *Dagbladet* essay warning Norway against a more American-style economy.)

Johan Norberg, a Swedish scholar, feels that the social-democratic establishment consensus is so significant a feature of Western European society that he's given it a name: "the one-idea state." Norberg (whose country has an even more lockstep elite than most) notes that "the social democrats' power over our minds, authorities, universities and media starts a process of adaptation from all sides, including the opposition, so that individualists and innovators are shut out." Precisely. Living in Norway, I saw that the media served up a carefully selected—and severely unbalanced—daily news diet, heavily dosed with artificial flavoring. Yet almost nobody seemed to realize it. One reason was that they were constantly being told by these same media what an extraordinary breadth of coverage and opinion they were getting—unlike Americans, whose media, they were assured, served only the interests of the White House.

In 2004, I followed the Sudan crisis for weeks online before seeing any mention of it in the Norwegian media. The same was true of the UN Oil-for-Food Program scandal: I'd read plenty online that made Secretary General Kofi Annan look very bad indeed, but for weeks the only mention of it in the Norwegian media was in a brief notice in *Aftenposten*. Then, in the summer of 2004 (thanks to a mischievous temporary editor who was obviously out to stir things up), I actually managed to publish an op-ed in *Dagbladet* about anti-Americanism, in which I noted that the Norwegian media, while obsessing over Abu Ghraib (since it made the United States look bad), had totally buried the Oil-for-Food story (since it made the UN look bad). Lo and behold, a couple of days later *Dagbladet* ran a full-page story on Oil-for-Food—which did a splendid job of leaving the impression that it was the United States, not the UN, whose hands were dirty in this matter.

America's rough equivalent to the Western European elite, which is sometimes labeled the "liberal elite" or "Eastern establishment," wields considerable power at many universities and at Hollywood film studios, at the *New York Times* and *Washington Post*, and at the news divisions of most TV networks. But this elite's influence in America is minor compared to that of its Western European counterpart. For America's elite, while controlling some powerful institutions, is not monolithic. No news channel in the United States is more popular, after all, than the conservative Fox News, and no newspaper more prestigious than the conservative *Wall Street Journal*. If liberals have the *New York Times* and *Washington Post*, moreover, conservatives have the *Washington Times* and the *New York Post* (not to mention the relatively new *New York Sun*). Even at the *New York Times* there are conservative columnists and, quite frequently, conservative op-ed contributors; many reporters' accounts, intentionally or not, challenge the opinions presented on the editorial page.

Similarly, America's political magazines range from *National Review* and the *Weekly Standard* on the right to the *Nation* and *Mother Jones* on the left (with the *New Republic* somewhere in between); its all-news networks range from Fox News to CNN; and its radio offerings range from Rush Limbaugh to NPR. Dozens of TV programs and radio call-in shows are devoted to fiery polemic by, or vigorous exchanges between, true believers at both ends of the political spectrum. Finally there are the Internet weblogs, whose politics are all over the map, and several of which, in the space of a year or two, rose from obscurity to positions of influence. Not long ago it could have been argued that America's liberal media had the power to bury or successfully spin major stories for political reasons. Now, Fox and Limbaugh and countless weblogs will be out there either setting the record straight or spinning the story their own way.

You have to be a regular media consumer in Western Europe for a while in order to understand just how dramatic the transatlantic difference can be. The European media can be stunning in the relentlessness and lack of nuance (that attribute supposedly revered in Europe) with which they disparage America and Israel, idealize the UN and EU, and sanitize fundamentalist Islam. Norway is probably more or less representative: a 2003 poll showed that no fewer than 69 percent of Norwegian journalists identified themselves as socialists, compared with 43 percent of the general population; the "populist" Progress Party, the only major party that represents a serious challenge to establishment philosophy, was supported by 22.5 percent of Norwegians but only 3 percent of journalists—and that 3 percent, I would wager, were more likely to be writing about local theater or school sports for regional weeklies than commenting on international affairs in Oslo-based dailies.*

Journalistic diversity in Europe is, then, largely illusory. In Denmark, it's true, *Jyllands-Posten* is rather more likely to be sympathetic to America or honest about the integration crisis than, say, *Politiken;* similar shades of difference exist between, say, France's *Le Figaro* and *Le Monde*, Spain's *El Mundo* and *La Vanguardia*, Sweden's *Expressen* and *Dagens Nyheter*, the Netherlands' *De Telegraaf* and *De Volkskrant*, and Germany's *Die Welt* and *Frankfurter Allgemeine*. But it's easy to overstate the differences. In Norway, some will tell you that *Aftenposten* is conservative, *VG* centrist, *Dagbladet* leftist, *Dagsavisen* even more leftist, and *Klassekampen* Communist. But the distinctions are considerably slighter than this categorization would suggest. (To be sure, in the last year or two, some "conservative" papers have admittedly strayed from political correctness to an unprecedented degree, either modifying their own see-no-evil views of immigration, integration, Islam, and terrorism, or at least making room for dissenting voices on these issues.) The only Western European country whose journalistic diversity approaches America's is Britain, where there are distinct and consistent differences between the *Guardian* and *Independent* on the left and the *Times* and *Telegraph* on the right.

Though there's not much journalistic diversity in Western Europe, there's a lot of talk about it—and a lot of tax money spent on (supposedly) ensuring it. (As Norwegian prime minister Jens Stoltenberg once ludicrously put it, journalistic diversity "is too important to be left up to the marketplace.") It's supposedly to ensure diversity that Norway's government, in addition to running two of Norway's three broadcast channels and most of its radio, subsidizes several major newspapers—a breach of the principle of media independence that would be unthinkable in the United States.† Yet despite this hefty investment of public funds, the Norwegian media rarely break out of lockstep on important issues. Edi-

---

*In Norway, at least, one reason for the lack of political diversity among journalists is that most of them are graduates of the journalism college at Volda, where the faculty consists largely of former members of the Maoist, pro–Khmer Rouge AKP (Workers' Communist Party). Norway's only professor of journalism at the university level, Sigurd Allern of the University of Oslo, was himself once head of the AKP.

†In Sweden, newspapers receive over five hundred million kroner a year (about $65 million) in government support.

torials take predictable lines, and the international coverage is blatantly ideological in its slant and in the selection of events and details.

In the United States, people from all walks of life write op-eds: I started contributing them to major newspapers when I was a graduate student in my early twenties; countless others without fancy credentials, but with something to say, have also gotten their voices heard in this way. This is relatively uncommon in Western Europe, where opinion pieces on key issues tend to be establishment boilerplate. To read most opinion pieces in Norway, indeed, is to gather that the authors' goal is not to introduce or debate fresh ideas but to remind the masses what they're supposed to think. The same holds true for most news articles, which routinely spin the news from the perspective of social-democratic orthodoxy, systematically omitting or misrepresenting any challenge to that orthodoxy—and routinely presenting the United States in a negative light. Most Norwegians are so accustomed to being fed only one position on important issues and events (such as the Iraq War) that they don't even realize there exists an intelligent alternative view.

Things are even worse in Sweden. During the run-up to the invasion of Iraq, the only time I saw pro-war arguments fairly represented in the Scandinavian media was on an episode of *Oprah* that aired on Sweden's TV4. Not surprisingly, a Swedish government agency later censured TV4 on the grounds that the program had violated official media-balance guidelines. In reality, the show, which had featured participants from both sides of the issue, had plainly offended authorities by exposing Swedish viewers to something their nation's media had otherwise shielded them from—a forceful articulation of the case for going into Iraq.

And yet Western Europeans are regularly told by their media that it's *Americans* who are fed slanted, selective news.

Over dinner with me, contrarian Danish journalist Lars Hedegaard accused his colleagues of arrogance: "They don't consider it their job to enlighten people about what's going on. They're out to educate. They think their readers need finishing school. They're doing missionary journalism. They have an incredible sense of moral superiority to their readers." This attitude, of course, is hardly unknown among America's media elite. The crucial difference is the attitude of ordinary citizens. Europeans, though not necessarily influenced by the press, are habitually deferential to it; by contrast, most Americans tend to view journalists (and professors and politicians, too) with skepticism or even scorn. Americans have a low threshold of tolerance for pretentiousness and posturing; though we greatly respect people with ideas, knowledge, and skills that are of practical value, we have little patience for those who want to be looked up to as authorities just because they can sling jargon or have been educated in some arcane subject. Americans have far more regard for common sense than for ideology. We care about what works, not what sounds good or impressive or credentialed. And we have a deeply ingrained belief in human equality—which translates into a respect for our own ability to make decisions about our own lives, and a resentment of anyone who tries to lead us around by the nose by pretending to be smarter than we are.

Europeans, by contrast, have been taking orders and listening to voices of authority for centuries. Living in countries that, compared to America, are ethnically very homogeneous, they're quicker than we are to find comfort in conformity. The media play a key role in this: if the American media tend to take a reflexively critical position toward political leaders, the Western European media are, to a remarkable extent, instruments of government. Perhaps it's no surprise that state-owned TV and radio news organizations present a worldview that reflects the government's guiding ideology and serves its purposes; but most of the Western European media organs that aren't state-owned tend to do pretty much the same thing.

Since 9/11, we've heard a lot about what "Europeans think." But do we really know what they think—ordinary Europeans, that is? Most of the opinions that are usually attributed to Europeans are in fact those of the journalists, politicians, bureaucrats, and professors who make up the European establishment. Of course, the European public has been raised on establishment views and trained to defer to establishment wisdom. The French writer Jean François Revel has noted that while his countrymen tend to "parrot . . . the received wisdom of their social milieux," Americans form their own views. "Too many Europeans," notes Tibor R. Machan, "live in the belief that government is their head of family." It's less common in Europe than in America, moreover, for young people to be taught to think critically about their history. Leif Knudsen recalls that when he attended secondary school in Norway, the curriculum "consisted of learning the authoritative rather than the critical interpretation of historical events." Thus is an acceptance of establishment views passed on from generation to generation.

In my experience, the habit of deference to elite opinion often results in an odd sort of ideological dualism. Many an individual who in a professional context will reliably echo the establishment line will, if you get him alone at a bar over a half liter of beer, express views at odds with that party line. This is not considered hypocritical or inconsistent: in Europe, unorthodox personal opinions that may slip out in an unguarded moment are one thing; an individual's "official" positions are another.*

In 1981, Einar Forde, a leader of Norway's Labor Party (and later head of NRK), said of himself and his fellow Norwegians: "We are all social democrats." It wasn't true then, and is even less true now (social-democratic parties, which once drew their strength from workers, are today largely the province of welfare-state bureaucrats), and in any case it wasn't for him to say. But few minded. The decades after World War II were, for Western Europe, a time of peace and prosperity, and most Europeans were content to let the elite run things pretty much the way it wanted to. Today, however, Europe's social harmony is increasingly being eroded and its affluence endangered by shrinking native populations and a growing immigrant population that's draining out billions in benefits. As this situation worsens, the masses will inevitably turn against their leaders in rising numbers. The danger is that, being enthralled for so long to social democracy, and having little understanding of American liberal democracy (which they might otherwise profit by imitating), they'll swing the pendulum too far to the right. This, indeed, is already beginning to happen in some countries. The prospect is not pretty.

Remember Weimar !

THOUGH IMMIGRATION and integration have become major points of contention in Europe, they weren't even open for discussion when I was first living in Oslo. On these topics, the "one idea" of the "one-idea state" was clear: Muslims in Europe were a colorful and enriching asset—period. In Norway, the expression on everyone's lips was *"fargerik felleskap"*—"colorful community." On the rare occasions when immigrants were mentioned on TV or in the press, you could be sure these words would figure prominently. Norwegian journalists, professors, and politicians loved to use the term. But from the beginning, I found it offensive. Its fixation on skin color mocked Martin Luther King's dream of a color-blind society, and its reduction of immigrants to their most superficial aspect turned them into mere window dressing—

*I'd already written this paragraph when I ran across a comment by blogger Frank Martin. "There are two Europeans," Martin observed. "The 'public Euro' and the 'private Euro.' They all passionately hate George W. Bush loudly in public. But later at the pub, at about the second beer, they all express quiet admiration for the man."

an outward sign of ethnic Norwegians' inner virtue. Often, hearing and reading comments on immigration by Norwegian establishment types, I nearly gasped at their grotesque condescension, their inability to see immigrants as individuals, and their view of the whole business as a morality play, with Muslims in the role of needy victims and Norwegians as heroic benefactors.

The kind of dishonesty in these matters that I encountered when I first lived in Norway is illustrated by an article on immigrants in Europe that appeared in *Time* Europe in 2000. Focusing on a few well-educated, successful immigrants, it argued that while Europe was receiving floods of newcomers eager to become loyal, hardworking members of Western society, racist native Europeans were trying to stop the flow. The words "Muslim" and "Islam" appeared nowhere.

Two years later, the *Economist* devoted much of an issue to European Muslims. The feature was a masterpiece of euphemism and evasion—a prototypical example of the way this topic has been handled in the European press.

Most Muslims in Europe, the *Economist* maintained, "live happily beside their neighbours." Of course they do. Because most of them live around *other Muslims*. Because they live in *ghettos*. The *Economist* explained that while "a few" European Muslims "believe that religious injunctions take precedence over temporal laws," the same can also be said of some Christians, Hindus, and Jews. Nonsense: only among Muslims would anything close to a majority place religious above secular law. "Individual Muslims flourish in western societies," the *Economist* continued, citing "the owner of the corner-shop, the prosperous tycoon, the eminent surgeon or the Aga Khan." As if the latter three examples were remotely typical! "Most work hard, hold strict family values and commit no crimes: model citizens, you might say." In fact, as we have seen, unemployment and crime rates are very high among European Muslims, and their "family values" are particularly "strict" for females.

The *Economist* acknowledged that some problems exist, but added that these problems also plague non-Muslim immigrants. What problems? Problem number one: "They often encounter xenophobia and discrimination, sometimes made worse by racist politicians." Yes, there's discrimination; but European Muslims suffer less from politicians' prejudices than from politicians' accommodation and appeasement of the prejudices of tyrants within Muslim communities. Problems two and three: "They speak the language of the wider society either poorly or not at all" and "They huddle in poor districts, often in state-supported housing." Omitted here is that both problems are caused by deliberate self-segregation. "In time," the *Economist* concluded, "most Muslims will integrate successfully into western societies, especially if common-sense policies like language-teaching, job-creation schemes and anti-discrimination programmes are promoted." In fact all these policies have been promoted, and an integrated Europe is still nowhere in sight.

As for concerns about Muslim attitudes toward gays' and women's rights, the *Economist* answered them in a remarkable way: by introducing immigrant Riaz Ahmad, who, having recently been elected mayor of Oldham, England, "could be forgiven for feeling a bit hurt" by attention to such matters, since he "had just started to use his new position to bring people together." Turning away entirely from the rights question, the *Economist* shifted attention to what Riaz "considers the main problems of everyone in Oldham," namely jobs and housing. In short, having raised the crucial question of Muslim attitudes toward civil rights, the *Economist* chose not to address it but rather to concentrate on the fact that raising such questions hurts the feelings of people like Mr. Ahmad. Such rhetorical sleight of hand is routine in European media coverage of immigrant communities.

The *Economist* feature was a letdown—but hardly a surprise. Since reading Esposito and LeBor, I'd come to see that their refusal to probe European Islam's problems, their indifference to Western freedoms, and their practice of contrasting Muslim virtue and piety with Western greed and decadence were par for the course among European journalists, authors, and professors.

One of the first prominent figures in Norway to take on the rosy establishment view of these matters was Unni Wikan, a professor of social anthropology and expert on Islamic societies at the University of Oslo. Wikan first publicly addressed immigration issues way back in 1992, when the endlessly reiterated establishment line was that immigrants "are entitled to respect." She turned around this meaningless mantra by pointing out that "it is disrespectful *not* to hold people to account." Invited to propose a government plan for immigrant families, she urged that attention be paid to the civil rights of women and children, an alien concept in fundamentalist Muslim communities; yet her recommendations were rejected on the grounds that it would be disrespectful to challenge the power of Muslim men.

Not only did the Norwegian government not want practical advice on immigrant issues; it didn't want solid information, either. Wikan has noted that "not much was known about the situation of immigrants in

Norway" before 1995 because "such knowledge was considered dangerous." Newspapers "were expressly forbidden to mention a person's ethnic or immigrant background in reports on criminal cases lest a bad
image be projected." (This in a land that regularly tops the list of nations
supposedly having the most press freedom.) If Norwegians were given
the facts, it "might trigger racist responses" and "our 'colorful community' . . . would suffer." One can hardly exaggerate the degree to which
Scandinavians fear being accused of racism—a word, Wikan has observed, that "pierces the heart of the well-meaning Scandinavian, whose
cherished identity is that of world champion of all that is kind and good."

Why should Scandinavians be so stung by accusations of racism if
they believe the accusations to be groundless? Here's why, I think. Until
a generation ago, Scandinavia was perhaps the most homogeneous—and
whitest—place on earth. At the same time, Scandinavians prided themselves on their absolute lack of prejudice. They made a point of telling
Americans, white or black, how much they adored Billie Holiday, Miles
Davis, and other black entertainers. They also touted their governments'
high level of aid to African countries. (The notion that direct humanitarian aid creates a dependency that forestalls real economic development
is alien in Scandinavia.) There was no doubt in their minds: unlike white
Americans, who were racists, Scandinavians loved black people.

Then, almost overnight, Scandinavia began experiencing large-scale
immigration from distant, and very different, parts of the world. Naturally, a degree of unease follows upon any dramatic social change; but the
average American could not easily imagine the culture shock involved
when Scandinavians, with no immigration history to speak of, suddenly
found themselves sharing seats on the tram with Pakistanis or Turks or
Iraqis. Though many aspects of this new situation made them uneasy,
they didn't know how to articulate, sort out, and evaluate their reactions.
Unaccustomed to living around dark-skinned people, many Scandinavians, when looking at their new neighbors, couldn't think of anything *but* race. Suddenly, their smug certainties were gone. For all they
knew, they *were* racists. What alternative was there, then, other than to
smother their misgivings and obediently echo the official enthusiasm for
the "colorful community"?

Few in Norway have influenced evolution of the immigration debate
more dramatically than Wikan. A slender, grandmotherly woman with
long white hair and wide, searching eyes, she's a complicated and often
maddeningly contradictory figure, sometimes sounding like a typical academic elitist—a priestess of PC—and sometimes piping up to quash re-

ceived opinions. (I like to think of her as embodying the tensions that exist between the establishment and the man in the street where these issues are concerned.) On the one hand, she's argued that it's not unreasonable to expect immigrants to integrate, learn Norwegian, and respect democratic values; on the other hand, she's invariably responded to criticism of any aspect of Islam with the flat assertion that it's a religion of peace, justice, and gender equality. If the Iraqi-Norwegian writer Walid al-Kubaisi calls Islam "an all-comprehensive world view," Wikan insists on attributing the worldviews of Muslims exclusively to their various national or tribal backgrounds; she seems determined to erect a firewall, as it were, between those worldviews and Islam itself.

On September 6, 2001, it was reported that 65 percent of rapes in Norway were committed by "non-Western immigrants" (a term that in Norway is essentially synonymous with "Muslims"); asked to comment on this alarming statistic, Wikan said that "Norwegian women must take their share of responsibility for these rapes" because Muslim men found their manner of dress provocative. One reason for this high figure, she explained, was that in the Islamic world "rape is scarcely punished," since Muslims "believe that it is women who are responsible for rape." Wikan concluded not that Muslim men in Europe needed to adjust to Western norms, but that "Norwegian women must realize that we live in a multicultural society and adapt to it."

Wikan often shows a different face, however. Comparing America's success with immigration and Europe's failure, she explains that the difference boils down to American realism versus European naïveté. The pillars of U.S. immigration policy are integration and employment; officials in Western Europe, by contrast, thought they were doing immigrants a favor by not requiring—or even encouraging—either. One might wonder why European authorities didn't try to learn from the spectacularly successful history of U.S. immigration. I've lived in Europe long enough to know why: they didn't *see* it as a success story. In the eyes of the Western European establishment, America is a fundamentally racist and materialistic nation that cruelly compels immigrants to shake off their identities and fend for themselves under a heartless, dog-eat-dog economic system. Accordingly, when large-scale immigration to most European countries began a generation ago, political leaders deliberately chose a non-American approach—one they saw as humane, sensitive to multicultural considerations, and respectful of other cultures.

In America, immigrants tend to make the switch to English relatively quickly; by contrast, many European children of immigrants are barely able to speak the language of the country in which they were born. Immigrants to the United States are, moreover, far more likely to enter the workforce—and are better paid—than are immigrants in Europe. Indeed, while immigrants to America are encouraged to become full members of society—and are rewarded for doing so—in Europe (where the native-born children and grandchildren of immigrants are actually called "second- and third-generation immigrants") the establishment prefers its minorities unintegrated. Why? The supposed reason is that it respects differences; the real reason, as I gradually came to understand, was a profound discomfort with the idea of "them" becoming "us." Immigrants to Europe are allowed to perpetuate even the most atrocious aspects of their cultures, but the price for this is that no one, including themselves, will ever think of them as Dutch or German or Swedish. Most Americans, I think, would be shocked to realize how far short of America Europe falls in this regard.

I've mentioned the Dutch history of *verzuiling*, or pillarization—the generation-by-generation separation of religious and other groups within society. When Muslim immigrants first began arriving in the Netherlands in large numbers, the government decided to extend *verzuiling* to include the newcomers as well. It was this policy, known as "integration with maintenance of one's own identity," that enabled Muslims to establish an extensive separate culture within the Netherlands, complete with government-funded schools, mosques, community centers, and other institutions. Policies were much the same elsewhere in Europe, even though other countries had no history of pillarization; what they had, rather, were histories of almost complete ethnic and cultural homogeneity. Naively imagining that they could admit immigrants on a large scale while at the same time preserving this homogeneity—the idea of a true melting-pot society being beyond their imagining—they, too, pursued a *verzuiling*-like process, encouraging newcomers to keep to themselves and making it extremely easy for them to do so. Establishment politicians, bureaucrats, journalists, and professors tirelessly drove home the message that the maintenance of a distinct immigrant subculture was a good thing; to think otherwise was, quite simply, to be racist. Indeed, it became a prime tenet of this establishment orthodoxy that any problem associated with immigration was rooted in European racism; keeping this precept at the forefront of the national consciousness became the task of private (but state-funded) agencies with names like SOS Racism and the Anti-Racism Center. This philosophy also shaped the way in which the police and courts operated. By definition, immigrants could not be criminals, only victims; if they did anything wrong, it was because they had experienced great suffering in their homelands or because of European racism.* The consequence of this belief was very passive policing of immigrant communities and incredibly light sentencing of immigrant offenders.

In many Western European countries, indeed, some laws are different for natives than for immigrants. For native Swedes, the minimum age for marriage is eighteen; for immigrants living in Sweden, there is no minimum. In Germany, an ethnic German who marries someone from outside the EU and wants to bring him or her to Germany must answer a long list of questions about the spouse's birth date, daily routine, and so forth in order to prove that the marriage is legitimate and not pro forma; such interviews are not required for German residents with, say, Turkish or Pakistani backgrounds, for it is assumed that their marriages have been arranged and that the spouses will therefore know little or nothing about each other.

Dilsa Demirbag-Sten, an integration expert in Sweden, notes that the situation for immigrant-group girls in her country is deplorable. But the government is next to useless because "the idea that no culture is more equal than another has long been a mantra in Swedish politics." Swedish leaders' notions about immigrants, she states flatly, "are out of touch with reality"; they deny "that certain cultures are more patriarchal than others." They dare not even acknowledge the fact of honor killing: after all, they argue, Swedish parents have been known to kill their children too. (The difference, of course, is that when Swedish parents kill their children, their community doesn't applaud them for it.)

European prisons, moreover, are overwhelmingly Muslim. In France, the figure is 70 percent. Across Europe, prisons have become centers of evangelism, where non-Muslims are converted to Islam and nonreligious Muslims are indoctrinated into fanaticism. In 2004, it was reported that over a hundred Muslim inmates in a Salamanca prison—some of them suspects in the Madrid terrorism of 3/11—were, in effect, in charge of the prison in which they were being held. Housed mostly in one wing of the facility, they'd turned the prison library into a prayer room and kept it off limits to non-Muslims. Prayer calls were broadcast

---

*This mentality is still alive and well. Commenting on the gay-bashing of Chris Crain in Amsterdam, a spokesman for Human Rights Watch said: "There's still an extraordinary degree of racism in Dutch society. Gays often become the victims of this when immigrants retaliate for the inequities that they have to suffer."

over loudspeakers, cell walls were decorated with pictures of Osama bin Laden, and nonpracticing Muslim inmates were being forced to pray. "The wing is theirs," the head of the prison officer's union told the *Guardian*. "The authorities have had no choice but to accept their demands." A member of the staff told *El Mundo* that entering the Muslim section of the prison was like crossing an international border: "We say that we're going to need to carry Maghreb [i.e., North African] passports."

If Wikan speaks of American realism versus European naïveté, one might, with equal validity, contrast America's respect for its immigrants with Europe's condescension to them. America views immigrants as potential assets, Americans in the making, the next wave of bearers of the American dream; Europe views them as needy cases, wards of the state. America treats them as individuals, who, though welcome to retain aspects of their cultures of origin, are expected to think of themselves as free, self-determining Americans; Europe treats them as members of an ethnic and religious group and is less interested in their self-realization as individuals than in the preservation, in Europe, of their group's customs.

Indeed, the European establishment has been reluctant to challenge even the most reprehensible traditions brought to Europe by immigrant groups. Female genital mutilation, for example, takes place in nearly every country of Western Europe; Sweden, Norway, Britain, and France have even passed laws against it. But like many such laws in Europe, they're never enforced. Only in one department of France have serious measures—namely, mandatory medical exams—been instituted to prevent mutilations; but though they've proven spectacularly effective, no other jurisdiction in Europe has adopted similar procedures. Only once, moreover—also in France—has anyone ever been put on trial for subjecting a child to such an operation. (The accused was given a three-year suspended sentence and three years' probation.) The establishment's indifference to such abuse was articulated in 2005 by Dutch politician Edwin van de Haar, who expressed revulsion at French-style proposals for mandatory medical exams: "As a liberal, you shiver" at such proposals, he said.

What about the dumping of European children in Koran schools? Denmark, at least, took action to stop this outrage after the problem was first reported in 2004. But the Norwegian government rejected a similar proposal, arguing that parents have a right to educate their children as they wish. In a country where the law makes it extremely difficult to open a private school (unless it's religion-based) and where state power routinely trumps the parental rights of ethnic Norwegians, this was an absurdly disingenuous line for officials to peddle—a clear affirmation of the double standard whereby ethnic Norwegian children are protected by the state while the Norwegian-born children of immigrants aren't. Erna Solberg, who until recently was Norway's minister in charge of integration, has even suggested that dumping has positive aspects, providing children with "knowledge of their own roots, family, culture, and language, the confidence of knowing 'who one is' and strengthened self-image."

As for forced marriage, the establishment position was succinctly articulated by a Norwegian journalist who, without a trace of irony, described the difference between Western-style consensual matrimony and forced Muslim marriages as a "collision between the individual-oriented West and the family-oriented East." The reporter, not surprisingly, expressed admiration for the "family-oriented" approach and even cited the low Muslim divorce rate as proof that the Muslim way was better— ignoring entirely the fact that wives who are forced to marry are hardly in a position to decide to divorce. (Indeed, Islamic law, while granting men divorce on demand, offers women severely restricted options for divorce.)

Then there's the widespread problem of wife beating. Some estimates suggest that 90 percent of European Muslim wives are physically abused. If an ethnic European husband beats his wife, the police know what to do; when the same police are confronted with spousal abuse in immigrant families, they're likely to see it as a cultural phenomenon that they don't have a right to intrude upon.

One of the most crucial resources for Muslim women and girls in Europe is the network of women's shelters that exists across the Continent. In 2004, four out of five residents at Oslo's main crisis shelter were non-Norwegian. Many had fled husbands who beat or raped them; some, the shelter's manager told *Aftenposten*, had been tormented by several relatives at once: "Uncles and mothers-in-law can be violent. Some have the whole family against them." A number of the women had lived in Norway for years but knew "nothing about Norwegian society." Several had found out about the shelter from their children (whose schooling gave them at least some contact with mainstream society) or from other immigrant women: "When the center takes in the first woman from an ethnic community that it hasn't been in contact with earlier, other women from the same community who are in need of help turn up quickly."

Many men in immigrant communities view such shelters with contempt. In 1999, a British Muslim named Faisal Bodi thundered in the *Guardian* that the shelters "tear apart our families. Once a girl has walked in through their door, they do their best to stop her ever returning home. That is at odds with the Islamic impulse to maintain the integrity of the family." (Bodi made certain to note—as if it definitively established the shelters' loathsome character—"the preponderance of homosexuality among members and staff.") Citing universal Muslim belief in "the shariah, the body of laws defining our faith"—which he described, disconcertingly, as "a sharp sword capable of cutting through the generational and cultural divide"—Bodi argued that British authorities must recognize the Muslim community "as an organic whole" and thus accord it a larger role in resolving conflicts over forced marriage.

Bodi's point was clear: when a Muslim girl or woman flees the tyranny of father or husband, the government should hand her over to a group of Muslim men—who, of course, will either return her to her family for "punishment" or "punish" her themselves. In short, British law should effectively be subordinate to Muslim law, with its insistence on the female obligation to obey and the male right to brutalize. Group identity trumps individual rights.

And honor killing? Here, too, moral equivocation prevails. Unni Wikan, who's written a book on the subject, sympathizes with parents who murder their children (as she does with parents who force their children to marry). For her, they're helpless cogs in a system that's "inhuman toward mothers and fathers." She envisions this "system" not as an ideology shaped by some individuals and subscribed to by other individuals, but as a power in itself, with a life of its own, against which mere humans are incapable of making independent moral decisions. One might in the same way maintain that a guard at Auschwitz was as deserving of pity as the children he shoved into the gas chamber, since he was, after all, a victim of Nazi ideology, compelled by the "system" to commit his crimes.

√ *Jewish lie!*

ALL YOU NEED to know about European authorities' faintness of heart in the face of even the most extreme provocation is the story of Mullah Krekar. The mullah, an Iraqi Kurd guerrilla leader whose real name is Faraj Ahman Najmuddin, entered Norway in 1991 as a "refugee"; his wife and other family members later joined him. In 1994, he founded Islamic Vision, a radical Muslim congregation that received 250,000 kroner—about $35,000—in Norwegian government support between 1996 and 1999. (Government funding for religious institutions is an established practice in Western Europe.)

The "refugee" did not stay put in Norway, however. On 9/11, he was in Iraq, where shortly afterward he set up a guerrilla organization called Ansar al-Islam. He and his fellow guerrillas attacked Iraqi villages, took control of them, and imposed theocratic rule. A resident of the Iraqi village of Biyara described life there after Ansar al-Islam moved in: "CDs were banned, music and songs were forbidden, picnics were banned, and you couldn't play backgammon in the tea shops," he told the *Christian Science Monitor*. "We weren't allowed to wear shorts to play soccer, and whenever they called for prayers, guards visited each house with an adult. Those who failed to go, they beat him hard."

Krekar's name first appeared in the Norwegian media on August 22, 2002, when it was reported that he was under investigation by Norwegian authorities because Ansar al-Islam was said to be developing and producing chemical weapons in collaboration with Al Qaeda. Follow-up stories stated that Norway planned to deport Krekar and his family. At the time, he was still in Iraq, or perhaps Iran. No one seemed to know for sure.

Then came a new angle. On September 1, *Dagbladet* ran an article headlined MY CHILDREN WAIT EVERY SINGLE DAY TO HEAR FROM THEIR DADDY and accompanied by a large close-up photo of Krekar's wife staring plaintively into the camera. It began as follows:

> Mullah Krekar's wife (39) is scared. For her four children, and for the future. A year ago, the family was to have gone on vacation. It didn't happen. Her husband went alone. "The only thing he said before he left was that he didn't know when he would come back, but that he had important work to do in northern Iraq," his wife told *Dagbladet*. His daughter, for her part, denied that Krekar was a terrorist, only "a good Muslim and a kind father."

This article—the first of many that were obviously designed to stir sympathy for Krekar—was followed on September 13 by the news that he'd briefly been arrested in Iran but had since been released and was now on his way to the Netherlands. The next day came news of his arrest at Amsterdam's Schiphol Airport on suspicion of terrorism. Jordan wanted Krekar on drug-smuggling charges (a year later, he and fourteen others were charged by Jordan with planning terrorist acts against United States and Israeli targets), and U.S. officials wanted to talk to him too.

But the Dutch, frowning alike on Jordan's indelicate treatment of suspected terrorists and on America's death penalty, would not extradite
him. Instead, they held him until January, then put him on a plane to
Norway on the understanding that he would be arrested at the airport in
Oslo. But Norwegian authorities—who shared their Dutch colleagues'
unwillingness to hand him over to either Jordan or the United States—
allowed Krekar to walk free.

Since then, the mullah has been a staple of the evening news. In February 2003, his passport was rescinded; in March, shortly after an interview in which he threatened the United States and boasted that he had
suicide bombers at his disposal, Norwegian police took him into custody,
only to release him after less than two weeks. An April 2003 report offered a glimpse of Ansar al-Islam under Krekar, recounting the torture
of a twelve-year-old boy on Krekar's direct instructions and a speech in
which Krekar called 9/11 "a gift from Allah." In September 2003 came
the news that Ansar al-Islam was suspected of being behind the destruction of the UN headquarters in Baghdad the previous month.

Yet such glimpses of Krekar's unpleasant side were rare in Norway's
mainstream media, whose treatment of him continued to be overwhelmingly benign. Gunnar Nyquist describes an August 2003 TV interview
in which "Krekar veritably chuckled in his beard over Norwegian tolerance, which allows terrorists to walk around freely." Krekar defined himself as a "jihadi," but the interviewer (from NRK) didn't ask a follow-up
question; Krekar's praise of bin Laden was on the record, but the interviewer didn't bring it up.

The European justice system has been equally friendly. In August
2003, a Dutch court awarded Krekar 4,970 euros in compensation for
having been imprisoned by the Netherlands; in April of the next year an
appellate court bumped the amount up to 45,000 euros. In mid-2004,
Krekar's Norwegian lawyer announced plans for a lawsuit against the
Norwegian government for malicious prosecution. Among those he
planned to call as witnesses was U.S. secretary of state Colin Powell.

Apparently under pressure from the United States and the Progress
Party, and aware that many Norwegians were tiring of Krekar's charms,
some elected officials sought ways to imprison or deport him—only to
be stymied by bureaucrats for whom no amount of evidence appeared
sufficient. In June 2004, Norway's public prosecutor dropped all out-
standing charges against Krekar, citing insufficient proof. This was a
timely gift: the mullah's autobiography, In My Own Words, had been
brought out a few days earlier by one of Norway's major publishing

houses; now the author—identified in the publisher's catalog as an "Islamic and Kurdish activist"—was able to do PR for his book without the threat of prosecution hanging over him.

Krekar's book (a combination autobiography and primer on Islam) was widely reviewed, and by European standards some of the notices were surprisingly sensible. Tore Rem noted in *Dagbladet* that while the book strengthened the author's image as "a good-natured Teddy Bear," it also reminded readers that "Uncle Mullah . . . is an extreme Islamist with jihad on his agenda." In *Dagsavisen,* Tarjei Skirbekk zeroed in on the book's central paradox: that Krekar, while praising the democracy that had given him shelter, also frankly admitted his desire to overthrow it and institute sharia, and thus embodied "the liberal dilemma of our times." A more familiar note was struck by NRK's reviewer, Tom Egil Hverven. For him, Krekar's book was important because it gave "a voice to a man whom the media and authorities in Norway, the Netherlands, and the U.S. have treated pretty roughly in recent years." Hverven admitted that it wasn't always clear what Krekar meant by "representative government" or "human rights"—but the same, he added, could be said about George W. Bush and then Norwegian prime minister Kjell Magne Bondevik.

Though Krekar's book sold poorly, he continued to bask in the admiration of passersby on the Oslo streets (where I've seen him myself) and to enjoy the support of groups such as SOS Racism and the Anti-Racism Center (which often seem dedicated less to the eradication of racism than to the use of the label "racist" to punish the politically incorrect).* Krekar's popularity got a boost when he took part in an anti–Iraq War protest in early 2003; a reporter wrote that immigrants and ethnic Norwegians alike stopped Krekar to shake his hand. When he gave a talk at a chic Oslo café, he drew an overflow crowd, mostly composed of ethnic Norwegians, and was applauded enthusiastically. The only discordant note was supplied by some fellow Kurds who, during the question-and-answer session, pointed out that Krekar is a murderer of his own people. "You talk about peace, but you kill Kurds!" one of them shouted. Yet this reminder apparently failed to dampen the audience's esteem.

How to make sense of this esteem? Multiculturalism, pure and simple. Ever since large-scale immigration to Europe began about three

*It was SOS Racism that organized a 2004 Kristallnacht commemoration in Oslo from which Jews were ejected for carrying Israeli flags.

decades ago, the European establishment has encouraged a romantic view of Muslim immigrants. In the establishment's eyes, they are, by definition, victims. To criticize any Muslim for any reason whatsoever is racist, and it is that racism that is the sole cause of any and all immigrant-related problems. As a rule, the establishment strives to overlook the fact that being a Muslim is a matter of holding certain beliefs and living (and dying) by them; it prefers instead to think of Muslim identity as having to do with cuisine, clothing, and skin color. Consequently there's an automatic tendency to view the likes of Krekar not as someone whose beliefs are a challenge to Western democracy but as an opportunity to prove one is not racist. To the extent that the establishment does acknowledge the reality of such phenomena as intolerance, sexual inequality, self-segregation, spousal abuse, and forced marriage within the immigrant community, it chooses to view them as aspects of cultural difference that simply must be accepted in a "multicultural society."

Though cracks have begun to form in this ideological edifice, establishment orthodoxy still stands firm. Take historian Lin Silje Nilsen, who in June 2003 spoke out in favor of the proposal to establish a sharia court in Norway. Basing her position on the concept of "collective rights" and the right of minorities to "protect their cultural and religious identity," Nilsen argued that what mattered most was "the desire for a dignified life for all and sensitivity to differences"—by which, of course, she meant differences among cultures, not individuals. "Does individualism have its boundaries?" she asked. "Is it right to ask questions about rigid enforcement of universal, individual rights?" Her implicit answer: yes. This is European establishment thinking in a nutshell.

Marching in intellectual lockstep with Nilsen was the religious scholar Jeanette Sky, who reflected as follows:

> In Oslo, there is doubtless someone who has lived directly over or under Mullah Krekar. Someone has perhaps picked up an orange just as it rolled out of his shopping basket in [the predominantly Muslim neighborhood of] Tøyen without thinking that the man could be a possible terrorist, and the orange, in another connection, a grenade. Or perhaps he is not some terrorist, perhaps he is only a peaceful Muslim out shopping for groceries? Are we in the process of creating make-believe visions of the foreigner?

The leaps of logic here were typical of establishment rhetoric. Sky pretended to criticize "make-believe visions of the foreigner," but this was precisely what she was proffering: against all evidence, she was reimagining Krekar as "a peaceful Muslim." Noting that conspiracy theories, science fiction, and fantasy often involve a dread of imaginary aliens, she suggested that perhaps our fear of the foreigners who live among us in today's globalized world is likewise all in our imagination. The problem, she proposed, is not terrorism but (naturally) America, which is engaged in a "neo-imperialism" that is as "invisible, unnameable, and omnipresent" as terrorism—the difference, of course, being that terrorism, unlike imperialism, may not be real. Sky concluded: "When the enemy is invisible, it is not good to know what is hidden in an orange in Tøyen. But it could well be that the enemy was an illusion and that the orange only offered sweet surprises."

Incoherent? Yes. But when you're in the business of dodging undeniable truths, clarity is your enemy. Sky wasn't trafficking in ideas; she was serving up a rhetorical smorgasbord of social-democratic comfort food. And the pièce de résistance was that most cherished (and condescending) of Norwegian establishment dogmas: that Muslim immigrants offer nothing but "sweet surprises"—exoticism, foreignness, a splash of color on the snow-white northern landscape. Oranges! To sustain this orthodoxy, Sky was obliged to write as if terrorists don't exist, aren't goaded on by mullahs like Krekar, and aren't cheered by millions of Muslims (many of them living in Tøyen). Her bizarre comments served as a reminder that in mid-2003, there were still places in the West where it was possible to insulate oneself intellectually from the reality of 9/11.

In Norwegian, *snill* means "nice," and clueless characters like Jeanette Sky are sometimes referred to (by those who dare to address such matters candidly) as *snillister*—politically correct types for whom the most important thing is to be seen as nice. The closest equivalent term in English is "do-gooder." Norway's *snillister* consider themselves pro-Muslim; yet their see-no-evil attitude toward the autocrats who run the Muslim community makes them, in effect, the enemies of those within that community who despise the autocrats' tyranny and wish to live as free, equal citizens of a Western democracy.

One such immigrant is Walid al-Kubaisi. Originally from Iraq, al-Kubaisi in 1996 published a splendid book, *My Faith, Your Myth*, in which he recounts a conversation with a classic *snillist* who ran a Norwegian "international cultural center." The center hosted activities by various ethnic groups, providing each with its own separate space; when al-Kubaisi criticized this arrangement for encouraging a "ghetto mentality," the director demurred, asserting his intention to showcase cultures and provide "exotic atmosphere."

> "But isn't it more important [al-Kubaisi inquired] for immigrants to learn about Norwegian culture and values than for foreigners to . . . provide you and other Norwegians with a little exotic atmosphere?"
>
> "It isn't our job to teach them Norwegian culture," he replied. "They can decide about that for themselves, if they wish. Foreigners have a rich culture. You mustn't think that way. It causes lots of problems. We have our culture, and you have your culture."
>
> "No, I'm thinking for example about values such as freedom of expression and religion," I replied.
>
> "Yes, of course these Norwegian values concern you Muslims also. We have religious freedom and this allows you Muslims to practice your Islam freely. . . . You can slaughter animals in a Muslim way in order to eat your Islamic meat. . . . You can make use of your freedom of expression to tell others about Islam and your fascinating culture; you can criticize Norwegian racists. . . ."

But what, al-Kubaisi asked, about the freedom of Muslims to criticize their religion—or even convert? The director was displeased.

> "You are a Muslim, Walid, and you must not lose your identity. If you become Norwegian, we will not see you as you are. You must be yourself."
>
> "But do you believe that I will lose my identity if I believe in freedom of expression . . . ?"
>
> "Listen. This is something you decide for yourself. But your attitude causes a lot of problems. We want to create a multicultural society, and we don't want to dissolve these foreign cultures. Your attitude alters all our plans. It creates conflicts between immigrants. I'm a culture worker, not a conflict worker," he said.

This cultural bureaucrat's remarks capture European establishment political correctness to a tee. If ethnic Europeans are viewed as individuals, even those Muslim immigrants who openly try to distance themselves from the Muslim community are seen as members of a group whose common identity is determined entirely by skin color, ethnicity, and religious background. If ethnic Europeans may choose to belong to any religion or none, but are expected to respect the law, Muslims are "religious beings by nature" and, as such, "cannot be expected to conform to European law and culture." As al-Kubaisi points out, such thinking "leads automatically to a view of Muslims as inferior"—and, one might add, not only works against integration but seems to view it as thoroughly undesirable.

For al-Kubaisi, that conversation with the "culture worker" was far from unique. After publicly criticizing slavery and female genital mutilation in the Islamic world, al-Kubaisi was attacked not only by an imam (who ominously compared him to Salman Rushdie) but by the head of a Norwegian government refugee office, who publicly supported the imam and reproached al-Kubaisi for hurting Muslims' feelings. On another occasion, a Norwegian writer, himself a vocal critic of Christianity, was angered by an essay of al-Kubaisi's that criticized Islam, for it would (he said) incite racism. The message of such anecdotes is clear: immigrants who embrace free speech and individual rights can expect harsh rebukes from the Norwegian establishment for criticizing or abandoning their culture or religion; immigrants who condemn democratic values in the name of culture or religion can expect to be congratulated for it.*

The Swiss Muslim scholar Tariq Ramadan is widely seen as the leading voice of European Islam, a bridge between European Muslims and non-Muslims, and the prophet and potential architect of a "Euro-Islam" that would involve a compromise of values on the part of both Muslims and non-Muslims in Europe. The usual argument for his importance as a bridge between cultures is that he's as liberal as one can dare to be and still receive a respectful hearing from ordinary Muslims. In 2003 Nicolas Sarkozy, France's then minister of the interior, challenged Ramadan to demonstrate his moderation by doing two things: one, tell Muslim women to remove their veils, and two, declare his opposition to the stoning of adulteresses. Ramadan refused the first request; in response to the second, he suggested a "moratorium" on stoning. "That way," he said, "you start a dialogue."

Ramadan (who's been denied entry into both America and France because of his alleged terrorist ties, but who in August 2005 was named by Tony Blair to a government panel delegated to help curb Muslim

---

*Alas, since the American invasion of his homeland, Iraq, al-Kubaisi has written several articles bitterly attacking the United States and characterizing the terrorist insurgency as a legitimate resistance movement.

violence) has written that European Muslims "are bound by the law in their country of residency to the degree that they are not thus compelled to act against their Muslim conscience." This tells us absolutely nothing. The question is, to what extent *does* their "Muslim conscience" compel them to violate European laws? Ramadan—who plainly seeks to do for European Muslims what Jerry Falwell did for American evangelicals— argues strenuously for their increased involvement in European politics. And how would he like European Muslims to use the power they ac- quire? The answer is implicit in his lament that while Europe gives Mus- lims the "freedom to believe 'whatever' in private . . . the public sphere's power of attraction, with its 'sacred values' based on individualism, money, and entertainment, is so strong that it seems illusory to think that any kind of opposition could be possible. It is as if we are imprisoned by freedom." This, then, is Ramadan's message: Western freedom is slavery; only within the confines of strict Muslim law and practice can Muslims find *true* freedom, in Europe or anywhere else.

COMPOUNDING ALL the problems I've enumerated here is a single colossal fact: Western Europe desperately needs immigrants. The native population is aging and its numbers are on the wane. In the years to come, more and more workers will be needed to keep national economies from shrinking and to help pay for mounting retirement ben- efits and hospitalization costs.

Yet there's no reason why the difficulties posed by fundamentalist Is- lam should prevent Western Europe from maintaining a steady flow of immigrants. Authorities must simply be more careful about whom they let in—and treat them differently when they do. They must stop think- ing of immigrants as charity cases and start thinking of them as equals who are ready, willing, and able to pull their own weight. They need not stop importing people from the Muslim world: millions of Muslims have no fondness for sharia law and, given the opportunity to live and work in a free country, would prove themselves valuable, loyal assets to their new homelands. And there are countless Christians, Jews, and Hindus (not to mention gays) who, though lifelong citizens of Muslim countries, have been treated like second-class citizens and would leap at the chance to live in the West.

Then there's the non-Muslim world. Many immigrants from East Asia, in particular, have proven themselves highly adaptive to Western ways, very skilled at starting businesses, and deeply appreciative of the blessings of democracy—not to mention hardworking and law-abiding. One evening, dining at a Vietnamese restaurant in Oslo, I saw the proprietress at a nearby table, helping her little girl with her homework. They spoke Norwegian—the mother's shaky, the child's fluent. It was a classic image of successful immigration. So was the sight of a man from India who, on the Norwegian version of *Who Wants to Be a Millionaire?*, answered a flurry of difficult questions correctly about distinctly Nordic subjects. I could make a long list of such moments when I've been vouchsafed glimpses of immigration success stories in Europe.

Time and again, moreover, I've encountered immigrants who've brought values and habits to Norway that the country needs more of. In our Oslo neighborhood, many of the local merchants—the counterman at the newspaper kiosk, the corner greengrocer—are non-Western immigrants. One of the first things I noticed after moving to Norway was how much friendlier they tended to be than Norwegians in similar jobs. They would smile, make chitchat, remember you on a return visit and greet you warmly. This was no surprise: in the countries that provide Norway with most of its immigrants—and certainly throughout the Arab and Muslim world—customer service is a veritable art form. Not in Norway. The concept of service is not indigenous in the land of the fjords; in order to be able to refer to it, the Norwegian language had to borrow the word "service," spelling and all, and Norwegians pronounce it like a foreign word. Yet many Norwegians, I've learned, don't quite understand its meaning: they often use it interchangeably with *tjeneste*, which means "favor." The idea that treating customers civilly is not a matter of doing them a favor but rather of doing one's job—let alone advancing one's own self-interest—can often seem an alien concept in Norway. The non-Western immigrants working behind Oslo's counters add a touch of genuine service-mindedness that strikes me as very positive; I hope some of it will rub off on the natives.

Europeans like to sneer about American friendliness, which they invariably describe as superficial or fake. They mock American tourists who, pushing their phone numbers on casual acquaintances, say "Look us up if you're ever in our neck of the woods." They can't possibly mean it, Europeans say. But they *do* mean it. Most Europeans can't conceive of people who let others into their lives and homes so readily. "New Yorkers have a reputation for being rude," the Dutch writer Stephan Sanders told me over dinner in Amsterdam. "But in fact they're very polite. And other Americans are *extremely* polite, especially in the Midwest. It's shocking, really. When I was first in Minneapolis and strangers on the street or in a shop would say hello and smile at me, I thought they were drug dealers or were coming on to me or something. In fact they were just being neighborly. To a Dutch person, it's amazing."

But Americans' readiness to invite people into their homes is of a piece with their history of welcoming immigrants and accepting them as fellow Americans. For if Europeans can't believe in the genuineness of Americans' willingness to open up their homes to near strangers, neither can they conceive of a country whose people, while proudly (and, in their eyes, excessively) patriotic, are also delighted to extend full and equal national identity to any foreigner willing to learn the language and get a job. Europeans, as I gradually came to understand, will allow immigrants into their country; they'll pay high taxes so that their government can dole out (forever, if necessary) rent support, child benefits, and so forth; and they'll refer to these newcomers piously as "our new fellow countrymen." But they won't *really* think of them as being Norwegian or Dutch. And something deep inside of them rebels mightily against the idea of immigrants living among them as respected, fully equal professionals.

It's this politically correct attitude that's helped turn educated, well-off young European Muslims like Mohammed Bouyeri into terrorists. To discourage the children and grandchildren of immigrants from identifying with the country of their birth and from bearing allegiance to its values is to encourage them to look elsewhere for something to identify with. Such multicultural conduct isn't an act of generosity—it's an act of cultural self-hatred and cultural suicide.

In English we have a word for fear of foreigners: *xenophobia*. It's a rare word, seldom seen in print, almost never actually spoken, and probably unfamiliar to most English speakers. Most northern European languages have words that mean the same thing. These words are frequently used in conversation and are familiar to every native speaker. In Norwegian, the word in question is *fremmedfrykt*. And while this word is often used unfairly to label anyone who criticizes any aspect of the immigrant communities, there is in fact a real element of *fremmedfrykt* among northern Europeans.

Indeed, it's not going too far to say that there's a species of bigotry, widespread in Europe, that trumps anything you can easily find in the United States. While living in the Netherlands, I began to see that despite their reputation for openness and tolerance, the Dutch were, by comparison with most Americans, intensely aware of ethnic differences. Yes, they respected the unwritten social code that forbade racial or ethnic slurs. But what people said in the public square and what they said to trusted intimates were two different things. And in fact the longer I stayed in the Netherlands, the more I noticed the words *binnenlands* (domestic) and *buitenlands* (foreign), as well as *autochtoon* (native) and *allochtoon* (foreigner), cropping up in all kinds of contexts. To the Dutch, it sometimes seemed, the single most important thing about you was whether you were one of them or not—and they could be surprisingly resentful of those (such as myself) who sought to cross the line from *buiten* to *binnen*.

At the hotel I stayed at in Amsterdam, one of the desk clerks surprised me by waxing moralistic about my desire to live in the Netherlands. "Every apartment being offered to a foreigner," he pronounced in a tone of profound moral censure, "is an apartment being denied to a Dutch person!" This was the same man whom I overheard cheerfully giving advice to hotel patrons as to how they might go about securing the paid sexual services of Dutch teenagers.

This attitude doesn't extend to immigrants from elsewhere in Western Europe, or at least not to the citizens of regional neighbors (in Norway, Swedes and Danes are not thought of as foreigners but as "cousins"). But it does extend to North Americans, as I discovered on my first visit to my new doctor in Oslo. An American who speaks several languages and has a degree from a leading U.S. medical school, he told me how he'd been turned down more than once for a license in Norway and had to sue in order to get one—this in a country starving for medical personnel. On a television program about immigrants, an Indian engineer with extremely impressive credentials (and fluent Norwegian) told of having applied for several hundred jobs with no success.

Walid al-Kubaisi tells of an immigrant from a non-Western country who left Norway for eight years to attend medical school and complete his internship and residency. On his return, he went to the social services department to ask for help in finding a job. (That's how things work in Norway.) He was told that they couldn't help him find a medical position—but that if he wanted to be a trainee at a grocery store, they'd be glad to be of service. And if he insisted on being a doctor? "Go to your country and work as a doctor there, but not here!" he was told.* Norwegians pride themselves on their humanitarian aid to wide-eyed children

---

*Hirsi Ali, now a member of the Dutch parliament, had a similar experience when she first arrived in the Netherlands as a Somali refugee. As Alexander Linklater wrote in the *Guardian*, "ponderous well-meaning labour officers . . . kept directing her to work she didn't want. The idea that she might go to university was dismissed."

in Africa—but something in them rebels against the idea of one of those children growing up to become a Norwegian doctor. Across Europe, that's the attitude: millions in aid, but not a penny in salary.

I thought about this when the Norwegian Nobel Committee awarded its Peace Prize to Wangari Maathai of Kenya. For weeks, Norwegian journalists and politicians heaped praise upon her. All I could think was this: if Maathai had immigrated to Norway thirty years ago, she'd have spent her life cleaning toilets. Europeans love celebrating a person like Maathai—as long as she's in the Third World.

I've had my own encounters with this mentality. After moving to Oslo, I began scouring the want ads. At first I just applied for the kind of work I'd done before—editing, teaching, writing. The opening for which I was most conspicuously qualified was a university position. In Norway, as part of the pretense that the hiring process is fair and objective, everyone who applies for a job in higher education receives a document outlining his and all the other applicants' résumés and publications. Looking at this document, I quickly saw that my qualifications easily outstripped those of all the other applicants, most of whom were very recent graduates of Norwegian universities. I also more than fulfilled the Norwegian language requirement. Nonetheless I was removed from the list of candidates without even being offered an interview, and officially labeled "unqualified." Given that the Norwegian university system is notorious for the low quality of its faculty, especially in my own field, it was obvious that I was being punished for that blue passport in my desk drawer.

Such treatment is standard practice in much of Western Europe. There's a powerful resistance to the idea of foreigners taking "good jobs"—or, for that matter, not-so-good jobs. (This is one reason why the most well educated—and thus, usually, most liberal and easily integrated—immigrants from the Muslim world go to America and the more illiterate, reactionary ones tend to end up in Europe.)

Like millions of other immigrants, I ended up learning a lesson: in Europe, generally speaking, only the most undesirable employment is available for people with foreign-sounding names or foreign-looking faces. This fact was demonstrated quite elegantly in the spring of 2005, when a Paraguayan immigrant to Norway told about the difficulty he'd had finding work. He'd spent two years applying for positions in the field of environmental therapy, but hadn't gotten so much as a nibble. Finally, in desperation, he legally changed his name from Lidio Dominguez to Nils Myrland. Myrland, he said wryly, became a "much sought-after man." He was called in for interviews, and less than three weeks after changing his name he had a job.

So it goes. In much of Western Europe, the less qualified native routinely wins out over the more qualified foreigner. As I've often said, Norway is a great place to be Norwegian, if your only ambition is to get by: unless you really work at screwing things up for yourself, the system will make it easy for you to slide along through life, whether you make an effort or not. You're not expected to have much in the way of a work ethic (indeed, too much drive can turn people off); the rates of sick-day absences in Norway and Sweden are the world's highest, and after a few months' employment (and this is true in the Netherlands and other parts of Western Europe, too) it's almost impossible to get fired, no matter how lazy or incompetent you might turn out to be.

Americans think of Europeans as being cosmopolitan, sophisticated, international-minded. Certainly Europeans see themselves that way. In fact, they're far more traditionalist and nativist than we are. Mauricio Rojas, a Chilean-Swedish economic historian, has described his adopted country as "a tribal society. . . . A *good* tribe! Very peaceful and nice! But a tribe." I would say exactly the same thing about Norway: despite the high level of Americanization (7-Elevens on every corner, American music playing everywhere), tribal customs predominate to an extent I never would have imagined before moving here. For example, though the great majority of Norwegians have stopped going to church or believing in anything in particular, confirmation remains a beloved universal rite of passage, far outstripping its role among Christians in America. Indeed, in order to accommodate fiercely antireligious Norwegian parents who refuse to allow their children to participate in a ceremony in such a backward institution as the Church of Norway, the Norwegian state offers something called "civil confirmation." It's a spectacularly meaningless concept—a nonreligious religious rite—but I've never heard anyone in Norway either criticize it or joke about it.

Confirmation is just one of many cozy old customs by which Norwegians define themselves. The spectacle on May 17 (Constitution Day) of men, women, and children parading up and down the main streets of their towns in the nineteenth-century folk costumes known as *bunad;* the claustrophobia of the Christmas season, from the jolly, aquavit-fueled preholiday employee dinners of *pinnekjøtt* (salted and dried ribs of mutton) and *lutefisk* (dried cod treated with lye) to the decoration of the tree (with, quite often, strings of little Norwegian flags) to the week of "home-coziness" between December 25 and New Year's Day; wedding dinners at which the bridal couple is honored with long Victorian orations—all these things are aspects of the experience of being Norwegian, and they're all things that Norwegians plainly don't want to change, and that they can't easily imagine immigrants, especially Muslim immigrants, becoming a part of. Indeed, they don't really *want* outsiders to take part in these traditions. Yet at the same time they think they believe in integration. The truth is that they don't understand the radical process that is true integration—a process that's been a part of American life for generations.

Not that Americans came by it easily. No, we learned it step by step. First the descendants of Britons learned to accept other northern European Protestants—Germans, Scandinavians—as fellow Americans. Then they had to become even more open and accept southern and eastern Europeans—Russian Jews, Polish and Italian Catholics, Orthodox Greeks—as Americans. Later still, they learned to accept Latin Americans, East Asians, and others. No step was without its problems. For many, alas, the hardest step of all was—is—accepting members of the non-Anglo-Saxon groups that were there before any others: native Americans and blacks. But acceptance has grown. And the result is a concept of American identity that's fluid and open to a degree that Western Europeans still don't get and fail to respect sufficiently and are nowhere near being able to emulate.

So it goes across much of Europe: the reflexive, inflexible clinging to native customs; the identification of nationality with ethnic identity; and the equation of membership in the society with an attachment to long-standing tribal traditions—all this is still part of the fabric of Europe, and it continues to make true, full, American-style integration next to impossible.

The more I thought about such things, the more I saw how American I was in my thinking about races and ethnic groups—and, by European standards, how radical. For most Europeans, a foreigner was unalterably foreign. An immigrant might live next door to you for decades, but he'd always remain, in some fundamental sense, an alien. This wasn't the way things worked in America. Growing up in Queens, I never for a moment thought of myself as part Polish, German, French, English, Scottish, Scots-Irish, and Welsh—I was an American kid, the product of a society that had rejected the European way of thinking about such things. One day, years after moving to Europe, I found the last names of my childhood neighbors and classmates rolling through my mind. Huber. Cino. Salholz. Friedman. Maurer. Kunz. Toohy. Conticelli. Fedorowich. Diaz. Schmiemann. Levine. Wojnicki. Ikeda. Timony. Paluszek. After years of living in Norway, I heard those names in a different way. I suddenly realized I'd grown up in the middle of a veritable United Nations of names. (A *real* UN, not that sinkhole of feckless bureaucracy on First Avenue.) And I'd never given a thought to it. It just *was*. And that was the beauty of it. The sound of those names—names that reached back through the generations to people of more primitive times who had hated, persecuted, enslaved, and made war on one another—was the music of America. It was one more thing I'd taken for granted all my life.

II

9/11 and After:
Blaming Americans and Jews

AT AROUND 3:15 Central European Time on the afternoon of September 11, 2001, I was writing at my desk in Oslo when I decided I needed to check a fact online. At the Yahoo home page I noticed a news entry dated only a minute or two earlier. A plane had struck the World Trade Center. I went straight to the TV and switched on CNN. Moments later, I saw the second plane strike.

For me, as for millions of others, the next few hours were utterly transforming—and clarifying.

Never had I felt more American. At the same time, I felt a new sense of urgency regarding the need for unity between the two continents I called home. Adherents of the extreme Islam that had gained a foothold in urban centers across Western Europe had now attacked my hometown—a metropolis that was the world's preeminent symbol of everything the West stood for and that fundamentalist Muslims despised.

I'd moved from New York to Europe as if from one world to another. Yet 9/11 made me realize I'd never left home. For in a larger sense, whether I was in America or Europe didn't matter. Together, America and Europe made up the West, the heartland of democracy; and both were now at war with a common enemy. Until 9/11, my encounters with fundamentalist Islam in Europe had seemed unconnected to my life in America. Now, in a matter of minutes, the world had been made smaller. New York and Oslo were one.

As I watched the day's events unfold, it seemed clear to me that such a provocation called for an overwhelming response. But others in Western Europe, it turned out, disagreed. Many, following the lead of their media and politicians, reacted to this atrocity as if it had been a natural disaster—an earthquake or tidal wave. This attitude would persist long afterward: routinely, the Western European press would refer to 9/11 as a "tragedy," never an act of war. Nor, I soon came to understand, did most Western Europeans see it as an attack on *them*. They couldn't—or didn't—want to recognize that an anti-Western jihad was under way; they wanted to believe that the attack was a statement of rage and despair about poverty (which was somehow America's fault) or U.S. imperialism or U.S. support of Israel. Thus, on the evening of 9/11, at our customary watering hole, friends and acquaintances all but stood in line to offer their heartfelt condolences to me, an American and a New Yorker. During the next couple of days, most of Europe seemed to share their sympathy. Headlines across the Continent proclaimed "We Are All Americans." Only later would I realize how shallow and contingent those expressions of solidarity were.

On September 12, a Palestinian who identified himself to a reporter as a member of Hezbollah stood outside the U.S. embassy in Oslo and cheered the carnage, his small son at his side. The Norwegian police reacted instantly—by politely asking him to go home.

Nothing, really, had changed. Yet for some time I believed—or hoped—otherwise. *All right*, I thought, *now the nonsense will end. After this, Western Europeans will see that we're all in this together. The free world is at war with religious fanatics who despise democracy. Not even the extreme leftists who sympathized with Communism can work up empathy for these murderous maniacs.*

But I was wrong. As the days and weeks went by—and as it became clear that America, instead of apologizing or engaging in dialogue or pretending that nothing had happened, was planning to react to 9/11 by invading Afghanistan—the response from many quarters of Western Europe was like nothing I'd ever seen. It wasn't just a matter of friendly disagreement about how best to respond to a common enemy. It was an increasingly vicious, irrational, and twisted howl of America hatred. In Italy, Nobel Prize–winning playwright Dario Fo accused the United States of killing "tens of millions of people with poverty" every year and called the mass murders of 9/11 "legitimate" for this reason. In Germany, composer Karlheinz Stockhausen described the attack on the World Trade Center as "the greatest work of art imaginable for the whole cosmos." And in Britain, the novelist Martin Amis accused America of having "destroyed at least 5% of the Iraqi population" through UN sanctions. The American writer Anne Applebaum, who was in London at the time, noted a shift in attitude after no more than thirty-six hours. In a September 16 column, she described a BBC talk show on which a former U.S. ambassador to Britain—who'd lost several colleagues in the attacks—was nearly brought to tears by the brutal anti-American rhetoric of his fellow guests.

Plainly, the Western European establishment, while loath to deal responsibly with real threats, was good at kicking its friends while they were down.

Was 9/11 "an attack on us all"? No, insisted bestselling author Jan Guillou in Sweden's *Aftonbladet* on September 17. "The terrorists were attacking U.S. imperialism. . . . The U.S. is the greatest mass murderer of our time." Dismissing the sentiment that "we are all Americans," they maintained: "we are Europeans. We are the only power on earth that can stand up against the Americans if they go ahead with their proposed plans to start a long and holy war. A war between the world's white people and the world's Muslims would, if nothing else, lead to a disaster of biblical proportions here in Europe, where perhaps 40 million of our fellow citizens are Muslims."

Norwegian author Gert Nygårdshaug agreed. "In recent weeks we've been fooled into thinking that we are Americans," he complained on October 6. "So wily and well-calculated is this Pentagon-directed act of deceit . . . that Norway's and Europe's population is now being scared into believing that the next time terror strikes, it can be at Oslo Airport, in Rome, or Copenhagen." Nygårdshaug wasn't buying it:

> Since the middle of the 1960s, the U.S. has more or less carried out a continual war against the world's poor people. . . . Travel around the world and ask! Talk to people in Latin America, in Egypt, Sudan, or Pakistan! . . . If you have the Stars and Stripes on your backpack . . . you're guaranteed to be met with openly hateful attitudes. But if you're wearing a Norwegian, French or Italian flag? Sheer goodwill and all smiles.

As Nygårdshaug wrote that, body parts were still being dug out at Ground Zero.

On September 21 a couple of Norwegian "peace scholars" named Birgit Brock-Utne and Gunnar Garbo complained in *Dagbladet* that the deaths of a few thousand people in New York were getting more attention than the million-plus that had died in the Iran–Iraq War or the hundreds of thousands massacred in Rwanda and Burundi. The answer to violence, they insisted, is not more violence; rather, "we must try to understand" what drove the terrorists to commit such a desperate act—namely, poverty—and not see them as inhuman. The authors stated (as if it were a universally accepted truth) that the Cold War had been based on mutual misunderstanding—neither side had really intended to threaten the other. For the United States after 9/11, the lesson in this was to do everything it could to avoid being perceived as threatening or demonizing others.

Four days later, it was reported that twelve Norwegian "professors, college lecturers, and other intellectuals" had issued a proposal that George W. Bush be nominated for the Nobel Peace Prize. The premise was that if he knew he had a chance of winning this glorious award—the pride of Norway—he wouldn't "set the world ablaze." I didn't know whether to laugh or cry. It read like a parody of provincialism at its most pathetic. History had taken a dramatic turn, and a dozen high-profile Norwegian academics (among them "peace professor" Johan Galtung) had proven beyond a shadow of a doubt that they were utterly clueless.

Afghanistan was invaded on October 7. Eastern Europeans, with their memories of Communism, had no problem understanding what it was about: hours after the invasion, Czech president Václav Havel proclaimed his "absolute support for this operation," which, he wrote, was "protecting the values of civilization." His colleagues in Western Europe, however, were more interested in playing moral equivalency games. *Dagbladet* journalist Line Fransson compared Bush to bin Laden: "Both use God to justify their actions. . . . And both say that they are defenders of the weak in society, and that justice will win in the end." Norwegian Parliament member Olav Gunnar Ballo equated the bombing of Afghanistan with 9/11.

The invasion occasioned demonstrations in every capital of Europe. And the media lost no time in describing it as a failure, a disaster, a quagmire. Less than three weeks after it began, *Dagbladet*'s editors, in their wisdom, decided that the time had come "to reevaluate the strategy against the Taliban and bin Laden." A day later Sweden's *Aftonbladet* condemned the NATO bombing as terrorism.

In November 2001 the Taliban fell—and none of those who'd used the word "quagmire" admitted their error. The focus simply turned to Iraq—and the anti-American fury just kept intensifying. I kept thinking it couldn't get any worse—and it just kept getting worse. It seemed as if every time I picked up a paper or checked out a Western European news Web site, I found somebody declaring the Atlantic alliance dead. For Norwegian journalist John Olav Egeland, the last straw was Abu Ghraib. Invoking an image of the Statue of Liberty using her torch as an instrument of torture, Egeland declared Norway's close ties to America broken at last: "Europe is a better alternative than Washington."

In all this, to be sure, there was a certain (shall we say) duplicity. Even as politicians and the media raged at America, most of the countries of Western Europe sent troops to help liberate Afghanistan, and several—Britain, Denmark, Spain, and Italy—took part in the invasion of Iraq. The situation in Norway was illuminating. Its government refused to help overthrow Saddam, and members of the Parliament and cabinet denounced America's "unilateral" actions loudly and often. At the same time, however, the unflappable, tough-as-nails defense minister Kristin Krohn Devold, a loyal friend of America (and a good chum of Norwegian-American Donald Rumsfeld), talked publicly as if the two countries were still solid allies and, one gathered, did what she could under the circumstances to aid the United States. Reading between the lines, one had the impression that across Western Europe, certain grown-ups in positions of responsibility (especially in regard to national security) who recognized the merit of America's position and the importance of NATO ties worked behind the scenes to preserve the alliance while the children cavorted onstage, doing their "Bush equals Saddam" act.*

Yet the fact remained that the European establishment, guided by what it obviously considered high principle, was dead set against George W. Bush's post-9/11 strategy. Indeed, it gradually became clear that the aftermath of that cataclysmic day's events had exposed a raft of fundamental philosophical differences between America and Europe regarding peace and war, freedom and tyranny. For me, as an American living in post-9/11 Europe, the cognitive dissonance was often through the roof. Europeans seemed to inhabit another mental universe—one where America was the enemy, Bush was a greater threat than Osama bin

---

*In 2005, "peace researcher" Stein Tønnesson complained about the Norwegian government's "Janus-face—one turned toward the U.S., one toward Norway."

Laden, and Israel, the only democracy in the Middle East, was the sole reason for that region's ills. As I traveled around Europe after 9/11, I found myself confronted again and again with these irrational views.

Yes, there were sensible arguments against invading Iraq—and those arguments figured significantly in the American debate. (For example, why go after Saddam, who had nothing to do with 9/11, when so many terrorists were citizens of our supposed ally Saudi Arabia?) But such arguments were hardly to be found in the Western European media. To believe most politicians, professors, and journalists in Western Europe, America was simply using 9/11 as an excuse to grab oil. Or to pursue its imperialistic goals. Or George W. Bush was being a cowboy.* Or he was making war for domestic political reasons. Or he was the mere puppet of a pro-Israel Jewish cabal that was out to destroy Islam.

The European media made little effort to support these claims. And they played a capricious game of mix and match, combining these theories or switching from one to the other with a breathtaking lack of seriousness. One got a distinct picture of an elite so removed from the realities of international affairs, and perhaps so irked by its own irrelevance in the global scheme of things, and most of all quite simply incapable of grasping the sentiments behind American rhetoric about freedom versus tyranny, that it could not see the Iraq invasion as anything more than an opportunity to hold up, like an Olympic torch, the European love of peace and dialogue and to contrast it tirelessly with the primitive American lust for war. Aging journalists who'd never gotten over the war in Vietnam—and who'd always seen it through a Marxist lens—leapt at the chance to echo the American left's line that Iraq would be another Vietnam. What bliss to be able once more to dig their claws so deeply into America's miserable hide! It was like being young all over again.

So it was that one day a few weeks before the invasion of Iraq, I received an e-mail telling me about something called the "Hello America!" campaign. It had been launched in Oslo on January 6, and it was "now being spread all over the world" to "carpet bomb the world with a message of support for all peace loving Americans." I was asked to sign my name to the attached message and forward it to my "friends and contacts," as well as to President Bush, Vice President Cheney, and several

*Cartoons of Bush as a cowboy were ubiquitous in the European papers. The idea was that he was an unimaginative fool—but what could be less imaginative than an endless succession of witless cowboy caricatures?

This charge has grounds!

U.S. news organizations, all of whose e-mail addresses were provided. And what was the message? This:

HELLO AMERICA!

The USA is on the brink of war. An aggressive and unpredictable leader is spreading fear and insecurity. His name is George W. Bush.

Mr. Bush possesses massive arsenals of weapons of mass destruction.

He claims he has the right to use them.

He was never elected by a majority of his people.

(32% of adult Americans voted for Bush. He got 539,989 less votes than opponent Al Gore)

He leads a regime, where he himself—and a rich elite—enjoy enormous wealth and growing privileges, while millions live in poverty and despair.

People of ethnic minorities are oppressed and humiliated.

His country ranks highest in the world with regard to *not* signing human rights treaties.

We thank you, America!

We know that most Americans want peace, prosperity and justice for all.

You are good people, like most people are, in Iraq, Israel, Palestine, Korea, Ukraine, Australia, Norway, Mexico, Canada, Germany, Indonesia, Brazil, India, Bolivia, Iran, Uganda, Portugal and elsewhere.

We thank you for giving us Abraham Lincoln, Bessie Smith, Elvis Presley, Franklin D. Roosevelt, Hank Williams, Martin Luther King jr., Toni Morrison, Jimi Hendrix, Jesse Owens, Woody Allen, Miles Davis, Ernest Hemingway, Helen Keller, Madonna, John Steinbeck, Jimmy Carter, Julia Roberts, Muhammad Ali and many more. *Add here patriot David Duke!*

If we can do anything to help you get rid of George W. Bush before he wrecks your reputation and messes up the whole planet, please let us know!

What a masterpiece of naive miscalculation! Though its authors were patently out to win Americans over to the antiwar side, their extreme condescension, and the audacity with which they presumed to lecture Americans about U.S. history, economics, and politics, seemed tailor-made to antagonize. The offer to help "get rid of" Bush was a dark touch: previous presidents (Lincoln, Garfield, McKinley, Kennedy) had been "gotten rid of," too.

What's more, if the document's authors were serious about listing America's contributions to the world, why hadn't they mentioned—along with Lincoln and Elvis—the role of Americans in such inventions and discoveries as airplanes, anesthesia, calculators, computers, DNA, compact discs, elevators, electric light, artificial hearts, helicopters, magnetic resonance imaging, the Internet, microprocessors, microwave ovens, motion pictures, nylon, pacemakers, phonographs, quasars, sound recording, sewing machines, mass spectroscopy, electric stoves, telephones, television, transistors, vacuum cleaners, washing machines, and the polio, measles, and meningitis vaccines—just for starters? If they were toting up Norway's special debt to the United States, why not acknowledge the liberation from the Nazis and the half century of protection from Soviet aggression?

Was the "Hello America!" campaign the work of misinformed youngsters playing at being radicals? Nope. The long list of signatories included one familiar Norwegian name after another—authors, journalists, professors, members of Parliament. From first to last, this infantile document was a product of the Norwegian establishment.

Nor was it an isolated artifact. Only yards from my door, on the steps of an empty building, was a three-dimensional variation on "Hello America!"—an array of candles, pictures, posters, and poems conveying the message that peace was good, war was bad, and America was no better than Saddam's Iraq. One poster read: "Babylon vs. Babylon: Don't Take Sides!" Schoolchildren had drawn pictures of airplanes dropping bombs on women and children. The victims' skin had been dutifully colored brown; the airplanes were labeled "USA." Apparently the kids' teachers had been happy to advise them on such details.

As it happened, that street-corner display faced the bus stop at which I regularly boarded the downtown bus. Riding it, I could read a *Dagsavisen* ad written by foreign editor Erik Sagflaat and headed "Among Bushmen and Saddamists":

> It's not easy to know whom one should believe in this world of Bushmen and Saddamists, where the truth is for sale and friends can hardly be distinguished from enemies. My job is to discover the connections and the histories that can be found behind, outside of, and beyond the TV cameras.

Once the bus reached downtown Oslo, there was a good chance I'd run into an antiwar march. They seemed ubiquitous that winter. Nor were the participants simply antiwar. They carried posters attacking the United States for everything from heartless capitalism to the death penalty. They carried signs on which a Star of David and a swastika were drawn side by side with an equal sign between them. They carried red banners with hammers and sickles. They carried Palestinian flags, Iraqi flags, and heroic portraits of Arafat. In these crowds I saw familiar faces from Norwegian TV—entertainers, politicians, journalists.

The more it went on, the more disgusted I grew. In American newspapers and political journals, I read intense, serious debates about U.S. policy in the Middle East. I also read accounts of Saddam's torture factories, his prisons full of children, his mass graves. In the European newspapers I read, I found nary a mention of these things.

In 2004, after the story of prisoner abuse at Abu Ghraib prison in Baghdad broke, Western European newspapers and TV news programs showed the same three or four pictures day after day for weeks. I was repulsed by the images and appalled that a few uncomprehending fools (at whatever level) had managed to damage the reputation of American servicemen and women; yet I was also disgusted by the cynicism of the European media. They had correspondents in Iraq who surely saw American soldiers doing good; but they never reported on—or took a picture of—any of it. The American media, though often slighting good news from Iraq, at least run the occasional story that shows the U.S. military in a positive light: for example, on June 19, 2005, the *CBS Evening News* ended with a report on a Wisconsin soldier who adopted an Iraqi boy with cerebral palsy. I've never seen a report anywhere in the European media that portrayed U.S. soldiers so sympathetically, so humanely. The coverage is consistently, flagrantly unbalanced. For European media consumers, Abu Ghraib *is* the U.S. presence in Iraq; Guantánamo *is* the war on terror. Make no mistake: any prisoner abuse is a disgrace to American values. But the fixation of the Western European media on Guantánamo and Abu Ghraib is pure hypocrisy: indifferent to far greater human rights abuses elsewhere in the world, they've harped on abuses by America out of sheer malice.

French author Philippe Roger has said of his country that "we keep creating a mythological America in order to avoid asking ourselves questions about our real problems. And they're problems that the Americans don't have much to do with." This is true of European anti-Americanism generally: its main purpose is to divert attention from the actual problems. After all, if you can talk yourself into believing that America genuinely is the greatest threat to world peace, you can be a very happy camper—for what a wonderful world it would be if America *were* the greatest threat.

The first weeks and months after 9/11 brought to a head my sense of the underlying conflict between American and European perceptions of reality—especially concerning our shared geopolitical interests. Instead of seeing themselves as part of Western civilization, all too many Europeans saw their interests as sharply diverging from ours—a circumstance that would seriously complicate the effective prosecution of the war on terror. In many ways, it was simply a return to a Cold War dynamic that I'd hoped—vainly, as it turned out—had been left on the ash heap of history.

I FIRST VISITED Europe in 1982. I was a third-year Ph.D. student, traveling with a German classmate—let's call her Magda—who'd invited me to fly home with her during our winter break and see some of her country. Our journey began in her hometown in the state of Hesse, where her stout, formidable mother drove us around and pointed out the sights. On a hilltop overlooking the town, the sturdy old widow stopped the car and nodded toward a neglected little monument that stood in a roadside patch of weeds. "For the Jews," she said in a flat, slow voice, "who were taken away." Her tone and facial expression were inscrutable.

From Magda's hometown we took the train to Tübingen, where she'd been an undergraduate. We stayed with a young couple, college friends of hers who, like us, were now grad students. Let's call them Gunther and Eva. They were attractive and amiable, and at first we simply made small talk, exchanging innocuous pleasantries about my country and theirs. But one thing led to another, and after a few minutes, although I'd done my best to obey Basil Fawlty's stricture—"Don't mention the war"—we somehow stumbled into that touchy territory.

Not surprisingly, the conversation's tone shifted dramatically. Gunther acknowledged that, yes, there'd been a time when Germany terrorized the world. The Nazi era was horrible: no doubt about it! But that had been long ago. The past was the past. Now Germany was a country to be proud of. Today, it was America that was the planet's number one force for evil.

Eva readily agreed. While Magda listened quietly, her friends piled on the evidence. I no longer recall the details. I know they brought up

What a lie!

Good observation; Both wanted to do good to their ∧ people!

Vietnam. And one of them mentioned President Reagan, who, they explained, was to our age what Hitler had been to his. In short, the great villain of the day was not the Soviet Union, which at that moment was holding the eastern part of their own country in bondage, but the United States, whose armed forces were all that protected the rest of Germany—*their* part of Germany—from the same grim fate.

What did I say? What *could* I say? I made it clear that I didn't share their views. No, my country wasn't perfect—far from it. Yet it didn't take a political genius to see that the global struggle between the United States and the USSR was a conflict between liberty and slavery, and that everything else was a footnote. From their reaction, it was plain that they found my point of view predictable, amusing, and undeserving of a serious response.

Our exchange reflected fundamental differences in the way Americans and Western Europeans of our generation were taught to look at the world. If Americans were brought up to be pragmatic, and to take it for granted that opinions about the world should (ahem) have their foundation in the world's sociopolitical reality, many Europeans were taught to be, for want of a better word, "sophisticated"—which meant holding opinions that had little or no connection to observable reality. For them, political opinions, by definition, inhabited a higher realm than that of mere experience. They were about ideas—ideals—ideology.

Yes, Americans were free and Russians were not free; Americans were, by any international standard, fantastically wealthy and Russians wretchedly poor. But my German hosts had been taught that to be sophisticated was to look beyond such black-and-white formulas. To be sophisticated was to learn to put words like "free" in quotation marks. It was to recognize that the Soviet Union, whatever its problems, had been founded on lofty ideas about workers' liberation and solidarity and the curbing of capitalist excess through the power of the state—ideas broadly consistent with the goals of European social democracy—while America (or so they had been taught) had been built on selfish ideas about competing with others, grabbing what you could, exploiting or being exploited, eating or being eaten.

One curious aspect of such "sophisticated" thinking is its selectivity. America's virtues are not to be taken at face value, but are to be deconstructed until they look like vices. By contrast, the notion of the United Nations, for instance, as the quintessential symbol and embodiment of all human goodness is never to be probed, tested, or questioned. Similarly, if young Western Europeans are taught to put quotation marks around the words "free" and "freedom," as if to suggest that there really is no such thing as being free—or, at least, that the reality is infinitely more nuanced than such crude language would suggest—they're never taught to look at, say, the word "peace" in the same skeptical way. So it was that in 2003, while the Western European establishment sneered repeatedly at the American argument that Iraq was being "liberated" (what typical stateside *simplisme!*), that same establishment consistently represented the invasion as a violation of Iraq's "peace"—as if the word "peace" could fairly be used to describe life in a country run by a mad tyrant who had murdered hundreds of thousands of his own people. In the same way, the Western European media mocked George W. Bush for calling Saddam Hussein and others evil, but had no trouble accommodating the view that America was itself Satan's own little lamb.

To be sure, if the Cold War anti-Americanism of people like my hosts in Tübingen was reality-denying, in a way it reflected a keen awareness of reality. For Gunther and Eva knew that however much mud they threw at America, U.S. soldiers would remain stationed in their country, ready to fight and die for them. America was a safe enemy—a phony enemy. Seen from a certain angle, indeed, Gunther and Eva's political views were nothing but a big game of pretend. It was as if America were a doting parent and they were its spoiled children, treating it with disrespect even as they enjoyed the security of knowing that they were under its absolute protection and would never be allowed to come to harm.

Ten years after my first visit to Germany, the Berlin Wall fell—thanks largely, of course, to the evil Ronald Reagan. When the Wall began to be demolished in June 1990, I was in Berlin, making a long-anticipated second visit to the country. It was extraordinary. You could feel the joy in the air, see it in people's faces. The long pretense that America, not the Soviet Union, had been the enemy seemed to have come crashing down to earth along with the Wall itself. Not only did anti-Americanism appear to have been forgotten; you would never have guessed that it had existed in the first place.

I traveled to Berlin by night train from Munich, riding in a cramped compartment with five other passengers, including an old woman and a boy of twelve or so, presumably her grandson. It was obvious from their worn but neat clothing and meek, timorous manner that they were East Germans. At one point during the night, the compartment door opened noisily, waking us all, and a formidable middle-aged man in uniform barked out a request for our tickets. The terror on the old woman's face at the sight of the uniform told me all I would ever need to know about life under Communism.

Later that night, I stirred from sleep and looked out the window to discover that we were pulling into a station in East Germany. It was grotesquely dilapidated: the light fixtures were primitive and battered, and large chunks of the platform—some parts of which were dark and others flooded with light—were simply missing. It looked as if a battle had taken place there earlier in the day.

No one was in sight. It could hardly have looked more sinister. It was like something out of a Graham Greene novel. (I wouldn't have been surprised to see a sign reading "Subotica.") Suddenly there appeared an old woman in a ragged, ill-fitting, preposterous uniform that she appeared to have been wearing for decades. Carrying a clipboard, she walked slowly alongside the train. Almost directly in front of our compartment window, she paused and painstakingly wrote something on her clipboard. I gathered that her job was to copy down, for reasons of security control, the numbers on the sides of the West German railroad cars. The Berlin Wall had already begun to come down, and this totalitarian functionary no longer had any reason to do what she was doing. Yet in a manner characteristic of bureaucracies everywhere, she continued to perform her now pointless task.

East Berlin proved to be a larger version of that crumbling train station. Crossing at the newly opened Brandenburg Gate from the western part of the city to the east, I left a grand, glittering metropolis for a place of endless gray—block after drab, depressing block of tumbledown buildings surrounded by rubble and riddled with half-century-old bullet holes. To all indications, the supply of paint and cleaning supplies had run out during the Depression and never been replenished. I didn't stay long.

The big thrill, during that remarkable time, was to walk the streets of West Berlin and see East Berliners catching their first awed glimpses of First World wealth. I'll never forget the gap-mouthed looks of amazement on the faces of men, women, and children alike as they took in the shiny buildings and cars and the abundance of clothing, appliances, and food in the stores. I'll never forget the ease with which I could tell the Westerners, with their healthy complexions, unscared expressions, and confident strides, from the gray Easterners, who, for all their delight, still bore the marks of their suffering—pallor, cowed postures, eyes tinged with angst. This, I knew, was the face of Communism's everyday victims. To deny its reality, or to try to find anything good in it, was obscene.

Standing beside the Berlin Wall at that brief, heady moment of history, and looking on in wonder as people chipped fervently away at the graffiti-covered concrete and gathered up the falling fragments, I thought: *Yes, now it's changed forever. Chic anti-anti-Communism is dead. America has been vindicated. The liberation of Eastern Europe has made the truth of Soviet tyranny undeniable. Those who defended it will hang their heads forever in shame.*

But no—the opposite happened. Once the Soviet Union was gone, Western Europeans didn't respond by cleaving gratefully to the country that had safeguarded them for decades. Instead, freed of the danger of Soviet invasion—and of the need for American protection from it—all too many of them allowed themselves to be persuaded by their academic, media, and political elites that the United States, now the world's sole superpower, was not a friend but a threat, and that Soviet Communism had, after all, had its merits, among them the fact that it had provided a necessary balance to rampant American power and capitalism.

This post–Cold War European attitude was certainly on display during our time in Amsterdam. The Dutch never tired of reciting America's past crimes—Vietnam, Chile, Nicaragua—and outlining the ways in which the United States was inferior to the Netherlands. ("You have a republic, we have a democracy!" my friend Bart told me one day. "Yes," I thought—but was too polite to say—"and you have a billionaire queen, too.")

One night I was having drinks at a seedy neighborhood bar with a couple of guys I'll call Niek and Tom when Niek decided to tell a joke. "What do you call someone who speaks four languages? A Dutchman. What do you call someone who speaks one language? A Frenchman. What do you call someone who speaks no languages? An American."

He and Tom laughed heartily at this witticism. When they had finished, I asked in a flat, unhurried, almost Dutch voice, "Why is it that so many Dutch people routinely insult Americans to their face, when an American would never do that to a Dutch person?"

Niek showed neither surprise nor contrition. Eyeing me levelly, he said that it might be because of such things as the Vietnam War and Chile. (By the latter, of course, he meant the CIA-engineered overthrow of Salvador Allende in 1973.) He brought up the fact that Americans— he meant American men—came to Europe and swaggered around and talked loudly. "They do this on purpose!" he said. "They know that they're citizens of the world's most powerful country and they're determined to remind Europeans of that."

"I know what you're talking about," I replied. I told them about visiting Cannes and noticing the contrast between American and European body language. "But you're totally mistaken," I continued, "to think that American men act this way in order to reinforce their image among Europeans. It doesn't occur to Americans to think about their image in Europe. It's just not a consideration for them. They couldn't care less. Rightly or wrongly, most Americans live their entire lives without ever thinking or caring for one moment about what Europeans think of them or their country."

Both Niek and Tom reacted visibly. For them, as for many Europeans, America was a virtual obsession. The idea that the fascination wasn't mutual was incomprehensible and traumatizing—it was too much for them to take.

"I'm not saying it's a good thing," I added. "I'm just saying that it's so."

They weren't silenced. They proceeded to argue that Europe was much more diverse and accepting of other races than the United States. (This, mind you, at a time when "ethnic cleansing" was under way in the Balkans and 27 percent of Austrian voters had just cast their ballots for Nazi admirer Jörg Haider's Freedom Party.) I acknowledged America's history of racial conflict, but also mentioned something Stephan Sanders had told me—that when he was in the States, Americans had accepted him as Dutch in a way that Dutch people never had, simply because he was dark-skinned. Both Niek and Tom—thrown a bit, I could see, by my evidentiary use of an anecdote told to me personally by a bona fide Dutch celebrity—admitted that Sanders had a point.

Inevitably, we got onto World War II. "To listen to Dutch people talk," I commented, "you'd think the United States had conquered the Netherlands and the Germans had liberated it." I mentioned the biography of André Gide that I'd been reading, and told them how struck I'd been by the reaction of Gide and most of his friends to the Nazi invasion: "They looked up, watched the soldiers go by rounding up Jews, and then went back to whatever they were doing." And Gide was one of the *good* guys! "As an American," I told them, "that boggled my mind."

"As an American," Niek replied, "you can't possibly understand what war is really like. No war has ever been fought on American soil."

"Yes it has. The Civil War."

He smirked. "The Civil War. But that was a civil war."

"So what? In any case, to me that's one of the remarkable things about America: that in World War II we weren't invaded and didn't have to get involved, but we did."

"Why keep talking about World War II?" Tom complained. "Why not talk about what America has done more recently? If the U.S. is such a great democracy, why has it done such terrible things around the world? What about Vietnam? What about Chile?"

"Europeans are always saying that Americans have no historical sense," I replied. "But when I talk about World War II, your reaction is that that was too long ago, let's talk about now." Regarding Vietnam, I told them that I had no intention of defending that war, but that it needed to be understood in the context of the worldwide struggle against totalitarian Communism. "And the main point about America in the twentieth century," I went on to say, "is that, whatever offenses it may have committed, it did save the world from both fascism and Communism. That's a fact, plain and simple."

"Yet it saved the world for what?" Tom asked, shifting the ground of the argument. "If America is capable of so many evils, how can you regard it as a force against tyranny, and not *for* tyranny?" He went on to complain, perversely, that "America is South America, and it is Canada, but people in the United States think that their country is the only America." (It's typical for Europeans to revert to the charge of American parochialism when they sense they're losing an argument.) Also: "The U.S. thinks it is such a big country when in fact it is a small country which could fit entirely inside of Siberia." I had nothing in particular to say to these inane comments.

"Besides," Tom maintained, "America only entered World War II for economic reasons. The capitalists demanded that Roosevelt bring America into the war because they were afraid of losing all their markets. And they wanted to make money manufacturing munitions. All American foreign policy is really domestic policy. America's entry into World War II had *nothing* to do with noble motives." I countered that this was all crap. "Americans went to war against Germany and Japan," I told them, "because they saw that freedom was being imperiled."

Tom sneered. "Freedom to what? Freedom to buy Nikes and Coca-Cola and big air-polluting cars? The idea that America entered the war to defend the cause of freedom is a fiction." That's true

I looked at both of them. They sat there smugly, actually believing and enjoying this nonsense that they had probably heard in a college classroom twenty years ago from a socialist professor (that was where *I* had first heard it) and that I suspected had given them a kind of comfort ever since. I argued with them, of course, saying that I'd agree with any criticism of the United States that I considered reasonable, that in fact I'd be the first to make the criticism myself, that this had been my stock-in-trade for many years now, but that if you really wanted to understand the United States you had to realize, first, that the Marxist analysis of America's involvement in World War II is utter bullshit, and that Americans, for all their idiocies and vulgarities, really do believe in fighting for liberty, even the liberty of strangers in faraway places with names they can't spell and languages they can't speak a word of and cultures they find ridiculous. In their view, to defend other people's freedom is to defend their own. I mentioned an uncle of mine whose racial attitudes I deplored and who probably despised me for being gay, but who as a mere teenager, while the Dutch were busy filling out Nazi ethnic-purity forms, joined the air force, took part in the D-day invasion, was shot down, and spent a year in a POW camp, and did it all for liberty—*their* liberty. Niek and Tom exchanged looks indicating that my sentimentalism about my war-hero relative was *exactly* what they had been expecting.

And yes, maybe that's what being an American does come down to—a sentimentalism, about liberty among other things, that many Western Europeans just can't fathom. If they're so quick to ascribe purely economic motives to America's involvement in World War II, perhaps it's because those are the only reasons they can imagine their own country—itself once a major colonial power—ever having for involvement in a faraway war, or any war.

Sitting there with Niek and Tom, I realized that they were genuinely unable to comprehend a land whose people take liberty seriously enough to die for it. Indeed, for these two men who had been born only a decade or so after the Nazi occupation, words like "freedom" and "tyranny" hardly appeared to have any real meaning at all. To talk of freedom, in their view, was simply to spout emotionally charged rhetoric that—either naively or with cynical calculation—sugarcoated the evil reality of capitalism.

I'd moved to Europe, in part, so I could better know and understand the world outside my own country. But Niek and Tom, neither of whom (they freely admitted) had ever been to the States, thought they already knew all they needed to know about it. They affected to despise it. Yet their pop culture was mostly American; the music that had helped define their generation was overwhelmingly American; and the very terms in which they reviled the United States had been coined by Americans, beginning with H. L. Mencken, Sinclair Lewis, and Theodore Dreiser.

As I got up to leave, Niek—whose flat we were subletting—urged me to "at least" read a book on his shelves entitled *Why There Is No Socialism in the United States*. Incensed at the implication that I needed to be educated by him either about my country or about socialism, I replied that I'd read that book, thank you very much.

"You know that book?" He seemed surprised.

"Of course I do! I have a Ph.D.!" I barked obnoxiously. I didn't shake their hands or say a real good-bye, and I was long past noticing or caring what anyone else at the bar thought of my raised voice. "I've read all that stuff already!" Needless to say, this wasn't true—and as soon as the words were out of my mouth, I regretted them.

I regretted, too, having thrown myself into defending a position that did, after all, simplify reality. I myself had often lamented the terrifying readiness of many young Americans to put their lives on the line in wars they didn't understand. I'd raged at the fact that it's America's poor and unconnected, not the members of its political and business establishment, who tend to lose their sons in wars. I knew there was much more truth in what I said about Americans' love of liberty than there was in Niek's and Tom's crude Marxist line, but when I reflected on the alacrity with which many young American men rush off to war (eager to save the world, to prove their courage and masculinity, to escape tedium), I found myself rather admiring Dutch youth, who were, generally speaking, too content with their lives to go to war out of boredom and restlessness, too cynical to be taken in easily by hyperbolic war rhetoric, too secure in their manhood to feel a need to prove it, and too aware of the preciousness of life (especially their own) to be willing to kill or be killed for anything less than profoundly compelling reasons. I wished I'd said something about that, too.

And September 11, 2001, was still two and a half years in the future.

That spring, the big news event was the NATO bombing of Kosovo. Its purpose was to halt Serbian strongman Slobodan Milosevic's repression of Kosovo Albanians, most of them Muslims. At the time, most of the European media opposed the bombing, which they saw as representative of gratuitous American brutality; the whole episode has since been recognized as a classic illustration of American resolve and European impotence in the face of despotism. Yes, European NATO members—including the Netherlands—participated in the bombing, but it took

America to spur them into action and put some muscle behind the high-falutin rhetoric about the EU's dedication to peace and justice in Europe. Kosovo showed that Europe, when left on its own, is hopelessly impotent in the face of tyranny in its backyard, unable to move beyond dialogue with murderers.

During the Kosovo bombing, the European newspapers told horror stories about Serb-engineered massacres and Muslim refugees; the numbers of people involved staggered the imagination. But that wasn't all: the papers also peddled plenty of stories designed to stir up readers' hostility—not toward the genocidal monsters in Serbia, but toward the United States, which was trying to stop them. For many European journalists, Kosovo was above all a wonderful excuse for facile America-bashing.

One night in the middle of all this, I was waiting in line for a taxi at Rembrandtplein when I overheard two Dutchmen further down the queue discussing the NATO bombing. "Fuck Clinton!" one of them said loudly.

"Fuck Beatrix!" I heard myself saying just as loudly. (Beatrix is the queen of the Netherlands.) The man who'd said "Fuck Clinton" laughed with delight—a quintessentially Dutch response.

For me, it made a huge difference being in Europe during the NATO bombing. Kosovo was closer, and *felt* closer. It is about the same distance from Amsterdam that South Carolina is from New York. Yet as the bombing proceeded, life in Amsterdam went on without any perceptible change. Nobody we talked to brought up Kosovo. Perhaps there was nothing to say.

In America, we feel obliged to do something about the Milosevics of this world. In a way, this need to set things right is, again, a kind of romanticism. What else (aside from a desire to avenge Pearl Harbor) can explain the alacrity with which we renounced the safety of isolationism in 1941 and committed ourselves to the fight against fascism in places far from home?

Western Europeans are different. For them, the Milosevics of the world, however monstrous, are also, quite simply, a fact of life. Nothing will ever end that. Get rid of one, and another will come along soon enough to take his place. They think of themselves as realists—but this isn't realism; it's fatalism. And (as I have since come to recognize, but didn't then) it can shade into a strange, disturbing respect for dictators, a respect rooted in Europe's own history of tyranny.

America had no reason to involve herself in Europes wars

IN THE SPRING of 2001, through a rather absurd set of circumstances, my understanding of European anti-Americanism took a great
leap forward.

One day, an editor at the *New York Times* travel section called me and
said she needed something in a hurry. They were doing a feature on
"farm stays"—working farms that accommodate visitors who want a
taste of the agricultural life—and were an article short. Could I find such
a place in Norway and write it up pronto?

It didn't sound like my cup of tea, but I promised I'd look into it.
Within an hour, I'd located a farm in Telemark that sounded suitable and
booked a room for my partner, his brother, and me.

A few days later we were there. High on a remote mountainside, it
was the opposite of what Americans think of when they hear the word
"farm": this was no patchwork of cornfields stretching to the horizon,
but a cluster of small, weatherbeaten wooden buildings surrounded
by rocky, scrubby earth, most of it far from horizontal, on which a
few dozen goats and chickens grazed. It was, admittedly, picturesque:
our room afforded a spectacular view of the valley and of a steep green
mountainside down which narrow waterfalls trickled, like tinsel
sparkling.

But the experience was ruined by the proprietor's behavior. Much of
the point of a "farm stay" is to watch the farmer farm—and our farmer
obviously hated being in our company, and seemed determined to make
his own company as unpleasant as possible. The three of us all came to
the same conclusion as to why he was treating us this way, but I'll keep
our speculations to myself; suffice it to say that I'd never encountered
such incivility on the part of an alleged host. We'd planned to stay two
nights but left after one.

Had there been time, I would've found another farm to write up; but
since the *Times* needed something right away, I did what I had to.
Though honesty required that I mention the host's conduct, this was a
travel article and not an exposé, so I tried to be as positive as possible. I
sent the piece in, and it appeared a couple of Sundays later. The next day,
Norway's newspaper of record, *Aftenposten*, ran a story summing it up.
Now, what I'd written wasn't remotely newsworthy; the only reason the
editors of *Aftenposten* thought otherwise was that Norway had been mentioned in the *New York Times*. The attention surprised me.

Even more astonishing was what happened next. The owner of the
farm, irked that I'd made a point of mentioning his rudeness, got his

revenge by telling reporters that I'd demanded McDonald's hamburgers for dinner instead of that most Norwegian of delicacies, reindeer steak. Though this was a transparent fabrication (his farm was in the boondocks, far from the nearest golden arches), the Norwegian press lapped it up. The story received high-profile coverage all over Norway and dragged on for days. After somebody at *Aftenposten* tracked down an essay I'd published in a Washington, D.C., policy journal, criticizing various elements of Norway's statist economy and praising the at least somewhat market-friendly Conservative Party, the newspaper ran an article helpfully explaining that I didn't just hate the farm in Telemark; I hated "pretty much everything about Norway."

Meanwhile our inhospitable host became an instant folk hero. The next weekend, he was accorded a cozy ten-minute segment on NRK's Sunday evening news show—the Norwegian equivalent of being profiled on *60 Minutes*. By the time the story had run its course, our unpleasant weekend trip had been transformed into a morality play about the threat posed by vulgar American urbanites to cherished native traditions. (Though two of our party of three had been Norwegians, we were referred to by more than one journalist as "the Americans.") I was flabbergasted. But my erstwhile host obviously wasn't: he knew his country; he knew its media; and he'd known, accordingly, that all he needed to do to spin events to his advantage was to breathe that talismanic word, McDonald's.

For me, the episode raised a few questions. Why had the Norwegian press paid so much attention to a mere travel article? Why had it then been so eager to repeat a cartoonish lie and obsess over it for days? Were these actions reflective of a society more serious, more thoughtful, than the one I'd left? Or did they reveal a culture—or, at least, a media class—that was so awed by America as to be flattered by even its slightest attentions, but that was also reflexively, irrationally belligerent toward it?

The more I came to understand Europe, the more clearly I recognized the Norwegian media's take on my farm-stay story as a perfect reflection of the European-establishment mentality—or, more specifically, of the neurotically conflicted attitude toward America that's standard issue for the so-called " '68-ers." It's the '68-ers—Europe's version of the sixties generation—whose formative experiences shaped the politically correct politics of today's European establishment, and who still make up the heart of that establishment.

Like their American counterparts, Europe's '68-ers were mostly middle-class university kids, children of postwar prosperity who came of age protesting the Vietnam War and decorated their bedrooms with posters of Bob Dylan and Jim Morrison (and, in some cases, Mao and Ho Chi Minh). The transatlantic similarities are many. But there are important distinctions. For one thing, the Europeans had another key formative event in addition to Vietnam: the May 1968 general strike by French students and workers, which paralyzed France and nearly brought down the government of Charles de Gaulle. This experience not only gave students an exaggerated lifelong sense of their own power and importance; it also established a postwar French custom of resorting to crippling, pointless strikes at the drop of a *chapeau* in response to just about anything.

The major differences between the American and European '68-ers emerged in the post-Vietnam years. Young Americans who'd raged against the evils of the American establishment grew up to become members of that establishment. In all but a relative handful of extreme cases, the pure, abstract oppositional ideology of their youth could not survive confrontation with the complex reality of America that was all around them and with the simple fact that America was their nation, their home, and—now—their responsibility. Indeed, for Americans in positions of power, the whole world was their responsibility.

That was not the case with Europe's elite '68-ers. As they grew older, their awareness of their own provinciality intensified, and with it their resentment and envy of the immense country on the far side of the ocean. America was the cultural hub; America was where it was happening. Americans of the Sixties generation had international responsibilities and an international audience. By contrast, as the European '68-ers progressed in their careers—as politicians, writers, journalists, teachers, professors, government bureaucrats—they became more acutely aware of the relative unimportance of what they themselves said and did and wrote, and could only look on from the sidelines, sniping and sneering at a country to whose people they were, essentially, invisible. This marginality and irrelevance had its impact on their views and their rhetoric: aware that their critiques had no effect, they continued into their adulthood to assume a posture toward America that was every bit as extreme and cartoonish as that of their youth.

Deep down, of course, the anti-Americanism of these '68-ers was rooted less in moral principle than in fascination. The same politicians and journalists who ranted about America visited it regularly; many of them had studied or worked there (and bragged about it); every now and then, between the lines of an article by an anti-American journalist or a

TV interview with an anti-American politician, you'd get a glimpse of his pride in his connections to America—a passing remark meant to indicate that he knew his way around New York or Washington or had friends in high places there.

After all, at the heart of the anti-Americanism of Europe's '68-ers lay a rather pathetic paradox: that the political philosophy by which they continued to live was American in its origins; the songs they cherished as generational anthems embodying that philosophy were mostly American (the others were British); and the writers whom they looked to as ideological lodestars were also American. To enrich the irony even further, these writers—left-wing extremists in the mold of Gore Vidal and Noam Chomsky—were people whose politics no one in the American mainstream took the slightest bit seriously. So it was that while most Sixties-generation Americans who found their way into positions of influence moderated their views and rhetoric and began to deal pragmatically with the real world's real problems, all too many of Europe's '68-ers, moving into positions of importance in their countries' establishment echo chambers, continued to think, and behave, like protesting teenagers, savoring their reflexive, petulant opposition as a badge of honor.

Underlying these contrasts, moreover, were critical differences on key issues such as the role of war and the meaning of freedom. American history is largely an account of the advancement of freedom through armed conflict (the American Revolution, the Civil War); by contrast, though Western Europeans owe their freedom to liberation from the Nazis in World War II, they've learned to lump that war in with the preceding centuries of pointless European combat that did nothing but wreak death and destruction. Given that the horror of World War II was a more immediate reality for Europeans than for Americans, and that those living on the Cold War's front lines felt more vulnerable than those across the ocean, it's not surprising that we've ended up drawing two vastly different morals from World War II. For Americans, the moral was that tyranny was evil and must always be resisted; for Europeans, the moral was that war itself was evil and must be avoided at all costs.

This focus on the evil of war and not the evil of tyranny proved decisive, leading many '68-ers to respond to the Cold War with a posture of moral equivalency, damning America and capitalism while as often as not finding ways to praise the Soviets and soften the image of Communism. This kind of thinking helped shape the guiding philosophy of the nascent European Union—a project that, to a remarkable extent, has been driven by the efforts of elite '68-ers and has relatively little to do with the values and opinions of ordinary Europeans. A creature of the establishment, by the establishment, for the establishment, the EU is the very embodiment of the establishment's reflexive political correctness, from its anti-Americanism to its long-standing unwillingness to confront immigration and integration issues. The EU also embodies the establishment's arrogant indifference to ordinary Europeans' views: its decision-making bodies are well insulated from the influence of the rabble—and thus, to a large extent, cut off from the grim realities of the post-9/11 world.

FEW EUROPEAN POLITICIANS have personified the EU and establishment ethos as consummately as Anna Lindh, the Swedish minister for foreign affairs, who was murdered in September 2003. While shopping at a Stockholm department store, Nordiska Kompaniet, she was attacked by a man—later identified as Serbian immigrant Mijailo Mijailovic—who stabbed her in the chest, stomach, and arms. Rushed to a hospital where surgeons worked on her for hours, she died the next day. Tributes poured in from every capital of Europe. For if Pim Fortuyn had been the European establishment's bête noire, Lindh, a cool, businesslike blonde with the air of a Nordic Hillary Clinton, was its golden girl.

Elected to Parliament straight out of law school, Lindh went on to hold several government posts and serve as chairman of the Council of the European Union. (From 1987 to 1989, she was also vice chair of the International Union of Socialist Youth.) During her political career she was a strong critic of the United States (in 2002, she condemned America for killing six Al Qaeda terrorists in Yemen), of the Berlusconi government in Italy, and (above all) of Israel, which she urged European countries to boycott. At the same time she maintained very friendly relations with Yasir Arafat and had very little other than kind words for Arab governments; few labored as actively as Lindh to tie Europe more closely to the Arab world. A strong EU advocate, she spent the last days of her life campaigning for Sweden to adopt the euro.

Posthumous honors abounded. Spain named a street after her; Harvard established the Anna Lindh Professorship in Global Leadership and Public Policy. And in May 2004, in recognition of her enthusiasm for Euro–Arab dialogue, the foreign ministers of the EU members,

Israel, Turkey, and eight Arab countries created the Anna Lindh Euro-Mediterranean Foundation for the Dialogue of Cultures. As historian Bat Ye'or noted, the report announcing the foundation's aims featured an upside-down map of the Mediterranean, with the Arab world at the top and Europe below—an all too fitting symbol of the EU's consistently self-effacing approach to Euro–Arab dialogue. The Lindh Foundation has promised to encourage European schools and universities to offer courses in Arabic, Islam, and Arab culture, as well as courses that "emphasize" Arabic influences on European culture. The foundation also plans to develop Arabic-language TV stations in Europe. Despite the failure of integration and the rise of extreme Islam on the Continent, moreover, the foundation supports the continued flow of Arab immigrants across the Mediterranean. There is little sign of corresponding efforts by the foundation—or by any official European entity—to encourage young people in the Arab world to respect democracy, to learn about Christianity, to tolerate homosexuals, or grant equal rights to women.

Indeed, just as Western European social democrats once soft-pedaled the sins of Soviet Communism—because it was the world's leading alternative to American-style capitalism—so now they wink at the intolerances of Islam, today's alternative. Recognizing this, European Muslims (despite their social conservatism) increasingly vote for socialist parties. In a *Spectator* article about this growing leftist-Muslim alignment—which he calls a "Black-Red alliance"—Douglas Davis writes that Socialist Workers' Party leaders "enforced gender segregation . . . at a demonstration in Trafalgar Square" and "ordered socialist women to cover their heads while demonstrating with their Muslim sisters outside the Israeli embassy in London." Such is the current state of liberal values on the European left.

AS THE IRAQ INVASION approached, I found myself thinking of Srebenica, the Bosnian town where the feebleness of the European elite's reflexive approach to murderous provocation had been all too tragically illustrated in 1995. The UN had designated Srebenica a "safe area," stationing two hundred Dutch "peacekeepers" there to protect local Muslims from Serbian aggressors under the butcher Slobodan Milosevic. Serbian forces, alas, didn't care about the UN's designations: they overran the town and murdered 7,500 men, women, and children. The Dutch soldiers—sent there by bureaucrats who seemed to believe that calling a place a "safe area" made it so—did little to resist. In April 2002, a report commissioned by the Netherlands Institute for War Documentation accused the Dutch troops of, in effect, "collaborating with ethnic cleansing"; the Dutch government resigned in disgrace. In the face of Saddam's provocations, one would have expected the Western European establishment to have learned a lesson from its passive response to Milosevic.

But no. French president Jacques Chirac and German chancellor Gerhard Schröder firmly opposed any invasion. On October 10, the same day that the House and Senate voted to support military measures, the Norwegian Nobel Committee announced the winner of the 2002 Peace Prize: Bush nemesis Jimmy Carter. Committee chairman Gunnar Berge admitted that the selection of Carter was meant as a slap at the current occupant of the White House. Not all European leaders were thumbing their noses at America, however. In an open letter dated January 30, Czech president Václav Havel and the prime ministers of Spain, Portugal, Italy, Britain, Hungary, Poland, and Denmark proclaimed solidarity with America; in February, ten Eastern European leaders issued a similar declaration. Chirac's furious comment that they'd "missed a good opportunity to keep their mouths shut" provided a fine illustration of how those who consider themselves Europe's kingpins deal with dissent.

On February 15, antiwar demonstrators—whipped into an anti-American frenzy by a daily diet of one-sided media reportage—filled the streets of London, Paris, Berlin, and other European cities. After the invasion began on March 19, the European media, predicting a long, tough struggle against Saddam's Republican Guard, mocked the suggestion that Iraqis would greet the invaders as liberators; when Baghdad fell less than three weeks later, and Iraqis did indeed welcome the foreign soldiers with open arms, the European media, rather than admit they'd been wrong, underplayed—or were silent about—this welcome. When the newspaper *VG* broke the silence in Norway by running a front-page picture of happy Iraqis waving American flags, its editors were condemned by colleagues at other news organizations for spreading pro-American propaganda. (Ironically, so convinced were Norwegians that the slanted war coverage they received was balanced that in a 2003 poll *VG*, in reality Norway's most nearly balanced news source on Iraq, got the lowest scores for media balance.)

Meanwhile, around the world, terrorism continued. On October 12, 2002, two Al Qaeda bombs destroyed a bar and nightclub in the town of Kuta on the Indonesian island of Bali. The death toll was 202; eighty-nine of the dead were from Australia, an American ally in the war on terror. The attack was called Australia's 9/11. (The Western media were quick to connect the atrocity with Australia's participation in the Iraq war, even though Osama himself explained that his principal grievance was Australia's leading role in the 1999 UN peacekeeping operation that delivered East Timor from the clutches of Islamic terrorists.) And in November 2003, terrorist bombs went off at two synagogues in Istanbul, taking twenty-five lives. A few days later, explosive devices at the British consulate and an HSBC bank in the same city killed twenty-eight, including British consul-general Roger Short.

The attacks were getting closer. Still, most Western Europeans slept peacefully, secure in the belief that the whole ugly business had nothing to do with them.

BAT YE'OR knew better. In a series of books and articles culminating in the sensational *Eurabia* (2005), she warned not only that Europe is on its way to becoming a colony of the Muslim world, but also that this is the result of European design, not neglect. For decades, there's been an extensive pattern of political, economic, and academic collaboration between the European establishment and Arab governments. At its center, for most of that time, has been a joint EU–Arab initiative called the Euro-Arab Dialogue (EAD). Ye'or argued that Europe's continued acceptance of Arab immigrants and its failure to integrate them have been intentional, the result of "special arrangements through the EAD for the preservation of the migrants' separateness, particularisms, and for maintaining them under [the] jurisdiction [of their countries of origin]." She documented how the EU—eager to win markets for European goods, secure oil supplies, and placate terrorists—has not only turned a blind eye to the tyranny of Arab regimes, but has provided them (and terrorist groups) with massive aid while leavening its side of the Euro-Arab "dialogue" with grotesquely inflated praise for them and their cultures (not to mention hearty denunciations of America and Israel). According to Ye'or, it's largely owing to the efforts of the EAD—whose meetings are closed, proceedings unpublished, and activities thus "shielded from scrutiny and democratic control"—that recent decades have seen the institutionalization in European media, schools, and universities of a strict political correctness that brooks no criticism of Arab governments or Muslim immigrants and that, in deference to Arab prejudices, promotes anti-American, anti-Semitic, and anti-Israeli attitudes.

Ordinary Europeans, Ye'or observed, have unwittingly endured "thirty years of constant indoctrination" in these prejudices, and while most European men and women "harbor no hate," a culture of hate has indeed been "imposed on them" and has, despite "the enormous gap between Eurocrat theorists and the European population," had an inevitable effect. Indeed, over the decades, Europeans have been encouraged by their establishment to, in essence, take on the role of *dhimmis*—the centuries-old term for non-Muslims whose lands had been conquered by Arab Muslims. *Dhimmis* lived in a permanent state of humiliation, their legal status inferior in every way to that of Muslims; they were not allowed to marry Muslim women, to have Muslim employees, to own land, to ride a horse or camel, or to defend themselves if physically attacked by a Muslim. (They were permitted to cry for mercy.) Those who accepted this status sought to survive "by flattering their oppressors"; those who refused to be *dhimmis* were killed. The European establishment's posture toward European Muslims today, maintained Ye'or, is precisely that of *dhimmis*.

Why should Americans care about any of this? If Europeans have accepted the role of *dhimmis*, why should we mind? The answer involves American power, American freedoms, and American culture. In America's struggle for democracy against the tyranny of Islamism, we have firm democratic allies outside of Europe—among them Australia, India, Japan, and Israel. But the strongest potential ally we have is Europe. The advent of fundamentalist Islam in Europe—and the eagerness of many Europeans to placate it—is a threat to American democracy and global supremacy. It's also a threat to what used to be called "Western civilization"—the cluster of societies, now spread across Europe and the Americas, that introduced the world to the concepts of human rights, religious tolerance, and individual self-determination. The entire premise of the Cold War was that Europe and America were, in a very important sense, a single entity, and that the survival of one was intimately and inextricably tied to the survival of the other. Europe's elite may have lost sight of that important truth, but many Europeans have not, and it's in our own best interests not to forget it, either.

AT TIMES, to be sure, even the most charitably minded American in Europe can find himself thinking: "You reap what you sow, people!"

Paris, November 2003. The tone of our visit was set immediately upon arrival at our hotel, a modest, rather run-down establishment in the neighborhood of Batignolles in the seventeenth arrondissement. While I waited on the curb with our luggage, my partner went inside and told the woman behind the desk—in English—that we had a reservation. *"Non!"* she snarled. "No rooms! No reservation! Full up! Bye-bye!" Or words to that effect. With a dramatic Gallic sweep of the hands, she gestured for him to leave.

He came back outside, stunned, and told me what had happened.

"Wait here," I said.

I went in. The woman was dowdy and middle-aged, and was padding around the shabby little lobby in a well-worn housedress. When she turned to look at me, I met her eye with a broad but firm smile that (I hoped) conveyed both courtesy and authority. *"Bonjour, Madame,"* I said in my best over-the-top restaurant French. *"Nous avons réservé une chambre pour deux personnes."* I told her our names.

She paused for only an instant, her eyes locked into mine. Then she leapt into action, hurrying to the front desk and running her finger down the page to which the huge, old-fashioned reservation book was opened. Then she looked up at me with an expression so full of manufactured delight that I almost thought she would clap her hands in a simulacrum of joy. *"Ah, m'sieur! Bienvenue! Bienvenue! Vôtre chambre est prête!"* Beaming with charm, she handed me the pen to sign the register.

It was the day after Thanksgiving. Bush had eaten his holiday meal with troops in Baghdad (and within a few days would be falsely accused of posing with a fake turkey). On Thanksgiving Day, it had been reported that French journalists, informed in advance of an insurgent plan to fire a missile at a cargo plane over Baghdad, had been in the company of the perpetrators during the failed attack. A few days earlier, a definitive article in the *Wall Street Journal* had outlined the massive French financing of Saddam Hussein—France's main reason, it turned out, for opposing the invasion of Iraq. French–American tensions were high: on the day we arrived in Paris, *Le Point*, which by French standards is wildly pro-American, was quoting Bismarck's comment that "God seems to have a special place in his heart for idiots, drunkards, and Americans" and was sneering at Americans' "curious inaptitude . . . to understand the . . . social milieux they encounter, their moods, their singularities. . . . Democracy is not exported like McDonald's."

After checking in, we walked down avenue de Saint Ouen and then avenue de Clichy toward central Paris. We passed discount shoe stores, cheap cafés, and one brasserie after another in which gray-faced men stood in their coats at linoleum counters, smoking cigarettes and sipping coffee from tiny cups. The people we saw weren't just French but a mixture of Europeans, sub-Saharan Africans, Asians. Yet I didn't see a single individual in distinctive Muslim garb. From place de Clichy we continued on down rue Amsterdam, where a couple of bespectacled schoolboys walked past, carrying violin cases under their arms.

We'd left our hotel at midday, and by now it was mid-afternoon. By the time we reached the hideously grand Gare Saint-Lazare, the rush hour was already beginning, and commuters were pouring into the station. A couple more blocks and we found ourselves in the midst of the Christmas-shopping crush on boulevard Haussmann, where the handsome façades of Magasins du Printemps and Galeries Lafayette sparkled with thousands of Christmas lights. Again, in all the crowds, we saw not a single man in *jellaba* or a single woman in *hijab*.

Late that night, hours after the *métro* had stopped running, we stepped out of a bar in central Paris and began trudging up a boulevard in the direction of far-off Batignolles. We were exhausted, our feet were killing us, an icy rain was falling—and there wasn't an available cab in sight. After we'd walked a mile or so, trembling in the cold, our light jackets soaked through (we had no umbrellas), a tiny pair of lights finally appeared in the distance: a taxi! We hailed it wildly as it approached. It pulled over. We rejoiced. My partner leaned down and, through the open window, smiling with relief, asked the driver politely—but in (horrors!) English—"Are you free?" She shot him a nasty look and pulled away, only to stop no more than five yards farther on to pick up a Frenchman who'd appeared out of nowhere.

MANY PUZZLING ASPECTS of contemporary French culture are rooted in the country's historical humiliations. Despite their defeat by Germany in the Franco-Prussian War, their occupation by Germany in World War II, their loss of empire, and their decline from great-power status, they're still raised to believe that their *République* is the cynosure of human civilization and their culture the pinnacle of sophistication. Charles de Gaulle, that ultimate personification of French national pride and hubris, set the tone of postwar French foreign policy: while Britain aligned itself strongly with the United States, in the interests of defending the free world against Soviet totalitarianism, France sought to position itself as a third force between the two superpowers. This had nothing to do with dedication to any moral principle; it was a purely strategic move designed to win for France a pivotal role that its own economic and military *puissance* could not, by itself, justify.

The development of the Common Market into an EU superstate was a product of this ambition; so was the Euro-Arab Dialogue. The EU, sold to politicians and journalists across Europe as a project dedicated to peace and political correctness, was in fact, as Bat Ye'or reminds us, viewed in Paris as a means to Gallic power. As Napoleon had once sought to bring all of Europe under French rule, and as his nephew, Napoleon III, had attempted to establish "an Arab empire stretching from Algiers to Turkey," so France's rulers now aimed to form a French-led European confederation with the entire Arab world as a protectorate. Ye'or predicts that as the Arab population of Europe rises, the dream of an empire straddling the Mediterranean will indeed come true. It won't be a European-led confederation of free peoples, however, but an oppressive Arab empire.

Certainly, if the French sought through the EU to establish their own cultural centrality in Europe, they failed miserably. France's visible influence on even its closest neighbors is negligible. While EU diplomats hail the cultural and philosophical unity of the European peoples, ordinary Europeans tend to be surprisingly indifferent to one another's cultures. Walking the streets of Berlin in 2004, I realized that although I'd overheard passersby speaking several other European languages, I hadn't heard a single person speaking French. Perhaps it was just a coincidence. But then I hadn't heard any German in Paris, either. Could it be that—no matter what the leaders of the EU's two largest members might want or claim—Frenchmen and Germans weren't really all that interested in visiting each other's countries, experiencing each other's cultures, or learning each other's languages?

Of course, the carefully coordinated joint opposition by France and Germany (along with Russia and Belgium) to the invasion of Iraq created an impression of a strong, principled entente between these two founding EU powers. But while Chirac and Schröder had a raft of reasons for forming their anti-American axis, principle wasn't one of them. Aside from the fact that Chirac wouldn't have dared risk angering French Muslims by participating in the ouster of a man—Saddam—who was a hero to millions of them, anti-Americanism was simply good politics in both France and Germany. Above all, both countries had too much to lose, both financially and in terms of reputation, if Saddam fell: as would later come to light in documents found in Baghdad, France and

Germany had both violated UN sanctions by supplying Saddam with arms and military equipment; Chirac, who often called Saddam his friend, had leaked confidential data to him right up to the eve of the invasion.

So much for French–German solidarity.

Indeed, notwithstanding the rhetoric of journalists and politicians, both France and Germany have closer cultural ties to the United States and Britain than to each other. Ordinary Frenchmen and Germans are far less familiar with each other's books, movies, and music than with America's. Walking around Berlin, I reflected that if the European establishment labors so valiantly to stir up anti-Americanism among the general populace, it may be largely because it's desperate to temper the ancient hostility, rivalry, and mistrust among their peoples (especially between Frenchmen and Germans) and to build a common European identity founded in part on shared hostility toward, rivalry with, and mistrust of America—the country to which the man and woman on the street are most likely to feel the strongest sense of connection.

Aside from a certain amount of literary cross-pollination, in fact, the cultural walls between European countries are remarkably high. People who are stars in one small country are totally unknown in the small country next door. (On a 2005 TV program in Norway, Swedes were shown pictures of Norwegian celebrities and asked to identify them. They couldn't.) Few Spaniards see Italian movies; few Frenchmen listen to Portuguese pop music; few Danes watch Dutch TV shows. In May 2005, Norwegian professor Geir Lundestad penned an inadvertently comical lament about American cultural dominance: "When did you last see a French TV program? And the cancellation of *Derrick* [a cop show] marks the end of German cultural influence." At the 2004 European Film Awards, one winner pleaded with viewers to watch more movies from other European countries. So far, it hasn't happened. When you come right down to it, each European country has two cultures: its own and America's. For all the talk of a shared European identity, the common culture of Western Europe these days is made in America.

IF THE ANTI-AMERICANISM in Paris was palpable, it was not ubiquitous. At a high-toned restaurant where we dined with a friend who sported a *Légion d'honneur* pin, the waiters treated us like royalty, their ingratiating smiles never fading. Sitting in that ultrachic restaurant, surrounded by modishly dressed young sophisticates conversing in a babel of tongues, one could easily have fooled oneself into thinking that Paris was still the same world capital of culture and style that had been celebrated in such movies as *Gigi* and *An American in Paris.*

But that Paris, I knew, was no more. Ditto the Paris of Proust, of Colette, of Hemingway and Fitzgerald and Gertrude Stein. *Fini!* Today, Paris is, more and more, a Muslim city. Of the more than five million Muslims in France, about one and a half million reside in Paris. Yes, the parts of the city frequented by tourists are still inhabited largely by beret-wearing, baguette-toting, wine-sipping Frenchmen; but away from the still glorious Champs-Elysées, beyond the still quaint streets of Saint-Germain-des-Prés and the Latin Quarter, outside the artificial boundary formed by the *boulevard périphérique* (Paris's beltway), sprawl grim suburban districts full of housing projects populated by North Africans. These areas, which are popularly known as *cités* and which have counterparts on the outskirts of virtually every other city and town in France, are expanding steadily as immigrants continue to arrive and as obedient, homebound wives continue to be fertile and multiply. The British physician Theodore Dalrymple has referred to these *cités* as "threatening Cities of Darkness" surrounding "the "City of Light." Few tourists notice them on the way in from the airport, but they're terrifying places where young men on government handouts loiter in the streets, returning one's gaze without "a flicker of recognition of your shared humanity." For these *beurs*—the universal term for the French-born progeny of North African immigrants—the meaning of life is derived from their hatred for French society.

These discontented young people—who don't think of themselves as a part of that society or as being subject to its laws—represent a looming challenge to twenty-first-century European prosperity, stability, and democracy. Thanks to them, explains Dalrymple, the great preoccupation in Paris these days is crime. Yet though people talk in private about the rampant acts of vandalism and theft, they hurry by wordlessly when encountering illegal acts in progress. (Only old people, remembering a more civilized era, stop to raise their voices in protest.) The police, for their part, rarely take action in such cases, knowing that if they did make arrests, the courts, strangled by political correctness, would turn the offenders loose anyway. As for the media, they cover up most transgressions as best they can, while government officials respond to those that can't be covered up by issuing brief, bland, ambiguous statements of censure.

In some urban areas in France, even non-Muslim girls feel now compelled to wear veils in public in order to avoid harassment by *beurs*.

Admittedly, Chirac's government took a tough stance early in 2004, when it imposed a ban on *hijab* in schools over the furious opposition of Muslim leaders. But to many observers, this action was too little, too late. A few days before our 2003 trip to Paris, a popular Jewish disc jockey was murdered by a Muslim neighbor who slit his throat twice, gouged out his eyes, mutilated his face with a fork, then said: "I have killed my Jew. I will go to heaven." The same evening, in a shoe store not far from our hotel, a young Jewish woman was murdered, stabbed twenty-seven times. (These crimes were not reported in the mainstream French press, and I didn't find out about them until much later.) The day after we left Paris, the *Jerusalem Post* reported on an eleven-year-old Jewish pupil at the Lycée Montaigne whose Muslim classmates repeatedly beat him up, saying, "We'll finish Hitler's job." (The school's headmaster responded by promising to "organize a debate on the dangers of xenophobia.") The next day, the *New York Times* ran a story on anti-Semitic offenses by French Muslims—thereby giving the topic considerably more attention than any major French newspaper. Many think France will be the first Western European country with a majority Muslim population—and thus the first to experience full-fledged sharia law. Yet as the crisis has progressed, the French elite's capacity for denial seems to have progressed along with it.

Nor is it just the French themselves who are guilty of denial. Take Adam Gopnik, who for several years in the 1990s was the *New Yorker*'s man in Paris, turning out a regular column about his family's day-to-day life in the City of Light. These columns gave his readers exactly what they wanted: the Ritz, the Pont Neuf, the Rive Gauche—the Paris they'd seen in the movies. In one column, Gopnik noted in passing the staggering demographic shift that's altered the face of the metropolis forever, changing it into a city of belligerent, unassimilable, and chronically unemployed young Muslim males (and their mostly invisible sisters back home in the kitchen); he also noted that his upscale Parisian friends preferred to pretend that this transformation had not taken place. Yet he quickly resumed his glittering portrait of the Paris of operas and cafés and dinner parties—for he was obviously aware that his own readers, too, preferred to ignore the unpleasant reality.

Why are the *cités* so full of alienation and rage? For the Western European elite, the answer is simple: poverty. Yet the young men of the *cités* are not poor: as Dalrymple points out, "they have cell phones, cars" (which, like those driven by young Muslim men in every other European city I know, tend to be BMW convertibles), and "they are dressed fashionably. . . . They believe they have rights, and they know they will receive medical treatment, however they behave." Whence the rage, then? Well, what else can one expect of young men who have been taught throughout their childhood that infidels are beneath respect, that Western women are whores, and that the only honorable response to the West's corruption and godlessness is the fury of jihad? Many of them, moreover, have received this unsentimental education in France—a country that, in the name of tolerating cultural diversity, has taken a hands-off policy toward every aspect of their upbringing. The French state might have given them a real education, taught them democratic values, and helped them grow up into responsible, self-supporting, and self-respecting French citizens; instead it's allowed them to be brainwashed into an ideology of hatred that teaches them to take what they can get from France, give nothing back, and applaud those who seek to destroy it.

The degree to which the inhabitants of the *cités* feel alienated from France didn't become clear to some Frenchmen until a soccer match between France and Algeria on October 6, 2001, only weeks after 9/11. Before the game, a number of young men in the stands—nominally French, but of North African origin—booed the French national anthem; and when the French team opened up a lead over Algeria that was too much for them to bear, they poured onto the field in protest, bringing the match to a premature end. It was an eloquent demonstration of loyalty to Algeria, not France, in the wake of the most colossal terrorist act in history. Other such episodes have taken place since; yet French establishment types continue to look away and cough into their hands and change the topic.

BY 2004, I thought I was inured to anti-Americanism in the European media. But Johan Galtung still managed to get under my skin. Galtung is widely recognized as the "father" of the international peace studies movement—which (not surprisingly) has flourished most impressively in the soil of his native Scandinavia. In the decades since his founding of Oslo's International Peace Research Institute in 1959 and the *Journal of Peace Research* in 1964, he's become an object of admiration, if not reverence, throughout the European political, academic, and media establishment, whose members have showered him with awards, honorary degrees, and appointments to international agencies.

Why all this celebration? Because Galtung, more than anyone else, has built an entire career on tirelessly reiterating the European elite's mantra that all international conflict can and should be resolved through dialogue—and that America's readiness to stand up to tyrants with force, if necessary, makes it not the world's paramount defender of liberty but the leading practitioner of "state terrorism" and thus the number one danger to peace. In 1999, at the time of the NATO bombing of Kosovo, Galtung wrote: "The world today has a major problem. That problem has a name. The name is not Milosevic, he is the small-town villain. The name of the problem is the United States of America." Galtung went on to accuse Norwegian officials of being America's "useful idiots," exploited by "the exploiters, murderers and torturists [sic] of America," and recommended that they ask themselves: "How could I let myself be fooled by the U.S.? What was my fault of intellect or conscience, when I could see the splinter in the eye of the Maoists, but not the wooden beam in my own eye?"

This obsessive focus on America as the planet's top troublemaker is the essence of Galtung's philosophy of "peace"—a word he's reshaped into a club with which to beat the United States. When, in May 2004, I ran across a *Dagbladet* op-ed by him, I knew that he was yet another left-wing crackpot who'd managed to parlay an unvarying line of B.S. into a successful academic career; but I wasn't quite aware of just how singularly appalling he was. In his op-ed, he likened America to Nazi Germany and the Soviet Union, pointing out that it had "attacked three countries" since 1999 in order to "expand its empire." In Galtung's world, there's no meaningful difference between Hitler's invading free countries to impose a brutal dictatorship and Clinton and Bush's liberating the oppressed, brutalized peoples of Milosevic's Bosnia, the Taliban-run Afghanistan, and Saddam's Iraq.

Galtung was, of course, opposed to the American-led ouster of Milosevic, arguing that "ethnic cleansing brought about the NATO bombing, the NATO bombing brought about more ethnic cleansing in a vicious circle of mutual causation." Never mind that countless lives were saved; never mind that a bloody tyranny was replaced by a democracy. For Galtung, no military action—and certainly not one carried out by America—can ever be acknowledged as having positive results. What approach did he recommend, then, in the case of Serbia? "I feel the problem of Yugoslavia can be solved, with more good will, more creativity, a little time and less dualism, less demonization," he proposed at the time. "Milosevic is very far from a new Hitler. . . . He is essentially an administrator of very unfortunate traits in the Serbian psyche, a megalomania and paranoia almost as high as that of the USA, about at the same level as can be found in Saddam Hussein's Iraq. In addition there are elements of the mafia boss, but they are ubiquitous in these globalizing days."

Vague talk of "creativity"; a refusal to call evil by its name; a systematic attempt to minimize the offensiveness of this or that dictator by finding some way to blame him on America (reducing Milosevic, for example, to just another baleful consequence of U.S.-driven globalization) and by stating that however bad someone may be, America's even worse: all this is part of the standard Galtung script. "Peace studies" sounds like something that's antiwar; in fact Galtung has hijacked the word "peace" and attached it to a discipline that is, at its heart, guided by a violent antagonism to America and to the defense of freedom. In the view of Galtung and other "peace researchers," it's the obligation of Western democracies to preserve "peace" not by strength or force but by sitting down with monsters and bullies, talking to them respectfully, and finding some way of compromising with them. In such negotiations, one is expected to put aside the idea that one is necessarily in the right and that one's opponent is in the wrong. Instead one must cultivate the idea that each of us has his own reality, and that we must seek to find a place in the middle where we can meet as friends. This is essentially the same philosophy of "peace" that Neville Chamberlain followed at Munich. Indeed, "peace studies" might thus more accurately be called "appeasement studies"—for if Galtung and company had their way, the world would be overrun by rogue regimes while democratic governments stood by, every now and then clearing their throats to respectfully request a meeting.

On a summer day in 2004, I went to the University of Oslo to attend a presentation by this man whose name is, for many, synonymous with the highest ideals of European civilization. Elderly and bespectacled, with unruly white hair, a rumpled jacket, and twinkling eyes that made him look like a professor from Central Casting, Galtung entered the room to prolonged applause and proceeded to stride energetically back and forth across the front of the auditorium, tossing out anti-American comments like firecrackers. There was no context, no continuity—only a series of wild, disconnected exclamations. On November 7, 2003, Saddam Hussein had offered to negotiate about oil, weapons of mass destruction, democracy in Iraq, and the Israeli–Palestinian question—but the Pentagon had said no! America killed 600,000 people in the Philippines in 1905! Eastern Europe is now in NATO! When the United States and Norway go to war in Azerbaijan to maintain existing borders, the French will not object, because they fear that if they support new borders their own Catalan and Breton minorities will want new borders too! America has killed twelve to sixteen million people around the world, six million of them killed covertly by the CIA and six million killed overtly by the Pentagon, most of them cooperative farmers and unionized workers! Kerry is no better than Bush—in fact, it's better to keep the idiot that everybody in the world already sees through than to switch to the smarter one, who in any case will only continue the occupation of Iraq. We must boycott American products (Coke, McDonald's), but we must also "girlkott"—that is, buy from *good* countries!

That wasn't all. Galtung maintained that after 9/11, Bush should have said: "This was reprehensible, but it's a signal to us that we've erred in our foreign policy." (When he proposed this, I unintentionally laughed out loud, drawing a few irritated stares.) Galtung insisted that a Truth and Reconciliation Committee was needed in Iraq—not to address Saddam's crimes, but America's. And he called for a Helsinki Commission in the Mideast. His presentation was in Norwegian, but after offering these suggestions, he said in English: "If you do this, terrorism will melt like snow in the early spring sunshine." Hearty applause. Indeed, the audience responded throughout in an entirely positive way, cheering Galtung's anti-American remarks and laughing delightedly at his "jokes." During the Q&A afterward, no one challenged him; all the questions presupposed the absolute truth of everything he'd said.

It was stunning: though Galtung's bizarre ramble was the sort of thing you might expect to witness in a psych ward, at the University of Oslo it passed for a serious lecture about international relations, and Galtung himself, by any objective measure a ridiculous crank, was regarded as a jewel in the Norwegian intelligentsia's crown. Indeed, in all his fraudulence, irresponsibility, and moral bankruptcy, Galtung was the epitome of elite European anti-Americanism.

Switching channels one day in June 2005, I came upon a documentary about Galtung. It followed him around the world, from one speaking engagement to another (where his America-bashing drew cheers) and from home to home (this raging anticapitalist owns lavish residences in several places, including Washington, D.C., Tokyo, and Spain). In the course of an hour, the worst thing that was said about him was that he could, sometimes, be arrogant. Otherwise the program was one long, shameless love letter, depicting Galtung as a wise and gentle man of peace, the Dalai Lama with a Norwegian accent. Young people in his audiences were shown staring at him in rapturous admiration; one interviewee after another called him a genius. Not one of Galtung's critics, however, was given an opportunity to say a word. By the time the documentary was over, I'd concluded that it must be the work of Galtung's own foundation: certainly this grotesquely flattering, one-sided portrait could not have been put together by any remotely reputable news organization. Even for the European media, it seemed a bit much. But I was wrong. It turned out to be a production of NRK—which meant that this piece of propaganda had been paid for with Norwegian residents' TV license fees, including my own obligatory annual $300. The realization made my blood boil.*

WHY ARE SO MANY members of the European establishment so vigorous in their misrepresentation and ridicule of America? One reason is that they're social democrats—and they recognize that the extraordinary success of American liberal democracy represents a threat to the system they prefer. After all, if Americans are doing so much better than Western Europeans, why not switch to an American-style economy? European politicians are well aware of the average European's cultural affinity for America; the danger, in their eyes, is that this attraction will translate into support for a more American-style polity with lower taxes and a smaller, less intrusive government. They've long since come to realize that the best way to forestall this possibility is to spread misrepresentations that pollute America's image in the minds of the European public.

This project has been under way for a long time. Jean François Revel recalls that his earliest opinions of America were formed by "the European press, which means that my judgment was unfavorable." (Those opinions changed when he actually visited America during the Vietnam War.) Decades later, he notes wryly, the European media still employ the

---

*One day months earlier there'd been a knock at my door. I opened it to see a brawny, unkempt man with a clipboard and an NRK identification badge. Without so much as a hello, he belligerently accused me of not having paid my license fee. I told him I'd always paid it. Poking a fat finger at his clipboard, he growled that I wasn't on his list of people who'd paid. I said he was wrong. We went back and forth a few times. I was firm but civil; he increasingly behaved like a bully—the very incarnation of statist arrogance. Finally he looked further down on his list and saw my name: I was mistakenly listed as living next door. He barked this information out at me, as if this, now, were some kind of deception on my part, then turned and left without either apologizing or saying good-bye.

same misrepresentations they did then, depicting an America plagued by severe poverty, extreme inequality, "no unemployment benefits, no retirement, no assistance for the destitute," and medical care and university education only for the rich. "Europeans firmly believe this caricature," Revel writes, "because it is repeated every day by the elites."

One feature of this daily barrage of anti-Americanism is the tireless reference to "American conditions." The term crops up again and again in reports on undesirable trends in European society. (Its connotations are *always* negative.) Is traffic getting worse? Are children getting fatter? Oh, no—we're being overtaken by "American conditions." The versatility with which the term has been used is impressive. When I recently googled its Norwegian version—*"amerikanske tilstander"*—I got 1,600 hits. I looked through the first hundred or so; most were newspaper articles about a wide variety of topics. Was money playing more of a part in Norwegian politics? American conditions! Was personal wealth increasingly determining the level of health care one received? American conditions! More people were working in temp jobs; lawyers were being more aggressive in child custody cases; more women wanted painless births; crime victims were being allowed to sue for damages—American conditions!

Googling away, I found the term equated with macho behavior, the prescribing of antidepressants to children, Internet spam, overpaid executives, long working hours, animal abuse, lack of sensitivity to the needs of convicts, the use of terrain bikes in heavy traffic, ponds being stocked with fish for "sports fishermen," interest-free financing on cars, schools advertising for students, and the "chaos" of having many commercial radio and TV stations instead of one nice, tidy government-owned station. Perhaps the most outrageous examples I found were an article equating "American conditions" with "long hospital queues" (sorry, that comes under the category of "European conditions") and another article claiming that "Rupert Murdoch controls the American presidential election through Republican propaganda on Fox News" and asking whether Norway's wonderfully objective media might someday fall victim to such dastardly ideological control.

America has a long tradition of energetic social criticism—not just in political nonfiction, but in literature, film, and other genres. *Citizen Kane* is social criticism; so are *The Godfather,* John Updike's *Rabbit* novels, *All in the Family, South Pacific,* and *The Simpsons.* Sometimes the criticism is intelligent and constructive, sometimes exaggerated and cartoonish. The Western European establishment has reacted to this tradition not by imitating it and encouraging Europeans to think critically about their own societies, but by echoing Americans' criticism of America—especially the more exaggerated and cartoonish examples. Noam Chomsky, a crank in America, is a sage in Europe. Michael Moore is as ubiquitous in Europe as he is in America; but while American critics have done a first-rate job of exposing his misrepresentations, for Europeans he remains an untarnished truth-teller.

Walk into almost any European bookstore and you'll find books by Moore, Chomsky, Vidal, and other Americans who preach that the world's major problem today is American power. But if you're looking for American books that take a more positive view of the United States, forget about it. Michael Moynihan, an American writer based in Stockholm, has listed the English-language political books translated into Swedish since 9/11. The authors on his list include not only Chomsky (with three titles) and Moore (with four), but also *New Left Review* editor Tariq Ali, "Holocaust industry" critic Norman Finkelstein, antiglobalist Naomi Klein, Communist historian Eric Hobsbawm, bilious anti-American journalist John Pilger, and many others. All but one of the authors on Moynihan's very long list are leftists.

Similarly, if a prominent American newspaper runs an op-ed by Vidal or Chomsky or one of their acolytes, chances are very good that it'll be translated and prominently reprinted in newspapers across Europe; by contrast, opinion pieces that challenge the European establishment's view of America—and that might actually give European readers something to think about, instead of simply reinforcing extant attitudes—are virtually never picked up by the European press.

The irrational extremes to which European anti-Americanism can go were demonstrated in 2002, when a grotesque book by author Thierry Meyssan shot to the top of the French bestseller lists and stayed there for weeks on end. Titled *9/11: The Big Lie* in its English translation, it presented an elaborate conspiracy theory about 9/11 that was, quite simply, nuts. The 9/11 attacks, according to Meyssan, were not the work of Al Qaeda but of persons high up in the U.S. government or armed forces. There were no hijackers; Meyssan suggested, rather, that the planes that struck the World Trade Center may have been guided to their target by remote control. Meyssan also claimed that American Airlines Flight 77, which struck the Pentagon, never existed, and that the Pentagon was in fact damaged by a missile.*

---

*"Nearly one-third of Germans under 30," writes Karl Zinsmeister, "say that the U.S. government ordered the 9/11 attacks."

The extraordinary success of Meyssan's book—not only in France, but in many European countries—was a window into the psychopathology of European anti-Americanism. The fantasy Meyssan peddled seemed, on the face of it, disturbing; but in fact, for the kind of mind that is drawn to such books, he provided a bizarre kind of comfort, erasing the unsettling reality of the terrorist threat and enveloping the reader in the familiar, soothing music of anti-American paranoia. Nor was Meyssan alone in profiting from rabid anti-Americanism: in recent years, French bookstores have been crowded with titles like *No Thanks, Uncle Sam*; *American Totalitarianism*; *Who Is Killing France: The American Strategy*; *The United States, Policemen of the World*; and *Fifty Good Reasons to Hate America*.

In summer 2005, Swedish TV ran a series of "documentaries" about America. It kicked off with—what else?—Michael Moore's *Bowling for Columbine*. (Swedish TV's enthusiastic online account of the film did not mention that it had been shown to be full of lies and fabrications.) Also included was a sympathetic account of the Stalinist atom spies Julius and Ethel Rosenberg, whom Swedish TV described as having been "executed in 1953 for their Communist sympathies." Then there was *Why We Fight*, which explained American military actions as being motivated by the avarice of military contractors.

During the same summer, I met an American tourist who was visiting Oslo. Like many Americans traveling abroad, he sprinkled his conversation with casual putdowns of his country and countrymen, the unspoken assumption throughout being that they were infinitely more parochial and less informed about the world than Europeans. He didn't seem passionate about this belief—indeed, he hardly seemed aware of what he was doing. I finally called him on it, in a friendly way. "Don't get me wrong," I said. "It's good for us to criticize our own country. It's what made it what it is. But it's strange to hear, when you live over here, because Europeans *never* talk about their own countries in this way. And they've got at least as much worth criticizing as we do." Once I'd made my own position clear, he felt free to drop the casual anti-Americanism and open up about his own honest impressions of Norway—mainly, his surprise at the proliferation of women in *hijab*.

THE INTENSITY of the European establishment's anti-Americanism is matched only by the intensity of its nostalgia for the good old days of Soviet Communism. Few politicians, professors, or journalists will admit to missing Communism. But most of them are awfully quick to say that, well, at least when the Soviet Union was around, it provided a counterweight to American power. This despicable, but now standard, line turns Cold War history on its head.

The first of May used to be the day on which the Soviet Union celebrated its Communist system. Though the Soviet Union is history, May Day remains a public holiday in Finland, Norway, Sweden, Germany, Belgium, France, Spain, Portugal, and Italy. In Oslo, the annual parade always begins in Youngstorget, a dreary square dominated by the Socialist Realist–style headquarters of the Labor Party and the rusty-metal headquarters of the all-powerful Norwegian Confederation of Trade Unions. The marchers are always mostly young—too young to have any meaningful memories of Soviet Communism. On May Day 2005, it took over an hour for the parade to file past. While the dozens of marching bands played a bizarre mixture of creaky old Communist anthems (such as "The Internationale") and kitschy homecoming-parade fare ("Hello Dolly"), participants waved red flags and carried huge banners that read: "Stop occupation and terror—stop the U.S. and Israel!" "Reject globalized capitalism—yes to socialism!" "Non-socialist politics is greed reduced to a system!" and "We are eternal optimists and proud socialists!"

In early 2004, NRK devoted a half hour of prime time to an affectionate profile of a once-prominent member of Norway's Communist Party. Though he's now a real estate tycoon in Spain, and admitted to voting for the conservative Partido Popular in Spanish elections (because they're the ones who support the presence of foreigners in Spain, and "we support those who support us"), he still considered himself a loyal Marxist. This loyalty was depicted as a virtue; nor was there any hint that being a Communist tycoon might involve a touch of hypocrisy or self-contradiction.

Later that year, *VG* served up a report on "the two faces of North Korea." The photo-heavy feature might better have been titled "the two sides of North Korean P.R." *VG*'s reporter, who of course had been kept on a short leash by North Korean authorities, had been taken to see the statue of the late dictator Kim Il Sung, and devoted two of his four pages to pictures of North Koreans paying tribute to the Great Leader's memory. And what was the other side of North Korea? The wretched poverty that's driven some to cannibalism? The tyranny that's subjected countless Koreans to torture and death? Guess again. "North Koreans live their lives just like everybody else!" *VG* assured us, and "proved" this with a splashy set of pictures of North Koreans at play—laughing, singing, strapping on skates, splashing around at the beach. Though *VG*'s reporter noted dutifully that the individuals depicted were members of the North Korean elite, that didn't keep him from passing along this vile Potemkin-village propaganda. The highlight of the feature was an amusement park where the main attraction was a ball-toss game. Its objective? To "kill the American." The reporter tried his hand, "killing" three out of five Americans—and winning a big hand from his new North Korean friends.

Far more common in the Western European media than celebrations of North Korea, however, are paeans to Cuba. The fact that Fidel Castro has ruled unelected for four decades, that he's imprisoned, tortured, and executed thousands of ideological enemies (and others who just got in the way), that Cubans enjoy no civil rights whatsoever (including the right to leave their own country or access the Internet)—all this is routinely glossed over. What's emphasized instead is the conceit that Cubans are an unusually happy people who, in a world of bland, cookie-cutter materialism, have taken a different path, retaining their magnificent, vibrant uniqueness and staving off the influences of the vapid "McDonald's culture" that reigns only ninety miles from their shores. (The fact that many Cubans have perished while trying to reach that vapid culture is, of course, invariably ignored.)

Until his death in 2002, the most famous living Norwegian was probably the explorer Thor Heyerdahl, who proudly boasted of his friendship with Castro. A few months before he died, Heyerdahl visited his comrade, whom he lauded in an interview (a clipping of which is on display at the Heyerdahl Museum in Oslo). "Fidel is not a dictator who thinks of himself," said Heyerdahl. "He doesn't collect treasures. He lives a spartan, simple life, and thinks only about doing what's best for the poor people of Cuba. I saw how terrible it was here before the revolution. There was so much poverty and misery that it was altogether too hellish. . . . Politics can be medicine for the people. For Cuba, Communism was the medicine they needed." (Apparently Heyerdahl was not asked about the fact that most other Latin Americans, who also lived in poverty under dictators a half century ago, are now far more prosperous than Cubans—and free, to boot.) Following Heyerdahl's death, his son, Thor Jr., picked up the torch. "Fidel Castro has a totally irresistible charisma when you meet him in private," the younger Heyerdahl told a reporter. "An almost uncanny glow."

Follow the media in just about any Western European country, and you'll find yourself regularly inundated with positive images of Cuba. In early 2004, NRK broadcast *Habana Libre*, a Norwegian documentary advertised as providing "a glimpse of the joy in life and the human spirit that breathes through an expressive culture that we usually experience only in fragments . . . here in the market-driven West." Produced with Norwegian government funds, the documentary, which followed several Havana residents through their daily lives, and which had been screened at a 2003 film festival in Cuba, was unadulterated Communist propaganda. Not a single negative aspect of life in Cuba was hinted at. The island's economic problems were blamed on the United States; but it was made clear that prosperity didn't matter to Cubans, anyway. The rest of the world might grimly struggle for loot and lucre, but Cubans spend their days singing and dancing and laughing together. They love life, they love one another, and they love their country. Cuba, we were told, is the only country in the Americas that still has a soul. Nor was the title's meaning ambiguous: whatever those *norteamericanos* might say, Cubans were *libre*—free.*

For the Western European establishment, the obvious attraction of Cuba is that, close as it is to America's shores, it remains a bulwark of anti-Americanism. Where Cuba's concerned, the media turn just about everything inside out. For them, Castro's not a tyrant—he's a heroic underdog protecting his people from American hegemony.

In November 2004, forty-three members of a Cuban theatrical troupe that was in Las Vegas to perform its "Havana Nightclub Show" requested asylum in the United States. German journalist David Kaspar noted that the troupe had appeared in his country a couple of years earlier, and that the members' devotion to Castro had been celebrated at the time on the German public television station ZDF. In a report that resonated, in Kaspar's words, with "a sly admiration for Cuba," ZDF made sure to mention the gift of a piano to one of the performers by Fidel and observed that the lack of defections from the troupe reflected the entertainers' "pride in their own homeland, in its attitude toward life and its culture, which for most Cubans cannot be outweighed by money." ZDF

---

*Shortly after seeing *Habana Libre*, I came across an enthusiastic article in a Norwegian film magazine about a similar-sounding film. Reporting from the Havana Latin American Film Festival, Audun Engh hailed director Fernando Perez's *Suite Havana*, a "poetic meditation about daily life in Havana" that "follows twelve residents of Havana in their varied daily lives from morning to evening." Engh overtly celebrated Castro's dictatorship and sneered at his nemesis to the north. " 'The Land of the Free,' " Engh noted darkly, "prohibits its own citizens from visiting Cuba. Sky-high fines and prison terms await Americans who travel there illegally." Engh neglected to mention that the official punishments for Americans visiting Cuba are never actually imposed, while Cubans who are caught trying to *leave* their country face torture and execution.

appears not to have covered the mass defection in Las Vegas. Nor did *Dagsavisen*'s Erik Sagflaat, who in 2005 asserted that "the most serious human rights violations" on Fidel's island were the ones committed by the United States at Guantánamo.

FOR SCANDINAVIANS WHO CAN'T swing a trip to Cuba, the next best thing—and right in their own neighborhood, too—is a little corner of Copenhagen known as Christiania.

One afternoon in June 2004, in a light drizzle, my partner and I crossed over a bridge from the fairy-tale setting of central Copenhagen, with its cobbled streets and stately old buildings, into a prosaic neighborhood of low-rise brick apartment buildings that reminded me of Forest Hills, Queens. A few blocks' walk brought us to a crude stone archway. Walking under it, we entered what might almost be mistaken for—yes—a Cuban village: there were no cars, trucks, or buses, and only one honest-to-goodness street (sans sidewalk), but there were plenty of old, rusty bicycles and a profusion of cats and dogs roaming freely among the ubiquitous trees and bushes and wildflowers. This was the "Free City" of Christiania, a place that's at once a dramatic departure from the reality of today's Europe and a bizarre embodiment of the ideals of today's European establishment.

Founded in 1971 by hippies, artists, and activists on a site newly vacated by the Danish army, Christiania is the permanent address of approximately one thousand people who don't pay Danish taxes but whose communal expenses are covered by Danish taxpayers and whose security needs are attended to by the Danish police. Despite this dependence, the residents of Christiania enjoy pretending that it's an independent state, a "free city" in the middle of Denmark, like Monaco or the Vatican (only purer in spirit). As if this conceit weren't ludicrous enough, they bite the hand that feeds them, scrawling on their fences and houses such slogans as "Fuck Fogh" (the Danish prime minister) and "Fuck the cops." In short, Christiania is the quintessence of European socialism at its most puerile: just as the Continent's elite routinely mocks and insults its long-time guardian, the United States, so the spoiled brats of Christiania mock and insult their protector, the government of Denmark. In true Sixties-anarchist fashion, they think of themselves as rebels against the state when in fact they're its wards.

We followed a path through Christiania's commercial section, which consisted of several small, ramshackle shops, all surrounded by wildflow-

ers; a few cafés; a tiny, old-fashioned general store; a bike shop; and an
outdoor flea market crammed with racks of Beatles and Santana T-shirts.
Taped in one shop window was a sheet of paper that spelled out "Christiania's common law" (e.g., "no weapons," "no private cars"). At a beer
garden we bought two bottles of Tuborg. There were picnic tables, some
of them under canopies on which were printed (in English) the words
"Say no to hard drugs." Since drugs had been one of the original reasons
for Christiania's existence, I figured this slogan must be an attempt to
pacify Danish authorities.

For there are those in the Danish government who want to put an
end to Christiania. This effort dates back to its beginnings, though the
Free City has been rescued every time through the intervention of people for whom it symbolizes love, peace, flaming youth, and hopeful hip-
piedom. As a result, the Danish parliament, which in the 1970s actually
voted to clear out the squatters—this being the correct term for the people of Christiania—was by 1989 satisfied with simply compelling them
to conform to Danish law (by, for example, obtaining building permits
and liquor licenses). After the conservative government of Anders Fogh
Rasmussen took office in 2001, efforts to close the place down intensified—but so did the shows of support. On May 22, 2004, several thousand demonstrators protested a proposal, then before the Danish
parliament, that would have denied Christianians any collective rights to
their community; on July 2, only a few days before our visit, the first
steps had been taken toward turning the Free City's five-hundred-odd
homes into an ordinary residential association. Though most Christianians accepted the arrangement, they insisted on retaining the right to decide who could join them in paradise.

The light rain turned into a deluge. We waited it out at one of the
canopied tables, drinking our beers, listening to a group of young rock
musicians playing in a small band shell, and looking over our fellow patrons. They fell into two groups: the neatly dressed ones in their twenties (plus a few in their thirties or forties) were obviously tourists; the
ones over fifty who dressed like old hippies were obviously locals—either
residents of Christiania or people who hung out there. One Hispanic
man wore a Che Guevara T-shirt and a cap with a red star on it.

Eventually the rain tapered off. We finished our beers and ambled
down the main road into residential Christiania, a sprawling jumble of
cottages surrounded by wildflowers. Every so often we ran across memos
posted by neighborhood councils. I was amused to find that, despite
Christiania's anarchist pretensions, the memos were written in the same

stiff, impersonal style, and typed up in the same fussy, rigid format, as the missives we get from Norwegian government bureaucracies.

From the outside, most of the residences in Christiania looked like dilapidated shacks in some godforsaken bayou hamlet: they were desperately in need of paint and repair, and the yards and porches were, in many cases, piled with junk (broken furniture, old TV sets, jugs and jars and paint cans) that looked as if it had been accumulating for twenty years. Peering through the windows, however, we saw one room after another that looked like a picture in *Architectural Digest*—sumptuous living rooms with pristine white couches and elegant bric-a-brac, immaculate bedrooms with wide-screen TVs and computers. Bourgeois luxury! It was Western Europe in a nutshell—in public, condemning American-style materialism; in private, savoring it. Every now and then we caught a glimpse of a local—an elderly woman working in her garden; a man sawing wood behind his house; artists painting in their studios, the windows opened wide to let in the cool breeze. Shambling out of his house in a soiled sweatshirt and worn khaki pants, a gaunt, unshaven man of sixty or so picked up a junky old bike off the ground, climbed onto it, and wobbled away down the road, disappearing around a curve.

On a mailbox we saw a sticker that read, in Danish: "The coalition's murders in Iraq *are* terrorism." We turned off the main road and followed a little path through the woods. On the back wall of a shed in the middle of nowhere were painted the words "Fuck Fogh." What, I wondered momentarily, could be the purpose of scrawling such a graffito in such a remote place—especially given that everyone in Christiania already felt exactly the same way? But then, what else would one expect? The place is, after all, the embodiment of European establishment dreams; and if that establishment is about anything, it's about disguising docile conformity as courageous dissent.

One point that came through clearly as we walked through Christiania was that its rejection of Denmark proper is as aesthetic as it is political. Denmark is a clean, orderly little nation of smooth surfaces and minimalistic décors; of picturesque cobbled streets and tidy lawns; of pale yellows, off-whites, grays, and earth tones; and of freshly scrubbed people with neatly combed hair and well-ironed clothing. Christiania, with its wild hair and wildflowers, is a reaction against all that. It's grown-ups playing at being Thoreau. I have to admit it was fun to visit. Yet how can any responsible adult live there with a clear conscience, knowing he's living a lie, bumming off a nation he officially despises?

Christiania is a uniquely European place. But like so much else in today's Europe—especially on today's European left—it reeks of American influence. It's what Woodstock would have become if everybody had stayed. Walking around the Free City, I recalled that utopian communities—Brook Farm, Oneida, the Shakers—formed one of the more interesting chapters of nineteenth-century American history. Yes, few of those communities lasted as long as Christiania has—but then, they didn't get government support. Crackpot utopian ideas that may be passing fancies for marginal elements in America have a way, in Europe, of going mainstream and becoming permanent fixtures on the landscape.

THE HUGE WOODEN DOOR of the *pension* opened, and a young man with a Mediterranean appearance—Turkish, I guessed—eyed us steadily. "Deutsch? English?" he asked. "English," I replied, and after introducing himself he walked us through a small, dark dining room—the tables already meticulously set for the next day's breakfast—to our room. "You can check in," he said, unlocking the door, "after you've settled in." He left, and I made a beeline for the TV set, finding CNN Europe just in time to hear an anchorwoman say that they were now switching over to CNN-US for live coverage of Ronald Reagan's funeral at the National Cathedral in Washington.

Though we hadn't planned our trip to Berlin so that its timing would be symbolically appropriate, that was how it turned out—multiply so, in fact. For one thing, there was the funeral of Reagan, a pivotal force in the events leading to the fall of the Berlin Wall. Then there had been the commemoration, a couple of days earlier, of the sixtieth anniversary of D-day. For the first time ever, German leaders had been invited to participate in the official memorial events—a reflection of establishment politicians' desire to de-emphasize the transatlantic alliance and prioritize pan-European solidarity. Finally, there were the EU elections, scheduled for Sunday. They would test the degree of public commitment to the future of the EU, whose largest and most important member is, of course, the German Federal Republic.*

As I sat there watching the first moments of the Reagan funeral, however, my thoughts were not on the future but on the past. Berlin had starred in the two nightmare dramas of the twentieth century, Nazism

---

*The low turnout in those elections, and the strong response in Britain to the anti-EU message of the newly formed UK Independence Party, suggested that many voters were less than enamored of the European project.

and Communism. The United States had helped deliver it from Hitler, airlifted supplies when Moscow tried to cut it off from the free world, protected its western half from Stalin and his successors, and played a pivotal role in the liberation of its eastern half from Communist rule. Berliners had much for which to be grateful to America—and, especially, Reagan. Or so one would have thought.

The next day we came up out of the S-Bahn at Potsdamer Platz to see before us a breathtaking panorama of large, shiny new buildings of glass and steel, their architecture astonishing in its boldness and imagination. I felt like Dorothy beholding the Emerald City. And the spectacle wasn't complete yet: to our right, on the opposite side of the street—Ebertstrasse—a sea of cranes seemed to stretch to the horizon. (I later learned that this immense site was that of the future Holocaust Memorial.) The opening lines of an old Marlene Dietrich tune flooded into my mind: *"Amidst the ruins of Berlin, / Trees are in bloom as they have never been . . ."* Dietrich sang those words in *A Foreign Affair* (1948), set in Berlin in the immediate aftermath of World War II. That, too, had been a time of rebirth for the city, at least its western half. Now, nearly sixty years on, Berlin's eastern half was catching up.

The richness of architectural inspiration at Potsdamer Platz was awe-inspiring. And what deepened the awe was the awareness that until recently there'd been nothing there—the square (which, pre-Hitler, had been Berlin's Times Square or Piccadilly Circus) had throughout the Cold War been a gray, forsaken wasteland in the shadow of the Wall. Now it was a gleaming hub of international culture and free enterprise—the ultimate ad for democratic capitalism.

To be sure, as we walked around Potsdamer Platz on that day in June 2004, the German economy was no longer the powerhouse it had seemed to be a few years earlier. Despite high productivity, both France and Germany were plagued by low growth and rising unemployment, a direct consequence of welfare-state policies. Those policies desperately needed reform, but voters wouldn't hear of it. For decades, they'd been conditioned to view their social-democratic system as the consummation of human history and American liberal democracy as a primitive holdover from the Industrial Revolution. They've been fed a zero-sum understanding of economics—the idea being that there's only so much wealth to go around, so that the poverty of poor nations is the direct result of the "accumulation" of wealth by rich nations (with America, of course, the worst offender). Hence the perceived obligation of the West to pour aid money into the coffers of Third World governments. That wealth in fact creates wealth—and that the rich can best help the poor through trade, not aid—is a virtually alien concept in Western Europe.

I've mentioned the catchphrase "American conditions." Economically, it connotes robber barons and wage slaves—unbridled capitalism and a total absence of employee rights and protections. In Western Europe, it's generally believed that most Americans have no health insurance, that the uninsured sick are routinely denied medical care, that American workers who lose their jobs don't get unemployment benefits, that America has no free public schools, that retired people don't receive government checks, and so forth. In 2004, however, a German author, Olaf Gersemann, published a book entitled, of all things, *Amerikanische Verhältnisse (American Conditions)*, in which he turned the phrase around, suggesting not only that German fears of American capitalism are unfounded, but that a shift to a more American-style economy would provide Germans with greater prosperity, financial security, and economic justice.*

Gersemann disproved one flattering myth after another: that living standards are higher in Europe (nope), that the rich pay lower taxes in America than in Europe (in the States, the richest 10 percent account for 65 percent of federal tax revenue; in Germany, they account for 4 percent), that people in the States must take second jobs to make ends meet (only 1.5 percent have two full-time jobs), and so on. In no meaningful category, he found, did Europe's overregulated, high-tax social democracies enjoy an economic advantage over American liberal democracy.

A comprehensive 2004 report by Timbro, a Swedish think tank, similarly challenged the conventional wisdom, establishing that, on average, Americans are far wealthier than Western Europeans. Indeed, according to Timbro associate Johan Norberg, in the last twenty-five years the American economy has almost doubled, whereas the EU economy has grown by slightly more than half. The countries that have prospered the most have been those—such as Britain and Ireland—that have imitated the U.S. economic model. Yet the European media continue to serve up the same comforting "American conditions" clichés.†

---

*The American edition of Gersemann's book is entitled *Cowboy Capitalism*.

†When Hurricane Katrina struck America's Gulf Coast in 2005, the European media focused on the supposed Third World poverty of its victims and the alleged indifference of the U.S. government to their fate. "American conditions" indeed! In the end, 1,200 people died in this hurricane, one of the half dozen or so most powerful ever recorded; by contrast, no fewer than 11,000 Frenchmen perished in a 2003 heat wave—a far more explicit case of Third World conditions and official indifference that was nonetheless never described as such in the European media.

From Potsdamer Platz, we followed the rim of the Tiergarten, Berlin's Central Park, to Brandenburg Gate. The plaza on the gate's western side looked much like any other European square in summertime: tourists in T-shirts and shorts poured out of buses, cameras at the ready; a quartet of minuscule Mayans in colorful ponchos played drums and pan flutes. We passed under the gate, entering what used to be East Berlin. This was the same spot where, crossing from west to east fourteen years earlier, I'd seen nothing but broken-down, bullet-riddled old buildings. The sight that now greeted my eyes could hardly have been more different. Pariser Platz, the square on the gate's eastern side, was a showplace. Lined by sleek low structures of glass and marble—the French and American embassies, the Dresdner and DG banks, the Academy of Fine Arts, and the Hotel Adlon, all designed by major international architects—it had to be one of the most attractive and prosperous-looking spots in Europe. The symbolism could scarcely be improved upon: here where Communism had reigned—suppressing freedoms, controlling the economy, censoring artists, and restricting travel—what could be more appropriate than to be surrounded by the embassies of two Western democracies, the headquarters of two banks, an art school, and a hotel?

There was also a Starbucks. The largest Frappuccinos cost €4.30—about five dollars. (How long would a Communist-era East Berliner have had to work to earn that?) We bought two of them and sat in the sunshine to watch the passing parade. Hundreds of people walked by; none had that gray, haunted look I remembered from 1990. Many, in fact, were German teenagers. As one group of fifteen-year-olds swaggered by, it occurred to me that they'd been infants when the Wall came down. They'd grown up in a united Germany, in a free Europe; they knew nothing else. This, I thought, is what it was all for. It was for them—for the sake of these then unborn young people—that the West had stood up to Communism for so long and at such risk and expense. It was for them that JFK had come to Berlin and said, "*Ich bin ein Berliner*"; it was for them that Reagan had come and said, "Mr. Gorbachev, tear down this wall."

Yet what had these kids been taught about that history?

The question had barely formed in my mind when it was, after a fashion, answered. A second group of kids walked by, one wearing a Che T-shirt. Shortly thereafter, I saw another kid wearing one. This shouldn't have come as a surprise: in summer, Che is ubiquitous in the streets of Oslo. Why should Berlin be any different?

I sipped some more Frappuccino. Then, idly turning, I saw an army of Ches.

"Excuse me for a second," I said.

Taking my Frappuccino with me, I walked over to the souvenir shop next door. Piled up on metal shelves outside the shop was an immense selection of Che T-shirts. Some bore the slogan *Hasta la victoria siempre*—ever onward to victory.

These days, nobody who ever lived appears on more T-shirts in Europe than Ernesto "Che" Guevara, Castro's second in command during and immediately after the Cuban Revolution. The most fortunate thing that ever happened to Che (which simply means "Argentinian," as "Yank" means "American") was that one day he had a photo taken that made him look like the ultimate romantic revolutionary. Long after his 1967 execution in Bolivia, that one picture has kept his myth alive.

I should have been inured to Che's ubiquity by now. But it angered me to see his face in Pariser Platz, where his cause had once won a nightmarish, and seemingly irreversible, *victoria*. Some would argue that his reduction to an image used to sell leisure wear represented a "commodification" of Communism, and therefore a victory for capitalism. But looking at those shirts, I felt no sense of triumph.

My own awareness of the reality of Communism dated back to junior high school. In ninth grade, I was friends with a Cuban boy named José. We were the two top students in Spanish, and as graduation approached, our grades were so close that it was unclear which of us would win the school's Spanish prize. Then one day our teacher announced that it would go to me. At the end of the hour, José graciously told me, "It's right that you won. It's my language, and you did as well as I did, so that means you did better."

José's language skills were in his blood. His father had been a journalist under Batista. When Castro and Guevara came to power, they arrested José's father, tortured him, and put his eyes out. On the day I met him, in his modest ground-floor apartment, he sat in an upholstered chair in a book-lined room and spoke to me with a courtliness and respect to which I was not accustomed. Ever since then, every time I've seen a Che T-shirt on some clueless young person, I've thought of José's father sitting in his living room, surrounded by books he could no longer read.

Such cruelties were par for the course for Che and his gang. José's father was lucky—at least he got out alive. Many didn't. Some were just teenagers when Che—having identified them, often capriciously, as enemies of the Revolution—blew their brains out. Paul Berman, who describes Che as "an extreme dogmatist, instinctively authoritarian, allergic to any democratic or libertarian impulses, quick to order executions, and quicker still to lead his own comrades to their deaths in doomed guerrilla wars," calls the cult of Che "an episode in the moral callousness of our time." Though Che "achieved nothing but disaster," though he "presided over the Cuban Revolution's first firing squads," and though he "founded Cuba's 'labor camp' system—the system that was eventually employed to incarcerate gays, dissidents, and AIDS victims," this "enemy of freedom . . . has been erected into a symbol of freedom." And he is now the supreme idol of the youth of Europe.*

I remembered an NRK news report I'd seen about a family of North Korean refugees. The father had died in North Korea of starvation; his wife and son had escaped to the South. Though at first I'd been surprised by NRK's acknowledgment of North Korean tyranny, the report had ended in familiar NRK fashion. Standing on a hill overlooking a South Korean street full of garish neon signs and heavy traffic (familiar symbols, in the Scandinavian media, of "American conditions"), the refugee son—now in his early twenties—said that neither the current North Korean system nor South Korean–style capitalism held the answer to North Korea's ills. Where, then, did the answer lie? He'd found it—in Che. The report concluded with a shot of him standing there on the hill, reading a red book with Che on its cover, plainly transfixed by its contents, dreaming revolutionary dreams.

Che T-shirts weren't the only Communist-related items on sale next door to Starbucks. There were Lenin postcards, hammer-and-sickle wristbands, DDR and CCCP T-shirts. As I looked them over, an attractive store employee in her thirties stood nearby, presumably posted there to deter thefts. Noticing, I gathered, my displeasure, she met my eye with an embarrassed laugh. "Nostalgia for East Germany," she said in heavily accented English, her tone ruefully apologetic.

Leaving Pariser Platz, we made our way to the nearby Reichstag, a sinister Prussian bully of a building. Behind it ran a wide, smooth, spanking new pale-gray pavement that looked like marble. Down the middle of the pavement ran an inconspicuous line marking where the Wall had

*Watching the Eurovision Song Contest in May 2005, I was ready to be moved by the Ukrainian band GreenJolly's performance of their song "Razom Nas Bahato," the anthem of their country's "orange revolution." My enthusiasm took a nosedive, however, when one of the band members turned out to be wearing a Che T-shirt—Che, hero of the tyranny from which his country had just liberated itself!

been. We followed it to the banks of the Spree. At the river's edge, a row of white crosses was affixed to a fence; each bore the name of someone killed trying to escape to freedom.

Later, we investigated a shabbier part of the former East Berlin. Walking up forlorn, garbage-strewn Schönhauser Allee, we passed block after block of graffiti-covered buildings. On one run-down facade somebody had written, in three-foot-high orange letters, "Fuck the free world!" We saw a Socialist Party poster: *"Europa an der Seite der UNO nicht im Schatten der USA!"* (Europe at the side of the UN, not in America's shadow.) Eventually we came to Gleimstrasse, a narrow tree-lined street dotted with sidewalk cafés. It was charming, though many buildings were in terrible shape. The only visible twenty-first-century touch was in the windows of the Wall Street Institute, where slick, snappy, red-white-and-blue placards proclaimed (in not quite natural-sounding English): *Learn English a better way!*

That evening, at a bar near our hotel, we fell into conversation with a sardonic German of about thirty who turned out to work for the U.S. Army. Mentioning Reagan's funeral, I asked him what he thought of the late president. He shrugged, and said something apparently meant to be magnanimous: "What can you say? He's dead, let him rest."

The Western European media, too, had decided to be charitable. They were making a big show of generosity—giving Reagan full points for gregariousness and charm while denying him any great significance. A memorial article by Lisa Erdmann in the newsweekly *Der Spiegel* was typical. Predictably, she worked in a reference to Reagan's "cowboy stride"—but why, one might wonder, did her article's subhead mention his stint as a lifeguard? Here's why: because to the elite Western European mind, it's ludicrous that an American president was once a lifeguard. In Western Europe, young people who are destined for top positions in politics, academia, or the media don't work as lifeguards or paperboys; they go to the Sorbonne or Oxford or Tübingen, where they sit at cafés discussing Marx and Sartre and being waited on by their less privileged contemporaries. To Erdmann, Reagan's background as a lifeguard—and then radio announcer and movie star—is all part of one big American joke: only in America could such a low-rent "populist" type end up running a government.

The title of Erdmann's article said it all: "The Last Cold Warrior." She seemed to regard him as a member of some aberrant species that is now, thankfully, extinct. Like many establishment types, she'd prefer to think that the problem was never Communism but anti-Communism.

Indeed, she showed not a hint of appreciation for Reagan—not the slightest awareness that he had, perhaps, been more prescient in some matters than the transatlantic political elites who mocked him mercilessly. I say this as someone who, during Reagan's presidency, criticized him for taking his ideas about the world from the movies. When Communism in Europe imploded, I was as stunned as everyone else. While I still disagreed with Reagan on many things, I had to admit that on the great issue of the day he'd been absolutely right. And I saw, too, that despite my own firm anti-Communism, I'd allowed my view of him to be overly influenced by an American media establishment that, routinely treating Communism more gently than anti-Communism, lionized Gorbachev but never gave Reagan his due.

Journalists in Western Europe, of course, went even further than their American counterparts in prettifying Communism. Since its fall, moreover, they've done a first-rate job of rewriting the whole story of the Communist era. Just as they've oversold European socialism while fitting out American democracy with a fright wig, so they've retouched Communism to make it look friendly while emphasizing the ugliest excesses of Western anti-Communism. In doing so, they've turned the dramatic defeat of an evil empire into a prosaic tale of a perhaps somewhat too authoritarian government's reform—a reform that, in their retelling, would have taken place no matter what America and its allies did.

Such shameless revisionism is standard fare in Western Europe. From Lisbon to Helsinki, from Dublin to Rome, "peace" is the mantra; and nowhere is this more surely the case than in Germany. Today's Germans reflexively oppose war—war in Iraq, war anywhere, war against anybody for any reason whatever. For Germans today, the very idea of armed combat is tied up inextricably with Hitler, Nazism, the Holocaust, and a profound, implacable sense of national guilt. All these things are part of one nightmarish continuum—one evil, ugly bundle. Germans realize, too, that for the world around them, the very idea of war is bound up with images of Germans in uniform. For a German today, the simple act of putting on military dress recalls immense historical infamies and imposes a feeling of culpability too heavy to shoulder.

One can well understand why a German might feel that his country's only hope for redemption, given its history, lies in peace, peace, and more peace—at whatever cost—and in proclaiming at every turn the German people's repudiation of their forebears' crimes. So it is that Holocaust memorials abound in today's Germany. For example, at the center of Wittenbergplatz, a sprawling Berlin square ringed with restaurants and cafés that give it a gemütlich atmosphere, stand two high poles between which are suspended several wooden signboards, each bearing the name of a death camp. At the top of this memorial are written the words: "So that we will never forget."

But what does it mean for Germans to say that they'll never forget Auschwitz and Treblinka? The more closely one looks at present-day Germany, the emptier these declarations of memory and regret can appear. A serious Germany—a Germany interested in learning lessons from its history and acting responsibly on those lessons, rather than simply embracing the moral vanity of pacifism—would be determined to fight today's equivalent of the Nazi juggernaut. But Germans, like other Western Europeans, have been raised on ways of thinking that make it exceedingly difficult for them to take such action. Even if someone else makes war on you, as Al Qaeda did on 9/11, it's your obligation, if you're civilized and peace-loving, not to fight back.

In 2004, American writer Frank Martin recalled his own encounter with this way of thinking about war. While touring the military cemetery at Arnhem in the Netherlands, the final resting place of over 1,600 Allied servicemen who perished in the futile 1944 battle recounted in the film *A Bridge Too Far*, Martin was told by a tour guide that "the soldiers were fighting for bridges, how silly that they would all fight for something like that." Martin's reaction? "It was hard not to want to slap the crap out of [that] 17-year-old kid. . . . I tried to explain that they weren't fighting for bridges, but for his and his families' freedom." His conclusion: Europeans today think "the conditions they live in are normal, and that they have always been that way." Indeed, an alarming number of Western Europeans don't seem to grasp that freedom and prosperity aren't the default condition of the human species—and that when these things come under threat, a sanguine passivity isn't the best response.

EVERY YEAR, during the weeks before Christmas, Norwegians participate in a cherished national tradition: *julebord*. Groups of friends or coworkers book a table at a traditional Norwegian restaurant, where they share a traditional Norwegian meal. One evening I joined a friend of mine and a large group of his friends—strangers to me—at a *julebord* in Oslo. As is the usual practice, we all met beforehand at a bar to have two or three beers. I'd barely sat down when I overheard a man I didn't know saying how horrible New York was. It was the usual rant about

"American conditions." My friend interrupted the man's speech to tell him that I was an American. He turned to me. "Where are you from?" "New York." Swiftly executing a 180-degree turn, he proceeded to tell me how much he adored New York: he was spending a week there at Christmas and couldn't wait.

We went to the restaurant. Again, I'd barely sat down when I heard the man next to me—another stranger—say: "Americans can't speak English and they can't write it." Again, my friend introduced me and said I was American. Nonplussed, the man resumed his anti-American oration without missing a beat. Nobody seemed to find it rude or remarkable, and nobody argued with him. After a couple of sentences he said something I wanted to respond to: "American and English are two different languages!" (This is a claim often made by Norwegians when putting down Americans.) My friend agreed. I didn't. "The differences between American and British English," I said, "are much smaller than the differences between any two Norwegian dialects."

"*Any* two dialects?" he sneered. "Even any two *Oslo* dialects? There *are* several dialects in Oslo, you know."

"Okay, not any two *Oslo* dialects. But most of the dialects of Norway are much more different from one another than American and British English."

"That's true," my friend conceded.

Apparently deciding he couldn't win this one, the man returned to the topic of Americans' many deficiencies. When at last he finally paused long enough for me to get a word in, I said, "You're pretty anti-American, aren't you?"

"I'm *very* anti-American," he said firmly, almost fiercely, without a trace of self-awareness or anything remotely resembling good humor.

Now, in Europe, Muslims complain a great deal about anti-Muslim prejudice, as do elite journalists and politicians. But most Europeans are extraordinarily careful never to say anything to a Muslim that might remotely be construed as anti-Muslim. Anti-Americanism, however, is something else. Europeans who consider themselves good, decent people will say things to an American that they would never say to anyone from anywhere else. If I'd sat there and said that I was an admirer of Osama bin Laden, or a convinced Maoist, or a Holocaust denier, the man sitting next to me would almost certainly have treated me with more respect than he gave me for being an American.

The other diners that evening were all perfectly friendly. Yet the way they shrugged off the anti-American vitriol suggested that for them, it was not an irrational aberration but well within the bounds of acceptable conduct. Many Europeans are so used to this brand of hatred that they don't even recognize it as such. And how can one expect them to? They encounter these views daily on the evening news and in the newspapers. "I'm *very* anti-American," the man had said. I could have asked why. But I knew why: he'd been pumped full of America-hatred all his life by teachers, professors, politicians, and journalists. Since I didn't want to make a scene, or, alternatively, sit there taking abuse, I ate my meal quickly, paid, and left. The entire time, the man kept his back to me.

Despite the cold, and the late hour, the downtown Oslo streets were crowded. There was a particularly large throng outside the Grand Hotel. Middle-aged men and women, teenagers, and young children congregated in the street and on the sidewalks, many with cameras at the ready. I knew why. The Nobel Peace Prize had been awarded that day, and on the next evening the Peace Prize concert would take place. Doubtless many of the stars scheduled to appear were staying at the hotel. Most were Americans—among them Oprah Winfrey, Tom Cruise, Patti LaBelle, Tony Bennett, Diana Krall, and Cyndi Lauper. So it was that dozens of Norwegians stood out in the bitter cold December night in the hope that they might glimpse an American star. Such are the contradictions that define Western European attitudes toward America today.

ANOTHER dinner party in Oslo. There were about a dozen guests in all; a man I'd never met sat across from me. He was around sixty, and had the look of a serious professional. "So you are American?" he said to me in Norwegian.

"Yes," I said, forcing a smile and bracing myself for a snide comment about how surprising it was that an American could speak a second language, or, perhaps, a stale crack about the stupidity of George W. Bush.

"What state are you from?" he asked.

"New York."

"New York City?"

"Yes."

He paused, and seemed to look me over more closely. "Are you a Jew?"

In Norwegian, it was *Er du en jøde?* The similarity between the Norwegian *jøde* and German *Jude* only made the question all the more unsettling. It was not the first time I'd been reminded of a couple of important points: 1) for many Western Europeans, it still matters very much who is and isn't a Jew; 2) a Jew is still, in some deeply important sense, not one of us.*

The exception that proves this rule is the magnificent story of the rescue of the Danish Jews.

At the time of the Nazi occupation, the population of Denmark was about four million, including about 7,500 Jews, most of them well integrated into Danish society. In 1941, when Hermann Göring brought up the "Jewish question" with Danish foreign minister Erik Scavenius, he received the blunt reply: "There is no Jewish question in Denmark." Two years later, on September 28, 1943, Hitler directed the head of the SS in Denmark to begin rounding up Jews and deporting them to death camps on October 1. When Georg F. Duckwitz, a German military attaché, heard about the order, he got word of it to a member of the Danish Resistance, who then told the leader of Denmark's Jewish community. The news spread throughout Denmark, and the Danish people leapt into action, risking their lives to shelter Jews and transport them to coastal villages, from which freighters and fishing boats took them to safety in neutral Sweden. The Nazis figured out what was taking place, but it happened too quickly for them to respond effectively, and the Danish police and coast guard refused to help them.

Within a few days, the overwhelming majority of Danish Jews made it to Sweden. The Germans managed to arrest only 481 of them, who were sent to the internment camp at Theresienstadt. Somehow Danish officials persuaded German leaders not to send the Danish Jews to death camps; the Germans even agreed to allow inspections by the Danish Red Cross. Throughout the war, the people of Denmark continued to monitor conditions at Theresienstadt and to send food and clothing to the Danish Jews imprisoned there. As a result, most of the latter survived the war and were able to return to Denmark at war's end. And there's one last extraordinary detail: "Almost everywhere else in Europe," writes Louis Bülow, "returning Jews found their homes had been broken into, and everything of value stolen. When the Danish Jews returned, they discovered that their homes, pets, gardens and personal belongings were cared for by their neighbors."

---

*In Norwegian TV news coverage of "Jewish issues," the names of Jewish interviewees, when shown onscreen, are almost invariably followed by the hyphenated label *norsk-jødisk*, "Norwegian-Jewish," as if they were recent immigrants from some foreign country.

In many ways, Denmark is the country in Europe most similar to the Netherlands: both are small, flat, affluent, bicycle-riding maritime constitutional monarchies bordering on Germany; both, today, have generous social welfare systems. Yet how differently they responded to the Nazis' Jewish policies! The Nazis murdered 79 percent of the Netherlands' Jews; they got their hands on almost none of Denmark's. How did this happen? How was it that the gentiles of Denmark, in almost perfect unison, acted heroically, swiftly, effectively, and without hesitation to save their Jewish neighbors from the Nazis?

A few years ago, on three successive Sunday mornings, a historian presented the results of her research into that question at my parish church in New York. Part of the answer, she explained, had to do with geography and demographics: Denmark was a tiny nation with a relatively small Jewish population and was located across a narrow waterway from neutral Sweden, which made it possible for all the country's Jews to be gathered together in one place almost overnight and smuggled by boat to safety. Yet she stressed that this remarkable secret project, in which almost every last gentile in Denmark was complicit, carried dire peril for all concerned and would never have been conceived and carried out had the Danes, gentile and Jew alike, not had a powerful sense of themselves as one people, belonging to the same community. When the Germans tried to separate the Danish Jews from the Danish gentiles, in short, it just didn't make sense to the Danes; every cell in their bodies resisted it; they saw the profound wrong in it immediately, and resisted accordingly.

Such was not the case, alas, in the Netherlands. Jews had been a part of the Dutch national fabric for centuries, or so they doubtless thought; but to the Dutch gentiles they remained, to some extent, a people apart. Yes, the Dutch are passionate egalitarians; yet when they speak of equality, they mean *among Dutchmen.* And while Americans can generally accept almost anyone from anywhere as a fellow American, provided they're not freeloaders or troublemakers, the Dutch imagination is challenged by the idea that someone not ethnically Dutch is indeed a Dutchman. It's less a matter of overt prejudice than of habitual mental categories. We Americans have learned from our own racial history that "separate but equal" is an impossibility; somehow, however, the Dutch failed to learn from World War II that their separate-but-equal *verzuiling* mentality was a formula for social catastrophe.

The rescue of the Danish Jews is a wonderful story. But it was, indeed, the exception. Not only in the Netherlands but everywhere else in the Nazi empire, conquered Europeans aided in the work of the Holocaust, helpfully rounding up Jews and shipping them off to their deaths. Given Europe's long history of anti-Semitism, this was not surprising. The Nazi demonization of Jews did not emerge in a vacuum; it was the culmination of centuries of Jew-hatred rooted in the European preoccupation with ethnic identity as the basis of cultural unity.

After the war, guilt and shame kept European anti-Semitism in check—or at least sub rosa—for a generation or so. But then old prejudices began reasserting themselves. They took the form of what Bat Ye'or calls "Palestinianism." This "hate cult against Israel" is ubiquitous among bien-pensant Western Europeans: in their eyes, Israel is always the aggressor, Palestinians always the victims. During the first intifada, which began in 1983, the European media invariably portrayed rock-throwing Palestinian children as intrepid Davids confronting an Israeli Goliath. That intifada was ended by the Oslo Accords of 1993. But in the summer of 2000, Yasir Arafat rejected a settlement at Camp David that would have given him nearly everything he'd wanted. The stage was set for a new intifada, and indeed, after the visit of Israeli politician Ariel Sharon in September to the world's holiest Jewish shrine, the Temple Mount—which is also sacred to Islam—a second intifada broke out. Suicide bombings became routine in Israel—and to any sane observer, Arafat's involvement was obvious.

You wouldn't have known this, however, from the European media, which continued to treat Arafat as if he were Gandhi. Europeans didn't just wear Che T-shirts—they wore Arafat T-shirts. Among the young and trendy, Palestinian scarves were de rigueur. A media watering hole in Oslo called Stop the Presses, located in the *VG* building and across the street from *Dagbladet*, has for years displayed in its window a smiling portrait of Arafat looking every bit as benign and lovable as—well— Mullah Krekar. During Arafat's last years, European leaders made pilgrimages to his headquarters in Ramallah and proudly posed for pictures with the Great Man. They were lovers of peace and of the poor, yet— perversely—they embraced as a hero someone who'd pocketed billions in EU largesse while his people starved and quashed hopes of peace for no other reason, it seemed, than that he couldn't bring himself to stop sacrificing Palestinian children and murdering Jews.

The European media spun the second intifada relentlessly—and with little if any regard for the truth. The day after Sharon's Temple Mount visit, riots swept Old Jerusalem, and a picture of a Palestinian man crouching down and desperately shielding his twelve-year-old son from Israeli gunfire ran in newspapers across Europe, which also reported that the boy had been killed. Later, when it was established that the Israelis could not have killed the boy—and still later, when evidence mounted that the entire incident had been staged—the European press ignored these developments and continued to refer routinely to this "murder" by the IDF as if the facts had never been in dispute.

Then there was Jenin. In the spring of 2002, the refugee camp there was the site of fierce fighting between Israelis and Palestinians. After the PLO spread the tale that Israel had committed a massacre there, the European media fastened gleefully onto the story and wouldn't let go. Long after the report was exposed as a fabrication, many European journalists were still referring to "the Jenin massacre" as if it were a historical event. On the many massacres committed by Saddam Hussein, however, the same media were silent. Ditto the massacres then taking place in Sudan. As for Bush's decision to cut off ties to Arafat and his recognition of links between Palestinian violence and the war on terror, the European media considered it definitive proof that Bush was the tool of a Jewish cabal. The result of all this poisonous, fraudulent reportage? Anti-Semitism in Europe soared.

This took forms both big and small. On April 8, 2002, a man named Ingmar Tveitt was eating in the private restaurant at the Norwegian parliament when security guards ordered him to remove his jacket. According to *Dagbladet*, the guards "had received reactions" to the Star of David displayed on Tveitt's chest pocket. As Tveitt pointed out, "People walk around [in Parliament] with Palestinian scarves and other pro-Palestinian symbols without any reaction." This happened only a few days after several Nobel Peace Prize judges said they now regretted giving the 1994 prize to Shimon Peres (though none of them regretted giving it to Arafat). A few days later, the parliament was the setting for a pro-Palestinian rally at which children waved signs depicting a swastika and a Star of David with an equal sign between them.

By then, Europeans had grown accustomed to the idea that Jews were today's Nazis. In Spain, *El Pais* ran a cartoon depicting Ariel Sharon with a Hitler mustache. A cartoon in *La Vanguardia* showed a Jewish Holocaust Museum with a Palestinian Holocaust Museum being built alongside it. In Austria, a cartoon panel labeled "then" showed a Nazi soldier tormenting a Jew; beside it, a panel labeled "now" showed an Israeli soldier tormenting a Palestinian child. In France, a popular comedian dressed up as a rabbi on TV and made a Hitler salute while shouting "Heil Israel!" In Berlin, I toured the Jewish Museum, where the main exhibition traces the history of Jews in Germany—only to drastically shift focus at the end, where the visitor is confronted with a large poster that asks: "Do you think Turkey should be a member of the EU?" You're supposed to push a green knob for yes, a red knob for no. What did this question have to do with the subject of the museum? Obviously, it was motivated by the European elite's conviction that Islamophobia is the new anti-Semitism—that Muslims are now the victims, Jews the Nazis.

In 2005, Bill Dawson, an American living in Austria, reported on an episode of *Tatort*, a highly popular *CSI*-type program on German public TV. "The sympathetic character is a young lady," wrote Dawson, "who finds her boyfriend—her *Arab* boyfriend—dead and bloody on the floor of her apartment." She knows the CIA is responsible. Why? Because she knows her boyfriend knew that 9/11 was "a hoax perpetrated by Bush, Cheney, Perle and Wolfowitz [all of whom were specifically named]— and was in the process of revealing the hoax by releasing information over the Internet." Like NRK's obsequious Galtung promo, this despicable piece of slander was paid for with mandatory TV-owner fees.

At the commemoration of the sixtieth anniversary of D-day, Jacques Chirac was asked what he thought of George W. Bush's comparison of the liberation of Europe to the liberation of Iraq. "History," snapped Chirac, "doesn't repeat itself." Well, not in every detail. Yet there's truth in Santayana's observation that those who can't remember the past are condemned to repeat it. For Chirac to dismiss the idea of history's repeating itself in a time when echoes of the darkest era of Europe's history were growing louder and louder seemed to indicate a case of willful historical amnesia.

Indeed, since 2000, anti-Semitism in France has been epidemic. Synagogues have been burned down, schools vandalized, shops attacked, rabbis beaten, children assaulted, school buses shot at, gravestones knocked over and defaced with swastikas and the name of Hitler. At Muslim demonstrations, shouts of "Death to the Jews" have become common. (One thing I've noticed is that while Americans speak of "Jews" or, more often, "Jewish people," Europeans usually say "the Jews.") On March 29, 2002, a dozen or so young men in masks smashed two stolen cars into the doors of a synagogue in Lyon and set the cars on fire. That same weekend, synagogues in Strasbourg and Marseille were burned. Shortly thereafter, Molotov cocktails were thrown at several other French synagogues. In March 2003, three men in masks carved a Star of David into the arm of a Jewish girl in Aix-en-Provence. In the spring of 2004, a rabbi's seventeen-year-old son was assaulted outside his home in a Paris suburb by attackers shouting anti-Semitic slurs. A week later, an assailant shouting *"Allahu Akbar"* ("God is great") stabbed another seventeen-year-old Jewish boy in the chest in another suburb of Paris. The stabbing took place just as the young man was leaving a Jewish school. Perhaps the most striking thing about this news item was that it was based on information provided by local officials *"on condition of anonymity."* Note well: the officials in question were not offering their opinions on Islam or anything else—they were simply providing the basic facts of a criminal case; yet even in stating those facts, they would not go on the record.

The response of the French media to most crimes of this kind has been to ignore them. "When an anti-Semitic act is so disgusting it is impossible to hide it," writes Guy Millière, "journalists will speak of 'confrontation between communities.' " Or, as Michael Gurfinkiel notes, "intergroup friction." Such locutions make it sound as if the violence goes both ways, which it doesn't. This kind of mendacious rhetoric is also commonplace in Belgium, where a local observer recorded that an attack by an Arab gang on young Jews in Antwerp was described on television as "violence between two communities." For an example of this kind of misrepresentation, one need look no further than the Associated Press dispatch on the stabbing outside Paris. After underscoring that such attacks "have coincided with rising tension in the Middle East" (as if this somehow excused or mitigated them), the AP reporter, Pierre-Yves Roger, added—in an apparent version of the "intergroup friction" fiction—that "Muslims have also been the victims of racist attacks." The details carefully omitted here by Roger are (a) that Muslims in Europe have not been attacked by Jews; (b) that unlike anti-Semitic acts, which are encouraged and applauded by influential figures within the Muslim community, anti-Muslim attacks are isolated incidents that no respected person or institution approves of; and (c) that the number of anti-Muslim attacks is dwarfed by the number of attacks on Jews. Roger's elision of these facts is typical of Western European reporting.

Most often, the media haven't reported such incidents at all. Yet the problem eventually became so serious that even *Le Monde* felt compelled to take note. A January 19, 2004, editorial commented on a demonstration by the Parti des Musulmans de France (PMF) in Paris: "How can one help being revolted by a protest march in which men forbid their 'sisters' to speak to the press? By the anti-Republican manner in which a *'pseudo-democracy,'* that practiced by France, is called into question? And finally, by the unabashed homophobia?" Yet *Le Monde* too felt compelled to prettify reality: the editorial concluded with a plea to "France's Muslims" to "ensure that this party remains a tiny minority"—as if anti-Semitism, homophobia, and the suppression of women's voices were confined to the PMF.

Gurfinkiel makes another important point: that Muslim anti-Semitism is helping to revive a native French tradition of anti-Semitism. The nineteenth-century socialist Pierre-Joseph Proudhon advocated either expelling or exterminating Jews; de Gaulle, after the Six Day War, called the Jews "an elite, self-conscious, and domination-oriented nation"; and François Mitterrand, reportedly a private anti-Semite, was "close to radical anti-Semitic circles as a young man and remained for all his life a close and devoted friend of Pierre Bousquet, the head of the Vichy police during the war, and as such, one of the main organizers of the Holocaust in France." Gurfinkiel records that offensive anti-Israel remarks are very common among French civil servants, "especially at France's foreign office, the Quai d'Orsay." *Quelle surprise.*

Why is anti-Semitism so widespread in Europe? Though Americans have been taught to think of Europeans as civilized and worldly, the countries of Western Europe, unlike the United States, are not melting pots. Yes, France, for one, does have a revolutionary tradition of supposedly considering all Frenchmen equal—and equally French—regardless of race, ethnicity, or religion; many Frenchmen claim to cherish this secular egalitarian ideal. But in France, rhetoric often bears little resemblance to reality. The widespread collaboration of French gentiles in the Holocaust testifies to the shallowness of many Frenchmen's dedication to *liberté, égalité,* and *fraternité.* In France, as elsewhere in Europe, the same native traditions of anti-Semitism that led to cooperation with the Final Solution remain very much alive. In America, the nation of immigrants, the ability and willingness of Jews to integrate harmoniously into mainstream society and to champion American values has made them the most successful of ethnic groups; in Europe, that same ability brought them to the edge of extinction. Among Western European elites, I'd suggest, Muslims are more popular than Jews precisely *because* they insist on retaining their differences, keeping to themselves, and rejecting a European identity.

Polls indicate that up to half of all French Jews have either thought of leaving France or advised their children to do so. In mid-2004, the *Jerusalem Post* reported that the Jewish Agency in France planned "a campaign to persuade French Jews to immigrate to Israel to escape a wave of anti-Semitism." Shortly afterward, French Nazi hunter Serge Klarsfeld suggested that it would be best for Jews to abandon *la belle République:* "One of the lessons of the Holocaust is that even if you want to fight against a wave of anti-Semitism, the best [thing] is to leave if you can." Klarsfeld's entreaty was echoed by Ariel Sharon, who in an address to international Jewish leaders cited the steep rise in anti-Semitism in France and urged French Jews to move to Israel "as early as possible." Sharon acknowledged that it was his standard practice to encourage Jews in the Diaspora to move to Israel, but for French Jews, he insisted, moving to Israel is "a must. . . . they have to move immediately."

Did the French government react to this extraordinary announcement by taking anti-Semitism more seriously? Hardly. Rather, the French foreign ministry called Sharon's comments "unacceptable" and demanded an explanation. "There is irritation in France," reported the BBC, "at the idea that life for Jews there is becoming dangerous—especially as the government has made every effort to show that anti-Jewish acts will be severely punished." Note that carefully: there's irritation in France not over the rise in anti-Semitism but over the refusal of Jews to keep quiet about it. Here, once again, we may observe the French elite's penchant for uncoupling rhetoric from reality: they got irritated not about anti-Semitism but about Jews' reactions to it; they worry not about Muslim-perpetrated atrocities but about the possibility that these atrocities will cause an anti-Muslim backlash. This is fear, pure and simple.

What has the European Union done to combat anti-Semitism? Predictably, it ordered a report. Entitled "Manifestations of Anti-Semitism in the European Union," it was commissioned by a Vienna-based EU body called the European Monitoring Center on Racism and Xenophobia (EUMC) and prepared by the Center for Research on Anti-Semitism (CRA) in Berlin in cooperation with a number of Jewish groups.

When the report was submitted, however, the EUMC chose not to release it. The ostensible reason was that it was of "poor quality and lacking in empirical evidence"; the actual reason was that it was altogether too clear in stating who Western Europe's new anti-Semites were. Yet the report didn't stay buried. A copy was leaked to the World Jewish Congress, which posted it on the Internet; in January 2004 Edgar Bronfman, president of that organization, and Cobi Benatoff, president of the European Jewish Congress, coauthored a blistering op-ed in the *Financial Times* accusing the European Commission (EC) of "intellectual dishonesty and moral treachery" for having suppressed it. An angry Romano Prodi, president of the EC, reacted to the op-ed in the same spirit as the French foreign ministry: he suspended a planned conference on anti-Semitism.

Finally, on March 31, 2004, the EUMC, under pressure, released a new, more detailed report. This time the EUMC chose to spin it, writing in a press release: "Although it is not easy to generalise, the largest group of the perpetrators of antisemitic activities appears to be young, disaffected white Europeans. A further source of antisemitism in some countries was young Muslims of North African or Asian extraction. Traditionally anti-semitic groups on the extreme right played a part in stirring opinion."

As Ambrose Evans-Pritchard commented in the *Telegraph*, these statements "astounded experts," so far were they from the truth. The EUMC's press release blatantly contradicted its own report, which made it clear that the vast majority of perpetrators of anti-Semitic acts in the EU were young Muslim males.

The findings, wrote Evans-Pritchard, "had been consistently mas-saged by the EU watchdog to play down the role of North African youth." One might wonder why EU leaders—if they were so intent on suppressing the truth—commissioned the report in the first place. Were they so out of touch that they didn't already *know* that Muslims are by far the major perpetrators of anti-Semitic acts in Europe? Or did they expect that those preparing the report would compliantly cover up this fact? Could it be that they're so accustomed to swathing uncomfortable realities in silence, euphemism, and misrepresentation that it didn't oc-cur to them that the report would actually tell some awkward truths?

Here's just a sampling from the report's country-by-country catalogs of anti-Semitic incidents during 2002 and 2003.

• *Belgium:* During a two-month period, there were two instances of firebombs being thrown at, and one instance of machine guns being fired at, synagogues. During the same period, pro-Palestinian and anti–Iraq War demonstrations featured "antisemitic banners and antisemitic slo-gans." In Antwerp, "a group of Jewish youths aged 13 were threatened by a group of allegedly Arab youths. . . . One of them menaced the Jew-ish youngsters with a mock rifle and was subsequently arrested." (If he was arrested, why the "allegedly"?) There were several attacks on rabbis and Jewish young people. Some fourteen-year-old Jews "were attacked in a subway station by a group of thirty youngsters throwing stones at them. One of the Jewish youths was thrown on the ground, insulted as 'dirty Jew' and beaten." (No arrests?) Finally, "insults were directed against a Jewish funeral procession in Brussels. Children of a nearby school allegedly of North-African origin yelled insults ('dirty Jew,' 'death to the Jews,' etc.) as they noticed the Star of David on the hearse." (If they were known to attend a certain school, what happened to them? Were their parents called in? Was any kind of disciplinary action taken?)

• *Denmark:* "The President of the Jewish Community reported that he had been harassed by two Arabs, who followed him closely and stepped on his heels near his home." The Islamist group Hizb-ut-Tahrir handed out leaflets telling people to kill Jews. There were many instances of Jews being spit at on the street, of gangs of young Muslims harassing Jews, and of words such as *Juden* being written on walls, cars, and traffic signs.

• *France:* The long list of incidents includes physical assaults on Jews (often students), arson attacks on synagogues, and the desecration of graves.

• *Sweden:* In Stockholm, 100 to 150 participants in a large "anti-Israel march" attacked a small crowd rallying against anti-Semitism and Islamophobia. There was violence; some attackers shouted "Kill the Jews" and "We'll blow you up." An "Islamologist" named Jan Samuelsson argued in *Dagens Nyheter* that "Muslim hatred of Jews is justified." The report cited "a tendency in Swedish society to become more lenient towards the expression of antisemitic attitudes that could be related to the Middle East conflict."

• *Britain:* The report identified Britain as being less prejudiced "by a substantial margin" compared to Belgium, Denmark, France, and Germany. Yet here, too, there were anti-Semitic incidents. In an attack on a synagogue in London's Finsbury Park (location of the famous mosque), "windows were smashed, excrement was smeared on the floor, and swastikas painted on the lectern, beneath the Star of David." A Swansea synagogue was vandalized in similar fashion. If British leaders have failed to respond aggressively to such acts, the report charged, it's because they're "very anxious not to upset the Muslim community."

Many of these anecdotes recount incidents of abuse in schools: Muslim students calling their Jewish classmates names, threatening them, ripping yarmulkes off their heads and Stars of David from around their necks, pushing them around, following them home, and beating them up, sometimes while telling them that their people deserve to be exterminated. Frequently the assailants are not individuals but groups. As a rule, this isn't ordinary school bullying; it's a case of children repeating what they hear at home, in the mosque, and in the Arabic-language media. Though the worst list of school-related incidents seems to be from France, none of the major countries of Europe appears to be exempt. Many offenders escape punishment. The report notes, too, that teachers are skipping history lessons on the Holocaust in order not to rile Muslim students.

In Copenhagen, a teacher helped smuggle a Jewish ninth-grader out of school so that he could escape a beating by Muslim students from a nearby school. Nor is it just Muslim students doing the tormenting: at Birmingham University, a teaching assistant (whose ethnicity and religion went unmentioned) allegedly "threatened two Jewish students" and told one that simply by being Jewish "he was infringing the rights of Palestinians, and warning 'you'd better watch your back.' " A Jewish teacher at a Stockholm school was harassed by a colleague who told her that "Jews with their money rule." In this blizzard of accounts, there's almost never any mention of offenders being punished.

The report seems systematically to avoid pointing a finger at Muslim perpetrators. "Jewish and Hindu students in Manchester," we're told, "joined together at an event designed to foster closer links between the two communities and in particular between Jewish and Hindu students, two groups that experience harassment on campus." Harassment by whom? The report isn't saying. In Sweden, "the atmosphere in schools has . . . become more difficult for Jewish pupils." Because of whom? In Brussels, several pupils insulted and threatened a Jewish teacher, who left the school and required psychological counseling.* What was the students' background? What, if anything, was done to them? Were their parents called in? Why did the teacher have to leave, and not the students? In this and many other cases, the report raises more questions than it answers.[†]

The incidents itemized in the EUMC report are, of course, only the tip of the iceberg. Many Jewish children endure abuse by Muslim schoolmates silently, fearing that they would only make matters worse by speaking up. Some tell their parents, who, likewise fearing the consequences, decide not to go to school authorities. And some parents do complain, only to be told that it's in everybody's interest to leave things alone.

Not all of the children who are picked on by their Muslim classmates, moreover, are Jewish. In the Copenhagen district of Nørrebro, an eleven-

---

*Though the report doesn't mention it, it's also widely recognized that Muslim students torment gay teachers mercilessly and that the prevailing attitude is that nothing can be done about this.

†The report does mention, however, that in the fall of 2003, Mikael Tossavainen published a study entitled *The Denied Hatred*, about the rise of Arab and Muslim anti-Semitism in Sweden; Tossavainen's focus, the report acknowledges, was on schoolchildren, and his information was gleaned largely through interviews with teachers.

year-old boy named Stefan, after being threatened daily with beating by Muslim classmates, was pulled out of his public school by his parents and placed in an independent Christian school—not because they particularly wanted him to learn religion, but because they wanted him to be safe.

Stefan's Muslim classmates said things like this to him: "You shouldn't eat pork here! It smells! If you bring a lunch to school with pork in it, we'll disinfect both you and your schoolbag in the garbage container!" When Stefan appeared at school with a cross around his neck, an act which "created great anger among the Muslim pupils," one of the latter grabbed his collar and screamed at him, "We don't wear that kind of thing here!" Yet the school's principal denied that such bullying represented a major problem: "Children are children, and they tease each other."

In a few places, the EUMC report quotes, without corrective commentary, remarks by politicians and journalists in which the blame for anti-Semitic acts and statements is shifted away from Muslims. For example, the section of the report that deals with Britain mentions a 2003 Labor Party conference at which a cabinet minister "attacked the racist factions of the far right" and, with the support of Alan Travis of the *Guardian*, denounced the British National Party and UK Independence Party for anti-Semitism. The report also cites *Daily Telegraph* articles with supposed "racist connotations."

Now, the BNP is indeed famously racist, but the implication here is that the conservative UKIP and *Telegraph* are as well, and that anti-Semitism in Britain is essentially a phenomenon of the right. On the contrary, anti-Semitism in Britain is far more visible among Laborites than among conservatives, whether Tory or UKIP. No major newspaper in Western Europe, moreover, covers anti-Semitism and Muslim issues with greater candor than the *Telegraph*; the British newspaper that can most reliably be counted on to slant stories against Israel and provide column space to anti-Semites is, as it happens, Mr. Travis's newspaper, the left-wing *Guardian*. Indeed, in late 2003, columnist Julie Burchill wrote that she was leaving the *Guardian* because of its "bias against the state of Israel. Which, for all its faults, is the only country in that barren region that you or I, or any feminist, atheist, homosexual or trade union-ist, could bear to live under." The EUMC report contains no reference to Burchill's resignation.

Sweden shares two distinctions with France: a high percentage of Muslims in its population and a high rate of anti-Semitic crime. The Swedish media, which are even more inclined than most of their Western European counterparts to ignore such matters, have cloaked this

shameful fact in silence. In October 2003, however, the silence was spectacularly broken—and exposed—in *Dagens Nyheter* by history professor
Sverker Oredsson and researcher Mikael Tossavainen. "Arab and Muslim attacks on Jews," they reported, "are rising sharply in Swedish society." The problem had grown so serious that "Jews in Sweden today are
often compelled to hide their religious identity in public: necklaces with
stars of David are carefully hidden under sweaters, and Orthodox Jewish
men exchange their skullcaps for more discreet caps or hats when they
are outdoors. Jews in Sweden nowadays get secret telephone numbers to
avoid harassment. In Sweden. Today."*

In January 2004, Swedish anti-Semitism made headlines around the
world. The occasion was *Snow White and the Madness of Truth*, an art installation at Stockholm's Museum of National Antiquities that consisted
of a toy sailboat floating in a pool of blood in the museum's courtyard.
Serving as the boat's sail was a portrait of a beautiful, smiling young
woman—Palestinian suicide bomber Hanadi Jaradat, who a few months
earlier had killed twenty-one people in Haifa. Accompanying the installation was a text that alternated lines from "Snow White" by the Brothers Grimm with excerpts from news stories about Jaradat, who'd sought
to avenge her brother's death at the hands of Israeli security forces. The
intent of the "artist" was plainly to win sympathy for Jaradat and to
equate terrorism with legitimate national defense; the exhibition catalog
even described Jaradat as a "freedom fighter."

In short, *Snow White* was a predictable piece of left-wing political
art, romanticizing and aestheticizing Middle Eastern terrorism from a
safe distance. It would probably have remained obscure but for one simple act: at a reception celebrating the exhibition opening, Zvi Mazel, the
Israeli ambassador to Sweden, unplugged the three spotlights that illu-
minated *Snow White*. He was immediately escorted out of the museum.
When news of his action (which was widely characterized as vandalism)
got out, the Swedish foreign ministry rebuked him and the Israeli government cheered. Commentators around the world denounced Mazel,
some of them sounding more outraged by the unplugging of spotlights
than by the murder of twenty-one people. Largely lost in the controversy was the fact that the art exhibition was tied to a conference on
genocide that was supposed to focus on the Holocaust; apparently, at the

---

*On June 17, 2004, several months after this article appeared, Somali Muslim boys
playing in a Swedish soccer match against a team of Jewish boys yelled out "Death to
the Jews!" and "Long live Palestine!"

Stockholm art museum, as at the Jewish Museum in Berlin, it was impossible to contemplate the Shoah without invoking the conceit that the Palestinians are today's Jews and the Jews are today's Nazis.

One recurrent feature of anti-Semitic acts in Europe is the passivity of bystanders. Ilya Meyer, a Jewish leader in Gothenburg, Sweden, has said that while ethnic Swedes rarely commit anti-Semitic crimes, their reaction when witnessing such acts is one of indifference. Meyer told the *Jerusalem Post* about his fourteen-year-old son, Nadav, who had been "attacked on buses, trains and in the street by gangs of Muslim youth" for wearing a Star of David. "Only once," Meyer told the *Jerusalem Post*, "did a Swede come to his aid and hold off the assailants." The Swedes, Meyer insisted, "shy away from conflict."

It's not just Swedes, of course. My partner, after all, was attacked in the middle of a rush-hour crowd in Oslo without anyone's coming to his aid. The 2005 gay-bashing of American journalist Chris Crain in Amsterdam was also witnessed by dozens of people who did nothing.

How to reconcile this kind of unresponsiveness—this colossal lack of what Americans call civic responsibility—with all the proud rhetoric about "solidarity" and "community" that fills Western European political speeches and newspaper editorials? Well, I realized quite a while back that this rhetoric, far from having anything to do with cultivating among citizens a feeling of mutual support and neighborliness, was, quite simply, welfare-state sloganeering. Western Europeans have been brought up to think of solidarity with one's fellow man not as something they have to attend to themselves but rather as something mediated through state bureaucracies.

Take the 2004 murder of Anna Lindh. Lindh, who, following the 2002 death of *Pippi Longstocking* author Astrid Lindgren, was probably her country's most beloved public figure, was stabbed to death in the middle of a busy Stockholm department store, in the presence of many witnesses; but her murderer was able to flee the scene of the crime without any trouble. Onlookers just stood there, waiting for the authorities to do something. It was as if the very capacity for useful response had been bred out of them. Admittedly, one shouldn't judge individuals' behavior in specific incidents too harshly: sometimes it's not clear exactly what's going on; sometimes things just happen too quickly. But there does seem to exist in Western Europe a deadly pattern of passivity that derives from a habit—born of life in a welfare state—of expecting the government to take care of things. This fecklessness of individuals in the face of atrocious crimes is, I would further suggest, a smaller-scale version of their governments' passivity in the face of Al Qaeda's terrorism, Saddam's tyranny, and the rise of Islamism within their own borders.

According to Meyer, most Swedish Jews who are assaulted don't dare go to the authorities because they fear retribution. They also doubtless realize that even if they did report these incidents, little or nothing would be done. The police instructed Meyer's son, as they've instructed others, not to reply to taunts, to walk away quickly, and to wear his Star of David inside his shirt—in other words, to be a *dhimmi.*

Norway, too, has its share of anti-Semitism. On April 7, 2004, then prime minister Bondevik, apparently under pressure to address the problem, met with a Jewish girl and boy who'd been targets of abuse. Nineteen-year-old Julie told him about a Muslim family that had noticed her Star of David on the street. The father had asked Julie if her father was from Israel, and when she had replied in the affirmative, the whole family—including a four-year-old daughter—had proceeded to abuse her verbally, while two of the girls physically attacked her, punching her in the face and tearing off her Star of David. Julie told the father that he should learn how to bring up his children; as she walked away, he and his children called after her that they would kill her family. Though some of Julie's schoolmates called her "fucking Jew" and "Jewish whore" in the corridors, the authorities refused to let her change schools, while the principal suggested that she stop wearing her Star of David—it was too "provocative."

Bondevik's comment? That "it is unacceptable and intolerable for individuals to suffer for what other people do, such as happens, for example, when Muslims are badgered because some Muslims are terrorists." The assumption here—standard among Europe's elite—is that anti-Semitic acts by Muslims, while indefensible, are rooted in understandable anger at Israel. Bondevik's comment also implies that anti-Muslim acts are common; they are not. The plain fact is that Muslim adults in Europe do routinely harass Jewish children, while Jewish and Christian adults in Europe virtually never behave in this manner toward children of other faiths. Major European Muslim groups have even put bounties on the heads of certain European Jews. For Bondevik to ignore such facts was disgusting.

In August 2004, a group of fifty Jewish university students from Israel, Poland, and the United States was assaulted by three male students from France whose religious affiliation went unreported. What made this stand out from the usual run of anti-Semitic attacks was the venue: Auschwitz. The students were examining mock-ups of a gas chamber and crematorium when one of the Frenchmen, noticing the Israeli flag wrapped around the neck of one of them, charged at the group, telling them to "go back to Israel" and that they "should be ashamed to walk around with an Israeli flag." Another Frenchman grabbed a Jewish woman by the arm "and wouldn't let go," she told the *Jerusalem Post.* "I was afraid. I couldn't move and I didn't know what he was going to do." The woman, who was from Poland, added that although she'd often experienced anti-Semitism, it was startling to have such a thing happen to her at Auschwitz, where members of her family had been murdered.

Reflecting on this incident, Laurence Weinbaum of the World Jewish Congress commented that "in Western Europe there is sympathy for dead Jews; it's just the live ones that they cannot tolerate."* One of the Jewish students said that the experience had "brought into focus a small part of what it's like to be a Jew in the Diaspora today and a little bit about what it was like to be a Jew in the Diaspora during the Holocaust." Later reports added that no one, including the Auschwitz tour guides, had come to the aid of the Jewish students; the guide accompanying them had just "backed off" when the attack began.

Americans are supposed to be ignorant of history, Europeans drenched in it. A 2005 survey showed that half of Germans under age twenty-four don't know what the Holocaust was.

THEN AGAIN, plenty of Europeans who are well over twenty-four—and who have been working with these issues for decades—are hardly less clueless. One such individual is Kåre Willoch, a slight, elderly *snillist* who was once prime minister of Norway. He's so famous for his hostility to Israel that it came as a surprise, in August 2004, to see his name on an article entitled "Ugly Anti-Semitism." Could Willoch, of all people, actually be speaking up against Jew-hatred? As it turned out, no. After a rote condemnation of anti-Semitism as a set of "primitive attitudes" historically found among "weaker groups" and often based on discredited "race theories" and misguided Bible readings, Willoch moved swiftly to his main point: that in modern times the Jews have brought anti-Semitism upon themselves. For centuries, he maintained, Jews and Christians had

*In fact, dead Jews aren't treated too well, either: in Britain, 117 Jewish cemeteries have been vandalized since 1990. In a typical incident, in June 2005 eighty-seven graves were desecrated in a London cemetery, where swastikas were drawn on several headstones and the words "Jew Boy dead. Ha ha" were scrawled on a tomb.

been tolerated and allowed religious freedom in Muslim countries. (This line of argument, which is highly popular among European apologists for Islam, ignores the fact that Christians and Jews who lived in Muslim countries were *dhimmis*—oppressed, segregated, and without rights.)

"Only after the first Zionists came to Palestine toward the end of the 1800s," argued Willoch, "did this change." Hostility to Israel, he claimed, intensified after it occupied land beyond its borders in 1967. Willoch omitted to mention that one reason why there's so much anti-Semitism in Muslim countries is that schoolteachers and the media throughout the region peddle outrageous disinformation about Jews and Israel. (Many people in the Middle East firmly believe, for instance, that Israel was behind 9/11.) Nor did Willoch mention that the 1967 occupation was a result of the Six-Day War, in which Israel had been savagely attacked by Arab neighbors bent on its extinction.

Explicitly rejecting the right of Israel to exist, Willoch insisted that neither the past suffering of the Jews nor their holy scripture gives them any right to "seize others' land." (He forgot to mention that most of the Arab world, other than the Arabian peninsula itself, was gained for Islam through the seizure of land. This includes Palestine, which before the Muslim conquest was populated by Jews and Christians.) While Willoch agreed that Israel's actions were no excuse to hate individual Jews, his intention was plainly to blame European anti-Semitism entirely on Israel. Willoch suggested that if Israel would only pull back to its 1967 borders, it would "receive the massive support against remaining enemies that can provide endless peace to the Jewish state." The notion that the inculcation of anti-Semitism in the Muslim world would cease if Israel only returned to its 1967 borders was staggering in its naïveté—or duplicity. The sad joke is that Willoch is considered in Norway to be an elder statesman of great wisdom and distinction—yet of course such reputations, in Western Europe, are the result not of innovative leadership or courageous contrariety but rather of a lifetime of saying the right things and being applauded for it by journalists who agree with you.

September 11 was a nightmare. The one bright spot was the expectation that this blinding dose of reality would awaken Europe's establishment from its fantasy of America and Israel as the two great beasts stalking the planet, bringing agony where otherwise all would be joy. But the opposite happened. The elite retreated further into its comfortable fantasy and began clinging to a new one: that 9/11, when you came right down to it, had nothing whatsoever to do with them.

III

◆

Europe's Weimar Moment:
The Liberal Resistance and
Its Prospects

ON THE MORNING OF March 11, 2004, I was working at my desk in Oslo, half listening to the news on CNN, when the first reports came through of massive explosions in Madrid. Soon news cameras were on the streets of the Spanish capital, registering shock on the faces of *madrileños* as they took in the horror.

"Well," I thought, "it's happened. It's happened here."

I kept the TV on all day, switching between CNN and the BBC. As reporters told of images of death and devastation too gruesome to be broadcast, I kept thinking of our vacation in Madrid in August 2000, four years earlier. I'd loved Madrid's cosmopolitan feel and scale, its solid stone buildings and teeming crowds. Even at the height of the blistering summer heat there'd been an energy, an air of purposefulness about the city that reminded me of New York; yet at the same time there'd been a feeling of Latin fun and tropical ease reminiscent of Miami Beach. All this had come as something of a surprise, because I realized I'd still thought of Spain as a country stifled by fascist oppression and severe Catholicism.

I knew, of course, that Spain had changed. Generalissimo Francisco Franco, absolute ruler since 1939, had died in 1975, and his chosen heir, King Juan Carlos, had astonished everyone by establishing a constitutional monarchy. Spain's post-Franco metamorphosis is invariably described in superlatives. But to read about Spain's transformation was one thing; to experience it was another. I kept thinking back to our peach-colored room in a modest *pension* off the Puerta del Sol, to strolls down shady avenues on scorching afternoons, to cool evenings when we'd sipped strong, icy gin-and-tonics at sidewalk cafés on the Plaza de Chueca, the affable waiters pouring the gin into tall glasses until it nearly overflowed. I remembered the museums—the palatial Prado, the Thyssen, the Reina Sofía, all strung along the length of the grand, lush, tree-lined Paseo del Prado. And at the foot of that boulevard loomed the imposing white granite facade of the Atocha railway station. It was there that a commuter train had now been blown apart and pieces of what had been men, women, and children littered the tracks.

The atrocity had been carefully timed. At 7:39 A.M., the height of rush hour, four bombs concealed in backpacks had gone off simultaneously on a train in the Atocha station. In the train yard south of the station, near a street called Calle de Téllez, three bombs exploded on a train that should also have been in Atocha by that time but that had been held up by a red signal light. Total death toll: eighty-nine. Two minutes later, two more bombs went off in a train in the El Pozo del Tío station, two stops down the line. Death toll: seventy. One minute after that, a bomb blew up a train in the Santa Eugenia station, two stops beyond El Pozo. Death toll: seventeen. In all, nearly two thousand were wounded. Other, unexploded bombs were found in the trains at Atocha, Téllez, and El Pozo. Experts concluded that the bombs on the Atocha and Téllez trains had been intended to destroy the entire station. Near the station at Alcalá de Henares, five stops down from Santa Eugenia, police discovered a parked van containing detonators, audiotapes of Koran verses, and cell phones (which had been used to trigger the explosions).

As the day went on, the number of confirmed dead rose steadily. In the end, it would reach close to two hundred. At first Prime Minister Aznar, a firm Bush ally in the war on terror, attributed the action to the Basque terrorist group ETA. I was no expert in the fine differences between ETA and Al Qaeda terrorist methods, but it was hard for me to believe that this atrocity was not the work of Islamists. The West, after all, was at war. After 9/11, and after the attacks in Bali and Istanbul, it had been clear that it would only be a matter of time before Islamists staged a massive assault on Western European soil. The bombings in Madrid should not have come as a shock to anyone.

But many Europeans *were* in shock, because for years their media had fed them systematic untruths. Repeatedly, they'd been told that

America had asked for 9/11—that the atrocity had been payback for American militarism, neocolonialism, capitalist exploitation, and support of Israel. Western Europe, they'd been assured, was fundamentally different from America—more tolerant, more peaceful, more respectful of its fellow nations, more sensitive to the problem of poverty in the Islamic world, more supportive of the Palestinian cause. For these reasons, Osama bin Laden and company would never do to Europe what they'd done to New York and Washington.

Such were the illusions with which many Western Europeans comforted themselves prior to the attacks in Madrid. Yet as the day wore on, as the body parts began to be sorted out, and as it became increasingly apparent who was responsible, some Europeans seemed at last to pull their heads out of the sand. On 9/11, they'd offered brief tut-tuts of sympathy for America, only to settle back into a comfortable assurance that none of this had anything, really, to do with them. Now, some of them seemed to be putting away their toys. Among those who spoke with a new, firm directness was then prime minister Bondevik of Norway. Usually, when pronouncing on international affairs, Bondevik could be expected to make bland European-establishment noises about mutual understanding and dialogue; now, however, he broke all the rules of sophisticated Continental discourse and, in stunning American-cowboy fashion, actually called the Madrid terrorists "evil."

He wasn't alone. Across Europe, political leaders and media commentators described the bombings as Western Europe's 9/11. Finally, some Western Europeans in positions of influence were saying what their American counterparts had been saying for two and a half years: that democracy was under attack by enemies of civilization.

How gratifying it was to hear such words pass elite Western European lips. Democracy! Enemies! Civilization! Some even declared, unbelievably: "The Americans were right all along."

Watching television the day after the bombings, I was impressed by the size of the crowds in the streets of Spanish cities. From where I sat, every indication was that the people of Spain were mad as hell and determined to fight back. "Murderers!" read their signs. "Assassins!" In on-camera interviews, they didn't disguise their contempt for the terrorists. Nobody tried to turn the stark black and white of the crime into the usual, soothing Western European gray.

One thing was for sure: the timing had been no coincidence. While the invasion of Iraq had been controversial in Spain, as everywhere else, Aznar had backed Bush and Blair to the hilt, and had stood at their side when the start of the invasion was announced. As the body count had risen, Spain's establishment had been increasingly restive, and the Socialist opposition had sought to make the national elections a referendum on Aznar's Iraq policy. Yet Aznar held firm and pre-3/11 polls showed him leading the Socialists by a comfortable margin. By bombing Madrid three days before the election, the terrorists had manifestly sought to scare the electorate into voting for the Socialists. I'd long complained about European irresolution, but Friday's mass demonstrations appeared to be solid evidence that I'd been wrong. As on 9/11, it appeared, the terrorists had overplayed their hand and underestimated their victims.

That illusion lasted a good two days—until Sunday, Election Day. The verdict was clear soon after the polls closed: the terrorists had won. Spain's voters had caved. On that day, the message sent around the world was that in Western Europe, terrorism pays.

Spain's newly elected Socialist government quickly reaffirmed its determination to yank troops out of Iraq. Party leader José Luis Rodriguez Zapatero—who, perhaps even more than France's egregious Dominique de Villepin, seemed the very embodiment of Western Europe's decadent political elite—vowed to steer a more "European" course, loosening ties to the United States and strengthening bonds with France and Germany. (Zapatero's sneering reference to the United States would have sent chills of joy up spines on the Quai d'Orsay—had there *been* spines on the Quai d'Orsay.)

Naturally, Zapatero's supporters denied that they'd given in to terrorism. They had another explanation: Aznar had at first attributed the terrorist acts to ETA, the fanatical Basque separatist group that had specialized for years in senseless murders on Spanish soil; Aznar had even gone out of his way to phone top figures at several news organizations and assure them that ETA was responsible. This was described as suspicious. It was said that Aznar had lied, convinced that if the Spanish people knew they'd been attacked by Islamists, they'd vote him out of office.

Yet this explanation failed to take into account the fact that many Spaniards, in the three days between the terrorist acts and the election, began to blame Aznar, not just for attributing the terrorist acts to ETA, but for the murders themselves. At rallies on Saturday evening, protesters carried signs calling their prime minister an assassin. It was sheer irrationality. To listen to them, it was all Aznar's fault: without his support for America, there would've been no attack on Madrid; boot Aznar, and all would be well again.

For many, such delusions were easier to embrace than the truth—and the truth was that Spain had enemies, who were motivated not just by Aznar's deployment of troops in Iraq but by a deep hatred for democracy and by centuries-old grudges. Spain, after all, had once been a part of the Islamic world. The Muslims had conquered it in the eighth century, and for nearly five hundred years had controlled most of the Iberian Peninsula, which they called Al-Andalus, or Andalusia. Those had been centuries of struggle—of conquests and reconquests, of forced migrations and forced conversions. The era of Al-Andalus had not drawn to a close until 1492, a date at least as famous in Spanish history for the expulsion of the Muslims as for the discovery of America. For many in the Muslim world, that defeat still stings—and awaits vengeance, and reversal.

To Western Europeans, of course, such thinking is scarcely comprehensible. After all, they've made a point of putting their bloody past behind them. Western Europe, so we're told, has finally learned the lesson of war's folly, madness, and waste. Now Europe is one, a chorus singing hymns of brotherhood and eager to convert the entire world to its religion of eternal peace. Henceforth, the only international conflict Europe will experience will be collegial debates in Brussels about agricultural policy, packaging standards, and the like.

It's a pretty delusion. In reality, Europe is even now entering another chapter in its long history of violent struggle. The enemy can't be wished or talked away. And what's at stake isn't just the sovereignty of one or two nations but modern democratic civilization.

On the morning after the Spanish election, few in the Western European media saw things this way. One newspaper after another took the line that, simply by going out and voting, the Spanish people had cast a blow against terrorism. The consistency of the editorials was remarkable:

- *VG* (Norway): "The Spanish people have answered Thursday's meaningless terrorist act with a massive defense of democracy."
- *Expressen* (Sweden): "The high voter turnout in Spain represented a defiance of terrorism and an assertion of support for democracy."
- The *Guardian* (Britain): "The Spanish people once again responded in the best way possible to the bombing yesterday by turning out in record numbers in their general election."
- *De Volkskrant* (Netherlands): "Yesterday [Spain] chose the ultimate democratic answer: in spite of the mourning and the confusion the voters went in large numbers to the ballot box."

- *Dagbladet* (Norway): "In spite of all their ordeals, the Spanish voters have shown the will to defend their democratic institutions by streaming to the polls."

"Yes," I yelled at my computer screen. *"To vote for the terrorists' candidate!"*

- *Dagbladet* (continued): "Spain's voters have given a worthy answer to the frightful ordeals they are experiencing. They deserve both support and admiration from us all."
- *Aftenposten* (Norway): "Spain's voters have given the terrorists a clear answer."
- *VG:* "The message is clear."

"Yes," I cried out. " *'We surrender!' "*

To its credit, *VG* did acknowledge the need to defend Western values. But how? "We must continue to move about freely and speak freely. And we must defend democracy, as the Spanish have done in such an impressive way in recent days." In other words, simply by walking and talking and voting, we're defending democratic values from terrorism—even if we vote to cave in to it.

Even after Madrid, alas, most of the Western European establishment continued to embrace the pretense that Islamist terrorism was too complex, too ambiguous, and too nuanced a problem to make possible any direct, forceful response. "How can one fight against such a danger?" Jean-Marie Colombani pretended to ask in *Le Monde*. Not, he argued, in the American way, which was too big on *simplisme* and emotional appeals. Instead, he argued, "against the enemies of democracy, the only answer is more democracy." More democracy was precisely what America was attempting to bring about in Afghanistan and Iraq—but Colombani obviously didn't mean *that*. He didn't really mean anything. It was just a lot of Gallic jibber-jabber. French politicians and journalists were good at such rhetoric. For them, it was an art unto itself. It had nothing to do with action. On the contrary, it was a *substitute* for action.

Some editorialists saw the truth, yet shrank from its implications. "The main reason for the left's victory in Spain," the editors of Sweden's *Expressen* acknowledged, "was surely the act of terror." But instead of saying anything further about this alarming precedent, they quickly skedaddled into a more comfortable, familiar topic—white European racism. "In Spain, Muslims draw in a deep breath before they leave their homes, in fear of suspicious looks or worse from their non-Muslim countrymen." Nonsense. Muslims in Europe have much more to fear from other Muslims than from white Europeans, and they know it; for *Expressen* to suggest otherwise was utterly disingenuous.

Aftonbladet (Sweden) felt that Spain had simply paid the price for taking part in the Iraq war: "Aznar's decision to ally himself with the Bush Administration instead of with the leading EU countries has cost Spain a significant number of dead soldiers and has now also turned the country into a bloody target for terrorism." *Dagens Nyheter* (Sweden) agreed, but added that "Up against this blind terror we are all vulnerable. . . . We can never entirely shield ourselves." And *VG* chimed in: "We must live with the risk of new terrorist acts." Fight terror? No. The point was to "live with" it—to go on with our lives and hope that the next one didn't strike *us*. In France, *Le Figaro* suggested that "if Europe really exists, it must be mobilized to help Spain to find serenity." This, apparently, was the only kind of mobilization some members of the elite could accept: mobilization in the cause of Spanish serenity!

Reading one eloquently impotent editorial after another, I couldn't help feeling that those who have described Western Europe as doomed to succumb to radical Islam were right. In the face of an enemy that sought to destroy them, the Spanish had voted to appease—and all over Western Europe, they were being congratulated for it.

It was not certain, of course, that Europe would take the road of appeasement. An equally disturbing prospect was a resurgent right-wing nationalism of a kind that had not been seen since the defeat of Hitler. The failure of Europe's liberals to stand up to Islamic radicalism could only empower the far-right fringe, as it had in the 1930s when the threat came not from fundamentalist Islam but from international Communism. It seemed to me, in short, that Europe was once more headed for either cultural surrender or full-fledged civil war. Small wonder that European intellectuals preferred to embrace the fantasy that the problem lay with America and Israel instead of acknowledging and addressing the real troubles at their own doorsteps.

Yet there was hope. Before Madrid, many European journalists had treated terrorism as an American delusion, simplification, or exaggeration. Now many were at least calling it by its real name. Most admitted, too, that all of Europe was a potential target. And most had ceased fretting (for the time being, anyway) about terrorism's supposed "root cause" in Middle Eastern poverty, American exploitation, or whatever.

That was about as far, however, as most opinion leaders were willing to go. They might recommend "joint action"—perhaps even with "the Americans"—but there were few specifics. While ready to vilify America, moreover, few critized the Spanish electorate. In short, though they now admitted that Al Qaeda was at war with Europe, most still couldn't quite accept that Europe was at war with Al Qaeda. The very idea challenged many Europeans' self-image: as one poster on *Dagbladet*'s online message board put it, "I don't like the thought that many Iraqis associate the Norwegian flag, our national symbol and our people, with soldiers with weapons." *This isn't us! We're not warriors—we're peacemakers! We love everybody!*

The *Telegraph*, perhaps Europe's sanest newspaper, noted that if many Europeans thought withdrawal from Iraq or payoffs to Arab governments would end terrorism, it was because they couldn't grasp "the ideological nature of [their] foes," specifically Islamists' aim of "reversing the reconquista of the Iberian peninsula. . . . The desire not to take our enemies at face value, in word and deed, is the hallmark of much of contemporary Europe." Indeed, it had become increasingly obvious to me that in understanding the Islamist threat, Americans have one big advantage: we're surrounded by religion. In the United States, even if one isn't religious oneself, one is likely to have friends, relatives, neighbors, or coworkers for whom religious identity is not merely a matter of vestigial, nominal affiliation but of profound conviction; it's something that guides their major life decisions and shapes their conception of the universe. Since we know such people, we know how powerful (for better *or* worse) religion can be. Few Western Europeans who aren't Muslims have this kind of firsthand knowledge. Most come from Christian backgrounds but don't go to church except for weddings and funerals. If they do belong to a denomination, it's because they were born into it and have never bothered to remove their names from the membership rolls. Their supposed religious identity has little or no meaning for them, other than perhaps being related in their minds to the broad ideals of universal brotherhood, equality, and peaceful coexistence—ideals that they associate at least as much with the UN as with any church. It's difficult for them to conceive that someone can actually view this or that theological system as containing the ultimate key to the workings of the cosmos— and can be capable of acting on that belief in earth-shattering ways. It's also difficult for them to grasp the idea that a religion might be devoted to something other than the ideals set forth in the UN charter.

This failure of imagination is especially pronounced among the

Western European elite. The average German politician, French journalist, or Swedish professor simply can't imagine a life directed by religious belief. Confronted with the fact that it's indeed such belief—albeit of a particularly dark and twisted variety—that impels Islamists, their immediate impulse is to be dismissive: No, that can't be it. It must be something else. It must be something we can relate to—poverty, oppression, colonialism. The neo-Marxist analyses come easily. And from these misreadings of reality spring a host of colossally wrongheaded responses.

In the weeks after Madrid, the air in Western Europe was full of calls for an "alternative" to Bush's war on terror. But nobody actually had one. And nobody really meant it when they demanded one. Like the urgent entreaties for "more dialogue," the call for an "alternative" was simply a way of dodging the need to take action. If you keep on talking—and keep insisting on "nuance" and demanding an "alternative" and accusing others of "*simplisme*"—you don't need to decide or do anything. What seemed lost in these calls for "nuance," moreover, was the fact that for Islamists, there *are* no nuances. In a war between people who had rock-solid beliefs and people who are capable of nuancing away even pure evil, who has the advantage?

Two days after the Spanish election, I was walking in Oslo when I noticed a couple of dozen police officers milling around in the street alongside the parliamentary office building. This was unusual. I kept walking. When I passed the front of the building, I saw thirty or so young people, all in black, strolling away from it. On its doors, I saw, they'd just spray-painted, in large orange letters, the words BOYCOTT ISRAEL! Above the doors, they'd spray-painted: ISRAEL OCCUPIES, NORWAY ACCEPTS! The security guards had presumably stood by while this was being done; meanwhile, the police appeared to be under orders to keep their distance. I wasn't exercised about the protestors; in Norway, such conduct was as familiar as the winter snow. But the passivity of the uniformed officers was depressing. Those spray painters, after all, could have been terrorists. For cops to hang back obligingly while kids played at radicalism was classic pre-9/11 Scandinavian policing. In Norway, the authorities didn't seem to have learned much from either 9/11 *or* 3/11.

That evening, NRK aired a discussion of the question: "What should Europe do about terrorism?" Progress Party leader Carl I. Hagen insisted that Norway take the terrorist threat seriously. To my astonishment, both Prime Minister Bondevik and veteran diplomat Torbjørn Jagland actually agreed. Others, however, served up the usual meaningless Euro-drivel. "We won't solve this [terrorism] nationally or in the

EU, we can only solve it globally," said Center Party leader Åslaug Haga, who called for (guess what?) "dialogue between the Western and Muslim world." Asked to name the cause of terrorism, Bishop Gunnar Stålsett, at that time the ranking cleric in Norway's underattended and oversubsidized established church, managed to turn reality on its head: "One thing is for sure: it doesn't lie in religion. It doesn't lie in Islam." Where, then, did it lie? In "the great divide between rich and poor." The key to ending terrorism, he added, lay in "standing up to false fears and xenophobia"—as if Western xenophobia had killed two hundred people in Madrid. Ridiculous "peace activist" Erling Borgen agreed.

Prime Minister Bondevik, whom one might have expected to be maddeningly noncommittal, stated rather bluntly that the terrorists had, "in a way, been allowed to direct" the Spanish elections. (This angered the ever-predictable Stålsett: "It was democracy that won in Spain!") Bondevik added that despite the Madrid bombings, Norwegian peace-keeping troops would stay in Iraq. (Less than a month later, this decision would be reversed.) One of the hosts closed the program by saying that, of course, this was a discussion that would go on.

And on . . . and on . . . and on. Which, of course, was the problem. Madrid had woken up some Europeans. But most leaders still clung to the belief that the only civilized response to any crisis is to hold a con-ference. I felt I'd never been so far from America, where taking action was still a living concept.

Three months after 3/11, an Al Qaeda internal document surfaced. For those who still had any doubts, it established definitively that the terrorists' motive had indeed been to induce Spain to withdraw from Iraq. Written in Arabic, the fifty-four-page document included the fol-lowing overly generous estimation of Spain's resolve: "We consider that the Spanish government cannot suffer more than two to three strikes be-fore pulling out under pressure from its own people." Shortly thereafter, in a *Le Monde* interview marking his hundredth day in office, Zapatero declared, "I never talk about Islamic terrorism, but international terror-ism." As John Vinocur commented in the *International Herald Tribune*, Zapatero's refusal to name the fundamentalist Muslim enemy was "a bit like newspapers that avoid the word 'cancer' in obituaries with the expla-nation that they are sparing sensitive readers."

If one thing was certain, it was that Western Europeans could not be spared the harsh reality indefinitely. In the months after the Spanish capitulation, at least two major bomb plots targeting Spain were uncovered—giving the lie to those who named the Iraq War as the "root cause" of terrorism in Western Europe.

is not this, too, terror?

A WEEK AFTER the Spanish elections, Israel did the world the favor of getting rid of Sheikh Ahmed Yassin, the founder of Hamas. European media reports on this event were full of sympathetic references to Yassin's age, charisma, charitable work, and confinement to a wheelchair. He was repeatedly identified as the "spiritual leader of Hamas," which is rather like calling Hitler the "spiritual leader of Nazism." The British House of Commons devoted a minute of silence to his memory. In Norway, NRK broadcast a debate in which several participants did their best to morally equate Yassin's execution with his own terrorist attacks on innocent children.

But at least airtime was given to people who found such views repugnant. (This seemed to be a step forward.) Most cheering of all was the fact that the program's viewers, despite the unanimous condemnation of Israel's action by the Norwegian media, responded to the question "Was Israel right to take out Sheikh Yassin?" with a resounding "yes." (The margin was fifty-eight to forty-two.) One would have liked to think that this was a reflection of public opinion generally, though that conclusion seemed inconsistent with EU survey results showing that 60 percent of Europeans considered Israel the number-one threat to world peace. *It is true, St Paul, too, said so* Then again, Europeans who answer the phone to find a pollster on the other end, addressing them by name, know what they're expected to say and are likely to feel uncomfortable saying anything else, while those who anonymously call a program such as *Holmgang* in a rush of emotion are presumably more likely to say what they really feel.

In any event, after the Madrid bombings, it seemed more obvious than ever that Europe's elite was largely hopeless—and that the Continent's only hope lay in the people. For across Europe, I knew, there were men and women who saw the situation clearly, who were devoted to the preservation of liberty, and who had already begun to have their voices heard. These were, one could only hope, the leaders of tomorrow. I thought of them as the liberal resistance—a hodgepodge of writers, politicians, and activists who operated outside the control of the political and media establishment and were determined to save Europe from suicide.

The prophet and first martyr of this resistance was born in 1948 to a Catholic family in the small coastal town of Velsen in North Holland. In the Netherlands it's common for men to have several given names, all of which appear on official documents, but to be known generally by a simple, one-syllable nickname—Bas, Cor, Cees, Gert, Henk, Joop. Wilhelmus Simon Petrus Fortuyn was called Pim. He studied history, law, and economics in Amsterdam, earned a doctorate in sociology, taught at the University of Groningen, and then became a professor at Rotterdam's Erasmus University. After leaving Erasmus, he began writing prolifically. His first book, *Against the Islamicization of Our Culture*, published in 1997—the year I first visited Amsterdam—argued that the rise of a fundamentalist Muslim subculture in the Netherlands threatened democratic values and that the nation was doomed unless it acknowledged this threat and addressed it seriously. *Pim was right*

Dutch politicians and journalists responded to Fortuyn's book in predictable fashion: they accused him of inciting racism and xenophobia and compared him to the far-right Jean-Marie Le Pen of France. Fortuyn would continue to make the same arguments throughout his life, and the establishment would continue to label him a racist. His response was always that race had nothing to do with it: as he wrote in a column that appeared eight days after 9/11, "Islam is . . . not bound to one race." The problem, rather, was "an ideology that is hostile to our culture." That ideology didn't consider secular government legitimate; it didn't protect minority rights (even in relatively liberal Egypt, fifty-two homosexuals had recently been imprisoned "without any form of due process"); it didn't respect "freedom of opinion, of expression, and of religious and social conviction"; it didn't recognize women's equality, but forced them into subservient roles and kept them "out of public sight as much as possible"; and it didn't respect individual rights (in Islamic countries, "the family, the group, the tribe are the basic building blocks, not the individual"). Fortuyn did not turn away from the harsh facts: that integration had failed, that the imams who ran the Muslim ghettos were expressing antidemocratic sentiments with increasing boldness (in 2001, the imam of Rotterdam would publicly denounce homosexuality), and that—given the higher Muslim birth rate, continued immigration, and Muslim schools that inculcated prejudices the Dutch thought their country had long since risen above—the danger would only increase.

What did such developments mean for the future of the Netherlands—which Descartes had described as the only place on earth where one could find absolute liberty? What, for example, would happen to same-sex marriage when fundamentalist Muslims gained enough power

Yes, it should be eradicated

to eradicate it? Islamic countries not only prohibit gay marriage: they execute people for sodomy. Fortuyn—himself both openly gay and a devout Roman Catholic—knew that if many of his new countrymen had their way, such punishments would eventually be instituted in the Netherlands as well.

And what of women's rights? Within Dutch Muslim communities, Fortuyn knew, lived Dutch-born women and girls who were hardly freer than they'd be under the Taliban. The very idea should have outraged any believer in basic principles of equality. Yet most Dutch politicians, for all their professed support for feminist ideals, would not go near this issue. Fortuyn took it by the horns. In doing so he was not displaying intolerance but reacting responsibly to a looming crisis to which his country's political and media establishment had turned a blind eye.

Fortuyn's opponents claimed that he called for an end to immigration and the expulsion of Muslims from the Netherlands. What he proposed, in fact, was a firm policy of education, emancipation, and integration. The Dutch government, he argued, should stop issuing residency permits to imams who preached that Dutch women are whores and gay men lower than pigs; it should ensure that children in Islamic schools were taught to respect democracy and regard themselves as Dutchmen; and it should do everything in its power to liberate Muslim women from subservience. "There is almost no conflict in the world at present," he wrote shortly before 9/11, "in which Islam does not play a prominent role."

He was right

> During the Cold War, the free West knew exactly who threatened our standards and values: Communism in the Soviet Union, Eastern Europe, China, North Korea, North Vietnam, Cuba, etc. History has since proven us right. The role of Communism is nearly ended, but it has been taken over by Islam. In the free West we have seldom acted against Communist parties or prohibited organizations. . . . But we have kept an eye on them. . . . We must do the same with all the Islamic organizations and religious communities in our countries!

How did the Dutch government respond? Only days after 9/11, Interior Minister Zaken De Vries promised that Dutch counterintelligence would "pay sharp attention to persons who want to disturb the peace and conduct a cold war against Islam"; the reference was plainly to Fortuyn. De Vries's remark perfectly exemplified the twisted thinking by Western European governments at the time. Consider the context: on the day the

World Trade Center fell, Moroccan immigrants in the Dutch town of Ede rejoiced in the streets; that Friday, a TV report on Nederland 1 commemorating the victims of 9/11 was followed immediately by a Koran reading (supplied by the Dutch Muslim Broadcasting System) stating that "unbelievers were fuel for the fire"; and in a post-attack survey of Moroccan immigrants in the Netherlands, 21 percent admitted their support for an anti-American holy war.* At least one Dutch mosque, it emerged, was raising money by selling calendars featuring a picture of the New York skyline ablaze. Yet the interior minister of the Netherlands was worried about Fortuyn.

Fortunately, the Dutch public was wiser, and its reactions provided an early illustration of the growing rift between elite and popular opinion in Holland and elsewhere. In a post-9/11 poll by *De Volkskrant*, more than 60 percent of Dutch citizens said that Muslim immigrants who approved of anti-American terrorism should be ejected from the country. In a stunning editorial, the newspaper's editors spelled the message out bluntly: "The Netherlands doesn't accept anti-Western fundamentalist attitudes from Muslims. In the eyes of most Dutch people, integration means adapting to a humanistic tradition, to the separation between church and state, and distancing oneself from the norms and values of one's motherland." The poll results appeared to suggest that the Dutch—perhaps the most liberal people on the planet—had finally begun to face a crucial fact: that tolerance for intolerance is not tolerance at all.

Less than a month before 9/11, Fortuyn's concern about these issues—and the failure of Dutch politicians to address them honestly—had led him to run for parliament under the auspices of the newly formed party Leefbaar Nederland (Livable Netherlands); by year's end he was its head. In February 2002, in a private meeting, he made an impassioned statement to fellow party leaders. "It is five minutes to twelve," he began. "Not just in the Netherlands, but in the whole of Europe." Disaster was just around the corner, but the Dutch establishment was sleeping at the wheel. "Do you want all this to continue?" he asked in language both blunt and heartfelt:

I am defending and protecting this country that we've built up over five, six centuries. What we now have here, goddamn it, is a kind of

---

*In a similar *Sunday Times* poll, 11 percent of British Muslims were willing to admit to pollsters that they considered the attack on the World Trade Center justified.

fifth column. People who are capable of destroying and depleting this country. . . . I have no desire to defend their interests. That is why I tell them: you can stay here in this country, but you have to adapt. . . .

I refuse to hear repeatedly that Allah is great, almighty and powerful, and I am a dirty pig. "You are a Christian dog, an infidel." That's what they shout! And you accept this and keep silent. Until now I've been very calm and disciplined. I never spoke like this before. But you've made yourselves their doormat. You've let yourselves be bullied by them. I'm not with you anymore. . . . Because the people of this country are fed up and don't accept so-called political correctness any more. . . .

If I have to choose my words more carefully, that's fine with me. But this is about the future of your children and grandchildren; it touches on everything I strive for. There is no other issue. . . . If I must be silenced or eliminated, I accept that fate. But the problem and the threat will not disappear. . . . The people are sick of it, knowing what is going on. Goddamn it, in my town Moroccan boys, Turkish boys don't rob Turks and Moroccans, but you and me, and old ladies.

The police are invisible—they do nothing about it. And if you have the courage to tell them, they'll tell you right to your face: you're discriminating!

How did Fortuyn's fellow party leaders respond to these remarks? They fired him as head of Livable Netherlands. Fortuyn promptly started his own party, Lijst (List) Pim Fortuyn. Millions of ordinary Dutchmen were delighted to hear the well-tailored former professor saying things they'd often thought but never dared articulate. But the Dutch establishment didn't share their admiration: the more lustily the crowds cheered Fortuyn—who radiated an intellectual energy and moral determination that was utterly alien in the bland, bureaucratic, consensus-obsessed corridors of Dutch power—the more viciously the politicians and journalists condemned him. The list of those who contributed to Fortuyn's demonization is a veritable Who's Who of the Dutch establishment.

Paul Rosenmuller of the Green Left called Fortuyn "an extreme right-wing outspoken nationalist and isolationist populist"; Jan Marijnissen of the Socialist Party labeled him "a charlatan" and "a Pied Piper"; Wim Kok of Labor, who was prime minister throughout Fortuyn's political career, considered him "a danger to the country" who was "sowing the seeds of hate, discrimination, and discord"; and Hans Kombrink, also of Labor, said, "I see a parallel with the 1930s. Fortuyn is the beginning of Nazism and fascism." It wasn't just the socialists who spoke of Fortuyn this way: the Liberal Democrats' Gerrit Zalm said: "Fortuyn is a dangerous man. He deceives the people." (This is a Western European elite way of saying "He tells the truth and helps people see through us.") Liberal Democrat Bas Eenhoorn said simply, "Fortuyn is Mussolini," while his party colleague Frits Bolkenstein, reflecting the elite preoccupation with appearance rather than substance, worried that "Netherlands will look like a horse's ass with Fortuyn as prime minister." And the journalists agreed: Peter Storm of *De Socialist* described Fortuyn as "a fascist overlord"; both Bart Tromp of *Het Parool* and *Volkskrant*'s Jan Blokker compared him to Mussolini; and *Trouw*'s Marty Verkamman equated him with Hitler.

With few exceptions, the American media echoed the Dutch party line. In January 2002, the *New York Times* cited Fortuyn as exemplary of the supposed "rightward drift" of European politics; profiling Fortuyn two months later, *Times* correspondent Marlise Simons made sure to include references to fascists: "he flies into a rage when people call him a new Mussolini or the Dutch equivalent of the Austrian right-wing politician Jörg Haider." Summing up his message as "anti-big-government, anti-immigrant, anti-welfare and pro-law-and-order" (why not "pro-democracy and pro–women's rights"?), and citing Zalm's "dangerous man" comment, Simons claimed that Fortuyn's "message bears striking similarities to those of other right-wingers across Europe." To her credit, she at least quoted Fortuyn's observation that "in Rotterdam we have third-generation Moroccans who still don't speak Dutch, oppress women and won't live by our values." Yet her article bore the absurd headline "Proudly Gay—And Marching the Dutch to the Right." (Note the tendentious use of the word "marching" as opposed to, say, "leading.") On the contrary, by standing up against a fascist, female-oppressing ideology, Fortuyn was *resisting* the movement of the Netherlands to the right—and, incidentally, standing up for the right of women like Marlise Simons to have careers, travel freely, and walk around with their legs bare and heads uncovered.

No one who could read Dutch had any excuse for misrepresenting Fortuyn's views. His voluminous political writings made it clear that he was no Hitler or Le Pen, but a believer in individual liberty who recognized a threat to that liberty when he saw it. Yet the Dutch establishment didn't care what the truth about Fortuyn was. (They never mentioned,

moral sewer

for example, that his companion was Moroccan.) For them, *he* was the threat—for his truth-telling was an earthquake shaking up their placid political landscape.

As the 2002 Dutch elections approached, opinion polls predicted that Fortuyn's party would win thirty-eight seats in the parliament. That would make it the largest party in the Netherlands—and Fortuyn the next prime minister.

Then came May 6, 2002. That day's issue of *NRC Handelsblad* featured a furious screed by Folkert Jensma, the newspaper's editor-in-chief. Jensma bemoaned the fact that if Fortuyn became prime minister, then every year on the fourth of May—the day on which the Dutch annually commemorate World War II—it would be Fortuyn's job to lay a wreath at the memorial to the war dead in Amsterdam's Dam Square. "He," wrote Jensma angrily, "the man who says Islam is a backward religion!" Describing the Netherlands as a country whose people "do not discriminate, do not prefer one culture above another," and "try to keep the xenophobes and racists at bay," Jensma argued that it was "a huge disgrace, after sixty years, to have to remind a politician in our midst" of what had happened in World War II. But of course it was Fortuyn who was acting responsibly on the lessons of World War II, putting out the word that intolerance is intolerance, whether those preaching and practicing it are speaking German or Arabic.

The election was nine days away.

That afternoon Fortuyn drove to the national media center in Hilversum, outside of Amsterdam, to appear with other candidates on a radio show hosted by Ruud de Wild. When Fortuyn left the studio after the interview, he was approached by a stranger in the parking lot carrying a Spanish-made Astra A-100 pistol. The man shot six bullets into Fortuyn's head, neck, and chest. The time was 6:05. Fortuyn, age fifty-four, died quickly. The first person to tell the world what had happened was Peter de Vries, a reporter for the radio station 3FM, who ran out to the parking lot with a live microphone and cried, "Oh my God . . . we have to do something!" The killer was Volkert van der Graaf, a thirty-two-year-old animal-rights activist from Harderwijk whom a neighbor would later describe as "a quiet boy with a big heart for the environment." Van der Graaf would later explain that he considered Fortuyn a "danger to society." He found his views about Islam "stigmatizing," and said that he'd murdered him to deny him political power.

Many Dutch journalists sought—with spectacular dishonesty—to cast van der Graaf in the role of a lone madman. (Two and a half years later, they'd do it again with Theo van Gogh's murderer.) In fact van der Graaf was an active member of a significant political movement. His views would not have prevented his becoming a respected journalist or politician. Indeed, it was precisely the rhetoric of establishment journalists and politicians that had persuaded him that Fortuyn needed to be stopped. Convinced by the arguments of people like Folkert Jensma, van der Graaf simply did what he considered necessary under the circumstances. Who, after all, wouldn't have exterminated Hitler or Mussolini if given the chance?

It's strange to think that at this very moment, Fortuyn might have been his country's prime minister, leading the way in reforming—and rescuing—Western Europe. Instead, thanks to politicians and journalists who all but painted a target on his back, his remains lie hundreds of miles from the Netherlands, in the dark of a family tomb in the northern Italian village of Provesano.

THOUGH DUTCH JOURNALISTS and politicians emitted the obligatory sounds of disapproval about Fortuyn's murder, the most prevalent emotions seemed dismay and embarrassment at the fact that the peace-loving Netherlands, in a sudden eruption of "American conditions," had experienced its first political assassination since 1584. They would never have admitted it, of course, but one suspects that many of Fortuyn's enemies in the Dutch parliament and press corps found his sudden disappearance quite convenient and, all in all, a relief. The impact of the murder on the Dutch public, however, was something else again. On the night of May 7, protesters stood outside the parliament building in The Hague and shouted "Murderers!" Banners outside Rotterdam's city hall blamed Fortuyn's death on "the goading of politicians and the hounding of the press." Across the country, angry, tearful Dutchmen marched to protest his murder and honor his memory.

The defamation of Pim Fortuyn didn't cease with his death. Dutch accounts of the murder repeated the familiar calumnies, which were echoed throughout the European media. (The *Daily Mirror*'s headline was "Dutch 'Le Pen' Assassinated.") The U.S. media, too, fell into line. Adam Curry, an American broadcaster based in Amsterdam, later recalled that "all three major networks . . . labeled Pim Fortuyn as ultra-right and/or racist." Curry awarded points, however, to Marlise Simons, who in a posthumous article on Fortuyn represented his positions more honestly than she had before: "He said he found it shameful that foreign Islamic clergy here [in the Netherlands] used offensive language against gays in this country and that Muslim men tried to impose medieval rural customs in the Netherlands. 'How can you respect a culture if the woman has to walk several steps behind her man, has to stay in the kitchen and keep her mouth shut,' he said." It was curious that this quotation hadn't made it into Simons's profile of Fortuyn a few weeks earlier—but better late than never.

A few days later, the *New York Times* ran a piece by—of all people—Folkert Jensma, the editor-in-chief of *NRC Handelsblad* whose abusive essay on Fortuyn had appeared on the very day of his murder. Posthumously, Jensma's line was suddenly softer. Giving no indication that he'd ever represented Fortuyn differently, Jensma focused largely on Fortuyn's style rather than on the issues he'd raised. Fortuyn, he wrote, had "combined charisma with personal charm. . . . He had a talent for rhetoric and looked great on television. . . . Fortuyn was everything Dutch politicians are not famous for. He was not dull, he didn't use jargon and he was openly ambitious." (Yes, he was ambitious—to bring *real change*, not just to become a faceless party hack.) Jensma couldn't sidestep Fortuyn's political views entirely, but his account of them was maddeningly toothless: he seemed to be laboring to come off as speaking ill neither of the dead nor of Islam. Fortuyn's positions, he wrote, were "a curious mixture of right, center and left." "Curious"? "Mixture"? Fortuyn's politics were entirely of a piece; the fact that they didn't fit neatly into the political establishment's ridiculous categories was a reflection of the fatuity of that establishment and its categories, not of any inconsistency on Fortuyn's part.

Having vilified Fortuyn in life, Jensma now—if in a rather tentative, halfhearted way—admitted that Fortuyn had had a point when he worried about the rise of Islam in Europe. (The most popular name for baby boys in Amsterdam, Jensma noted, was no longer Jan but Muhammed.) But he didn't dare to praise Fortuyn's courage in taking on the political and media establishment; he didn't mention that that establishment (with himself front and center) had relentlessly demonized Fortuyn. While he largely avoided the usual inflammatory language about Fortuyn, moreover, he managed to draw the usual ugly connections: "Do Jean-Marie Le Pen's success in France, Jörg Haider's in Austria and Silvio Berlusconi's in Italy signal a trend?"

Van der Graaf was tried for the murder of Pim Fortuyn. In his

defense, echoing a long list of Dutch politicians and journalists, he compared Fortuyn to the Nazis. He was sentenced to eighteen years in
prison. He'll probably serve a fraction of that. And what will the experience be like? At a typical Dutch prison—where the goal (as Colin White
and Laurie Boucke note in *The Undutchables)* "is to provide the prisoners
with as normal a lifestyle as possible"—inmates are paid about $27 a
week, which they can use "to decorate and furnish their private 'cells'
with televisions, stereos, pets, and, of course, a *koffie*-maker. A special
private visitor's room—'sex cell'—is provided, complete with furniture
(including a bed), paintings and carpet. Other privileges . . . include
wearing one's own clothing, access to a kitchen to cook one's own meals
if so desired, the right to vote, freedom to speak to journalists and a system for expressing and debating complaints."

As a result of Fortuyn's murder, the Dutch taboo on discussing immigration, integration, and Islam fell. The Dutch government and media,
however, remained in the hands of the same elite that had demonized Fortuyn for talking about these things. So nothing much changed. Nor did
Fortuyn's murder have any appreciable effect beyond his own country.

It would take more than one assassination to bring about major
change in Europe.

NOT LONG AFTER Fortuyn's murder, a new star emerged in the fir-
mament of France's liberal resistance. But while Fortuyn preached to the
Dutch largely about immigration and integration, Sabine Herold was
preoccupied with the economy. Still in her early twenties, Herold was
one of the few prominent young Western Europeans to challenge social
democracy head on. Leader of an organization called Liberté, J'écris Ton
Nom (Freedom, I Write Your Name), Herold is everything a young
Frenchwoman isn't supposed to be: a forthright admirer of America and
American liberty, she's also a vocal critic of France's social-democratic
economy and its entrenched, out-of-touch political elite. She became
famous throughout France while still a college student, speaking out
against public-employee unions, whose endless strikes have won them
benefits well in excess of those enjoyed by private-sector workers while
inconveniencing generations of Frenchmen. Though the French had
long accepted these strikes as a part of life and bought the argument that
no perk is too much, Herold came along at a time when the destructive
effect of all this on the French economy had become clear to many, who
were finally ready to draw a line in the sand.

Herold—who in a few years has gained an increasingly large following—rejects the lockstep statism and reflexive anticapitalism of her country's political establishment: "I don't want to be a kind of apparatchik. I think if you're not able to do things for yourself, or show that you can help a company, how can you help the state?" The problem with the European political system, she has rightly observed, is that if you're a young person who wants to be "politically involved," you join a party and set about parroting its program; "there's no real forum to express your views," no place "to engage in both action *and* reflection." She's particularly fed up with France's two major parties, the Socialists and Chirac's Union for a Popular Movement: they've "produced *nothing* on an intellectual basis for more than twenty years." As for the French economy, one of its major problems (as is true of other European economies) is that the bureaucracy makes it very hard to start a company; by contrast, America is "a country where you can create and make yourself what you want to be." Unusual words indeed from a Frenchwoman.

Another French voice for the liberal resistance who emerged after the death of Fortuyn was Guy Millière, a professor of cultural history and legal philosophy at the Sorbonne who began to address the growth and self-segregation of France's Muslim population. In France, which prizes the idea of itself as a secular republic, one aspect of the situation that did offend establishment sensibilities was the increasingly familiar sight of girls wearing Muslim headscarves in public schools. In early 2004, in an attempt to preserve the ideal of secular equality, the Chirac government—over the furious opposition of many Muslims, who protested its decision in marches held not only in France but in cities across Europe—imposed a ban on headscarves in schools. For Millière, the ban was ludicruously insufficient. In a brief, intense jeremiad entitled *Who's Afraid of Islam?* and a number of articles, he spoke of France as having already crossed the line of no return. "Economically speaking," he maintained, "France is decaying, full speed. . . . The greater part of young people are Muslim, not integrated with French society, and almost illiterate. . . . the only things that are growing in France right now are crime and Islamism." Millière predicted that Muslims, who now make up about 12 percent of France's population, would in ten years account for "more than 20 percent. They will be mostly young, and non-Muslim French people will be mostly old." In twenty years, he believed, Muslims would be a majority. "And if nothing changes, they will be radical Muslims. The French government takes care of the present: it knows it

[handwritten in margin: Racial sacrilege]

cannot take care of the future because there is no future." He quoted a speaker from one of the Muslim Brotherhood's national congresses: "Be patient, be wise, time is on our side."

Yes, Millière's language is strong. (He's called Jacques Chirac and Dominique de Villepin "preposterous megalomaniacs," which sounds about right.) But he knows whereof he speaks: in addition to being a respected professor at the Sorbonne, he's the husband of a woman who was born a Muslim. ("She's not a Muslim anymore," he notes, "and because she left Islam, she risks being killed if she says it openly.") His prediction:

> France will become a Muslim country. French leaders know it. They will never take a decision that could make young radical Muslims angry. It's one of the reasons why they could not support the United States during the war in Iraq. The result would have been riots in the suburbs, and the French police is ill equipped to face riots. French leaders have no choice except to be the leaders of the Arab-Muslim world. They accepted too many things to go backward now. The rift between France and the United States will become bigger and bigger. France is already the main enemy of western civilization. The most dangerous enemy is always the enemy within, and France is the enemy within.

One can only hope that Millière is exaggerating to stir his countrymen to action. But it's true that since 9/11, France has often seemed to be doing everything it could to foil the war on terror and to curry favor with Arab and Muslim leaders at the expense of the West's security. (It's known, for example, that Chirac helped Saddam skirt UN sanctions and provided him with classified U.S. and UN data right up to the invasion of Iraq.) In part, France's actions have been cynical power moves, efforts to reinforce its position as the leading Arab-friendly Western nation in opposition to the United States and Britain; in part, they've been an attempt to insulate France from terror.* The French policy met a crucial challenge in August 2004, when two French journalists were taken hostage in Iraq by a group calling itself the Islamic Army in Iraq. The kidnapping seemed to indicate that for at least some Islamists, France's appeasement of their movement made no difference; as far as they were concerned, France was a Western democracy, and hence their enemy.

---

*France, like Germany and Russia, also had financial ties to Saddam Hussein that inclined its leaders to oppose his overthrow.

In addition to the two French journalists, Georges Malbrunot of *Le Figaro* and *Ouest-France* and Christian Chesnot of Radio France Internationale, the group had abducted an Italian reporter, Enzo Baldoni. In exchange for Baldoni's freedom, they demanded that Italy withdraw its forces from Iraq within forty-eight hours. Italy refused; Baldoni was executed. From France, they demanded a reversal of the ban on headscarves in schools, which was scheduled to be put into effect at the beginning of the school year. France, too, refused; yet this didn't end the matter. Chirac called in his chits: Foreign Minister Michel Barnier flew from one Muslim capital to another pleading for support. The leader of every single Muslim country, including Yasir Arafat, came through, reminding the kidnappers that France was a friend that had condemned America's invasion of Iraq. France's Islamic leaders, who had recently been up in arms with Chirac over the headscarf ban, also rode to the rescue, explaining to the kidnappers that they were doing French Muslims no favors and that the headscarf ban was now a "closed issue."

One might have thought this kidnapping would help Frenchmen see that all Western democracies were in this together; instead, the French government strove to get the message through to the hostage takers that in the war between Islamism and America, France was on the Islamists' side. *Le Monde* applauded this spineless tactic. While pointing out that no democracy—not even France—was safe in the holy war that had begun on 9/11, the newspaper's editors went on to celebrate (in typically flowery French-editorial prose) the fact that the hostage taking, instead of exacerbating tensions between French Muslims and non-Muslims, had instead "caused a movement of national communion, almost of sacramental union." Why? Because French Muslim leaders (who, practically speaking, could hardly have done otherwise) had unanimously denounced the nabbing of Malbrunot and Chesnot, expressed their loyalty to France, and sent envoys to Baghdad to help free the journalists. That's it: all it takes for the French intelligentsia to wax poetic about "sacramental union" and about "the Muslims of France" being "the first in line to defend the Republic" is for French Islamic leaders to be willing to dissociate themselves from a patently barbaric act.

The same tune was still being played two days later. With the safety of the two journalists assumed to be all but certain, *Le Monde* noted that if the episode had "ended tragically," it would have "demonstrated that even the foreign policy of France"—i.e., abject appeasement—"was not enough to protect it from irrational terrorism" and would have "risked opening up a dangerous fissure between the Republic and France's

Muslim community." (As if there weren't already a huge gulf between the two!) But happily, things turned out differently: "not content to denounce the taking of hostages and to proclaim, loudly and clearly, their attachment to the French community," France's Islamic leaders "went to Baghdad to plead directly for the liberation of the two Frenchmen." Already forgotten, apparently, was the fact that some of these new heroes of the Republic had, in their earlier denunciations of the headscarf ban, explicitly voiced their devotion to the Koran as the ultimate source of civil law. As Ivan Rioufol bravely asked in *Le Figaro*, where had these French Muslim leaders been when American journalist Daniel Pearl was decapitated, or when dozens of others, including Baldoni, were murdered "pursuant to the sentence of God"?

Le Monde was thrilled not only by the cooperation of French Muslim leaders, but also by the helpfulness of leaders across the Muslim world, which it described as "nothing less than spectacular":

> It is effectively without precedent for a Western country to benefit from the support and the proclaimed solidarity of nearly all of the governments of the Middle East, as well as the Muslim authorities, whether moderate or extremist. This unity testifies that the pleas of France will not have been in vain: against terrorism, policy can be, must be, more effective than war. It shows equally that France can make its singularity—the fact of its having and accepting the role of the first Muslim country of Europe—a peaceful weapon to surpass the logic of ideological and religious confrontation.

In other words, selling out pays off. France had made—or tried to make—a separate peace with an enemy that was making war on Western democracy. The editors of *Le Monde*—as well as politicians and journalists across France—found this "spectacular." They seemed not to understand that if the Islamist terrorists responded favorably to their overtures, it was simply because France's continued estrangement from the United States and Britain was in their strategic interest; nor did the editors seem to understand that if the terrorists did end up defeating the United States and Britain, France's usefulness would be at an end and its "policy" would no longer be able to protect it.*

There were several levels of delusion here—the delusion that an

---

*The French journalists, incidentally, were not released until December 2004, apparently in exchange for a $2 million ransom payment by the French government.

"understanding" between France and Islamist terrorists was something to be proud of; the delusion that French Muslims' help in this matter in any way mitigated their hostility to democracy and integration, or their determination to continue the Islamicization of France; the delusion that a successful outcome of the hostage situation would constitute proof of Muslim–Christian harmony in France, or of the wisdom of French "policy," rather than the Islamist terrorists' recognition that France was (in Lenin's term) a "useful idiot."

ON SEPTEMBER 1, 2004, the first day of the autumn term, about thirty armed men and women, most of them in ski masks, seized Middle School Number One in the Russian city of Beslan and took over 1,300 hostages. Russian police and armed forces formed a security cordon around the school, and for two days the hostages—most of them children—sweated in the intense heat while their captors denied them food, water, and medicine. On the third day, the authorities stormed the school. Chaos ensued. Children trying to flee the melee were shot dead in their tracks by the terrorists. When it was over, 331 civilians and eleven soldiers had died. After an investigation, the Russian government announced that the hostage takers had come from a variety of national backgrounds—not only Chechen but also Arab, Tatar, Kazakh, and Uzbek. Several had connections with Islamist terrorists. Beslan, then, could not be viewed in isolation from the larger picture of Islamist terror. It should have given French leaders pause to realize that while they'd been congratulating themselves on having forged friendly ties with terrorists, members of the same far-flung brotherhood had been shooting children in the back.

If after the Madrid bombings I'd felt a cautious optimism about the prospects for a new European realism about fundamentalist Islam, after Beslan I had the impression that many Europeans were simply becoming better at looking away. Everyone responded to the massacre with expressions of horror, grief, solidarity; but taking in the reactions by politicians and journalists, you'd almost think that all those children had died in an earthquake or hurricane. Western European television reports were filled with the passive voice—"the school was seized"; "the children were killed." It was as if, three years after 9/11, they had raised to a high art the ability to avoid saying who, exactly, had done what to whom.

Some chose to focus on the government of Vladimir Putin. In the view of these commentators, Beslan was simply a response to Putin's mistreatment of Chechnya and underscored the need for (what else?) dialogue. A handful actually concentrated on the perpetrators, though in most cases the thrust of their commentary was to deny any connection with other assaults by radical Muslims on Westerners. Hardly anybody seemed to get the point that even if Putin *had* mishandled things, even if Chechnya *had* been treated brutally, the fact remained that the massacre was the work of Islamists connected to Al Qaeda who saw the Chechnyan cause as part of the international jihad. Indeed, some members of the Western European elite proved that they could nuance into nothingness even the spectacle of children being monstrously gunned down as they ran or brutally murdered when they begged for water. EU foreign minister Bernard Bot voiced the attitude of that elite when he demanded that the Russian government explain "how this tragedy could have happened"—as if the children had perished in the collapse of a poorly constructed school.

Immediately after the Madrid attacks, Norwegian TV had aired a program on which leading politicians and activists discussed the bombings. After Beslan, more or less the same cast of characters was reunited on TV2's *Holmgang*. Even in the wake of this breathtaking atrocity, some of them managed to recycle the same empty rhetoric. Center Party boss Åslaug Haga instructed viewers that the true sources of terrorism were "desperation" and "poverty." (So much for the bin Laden family millions.) Peace activist Erling Borgen found it appropriate to compare the number of people killed in Madrid with those who'd died in recent fighting in Fallujah—his point being that the events in Fallujah amounted to a terrorist act by the United States. He quoted one of the Beslan murderers who, replying to a mother's plea not to kill her child, said, "They killed all four of mine."

When the subject of Islam finally came up, Borgen snapped that the "worst form of religious fundamentalism" is not Islamic fundamentalism but "market fundamentalism"—thus neatly summing up the establishment view that even Taliban-style Islam is better than American-style capitalism. Borgen stressed the importance of turning to Amnesty International and the UN, which alone, he said, had "legitimacy" in such matters. There was also plenty of talk about how the West needed to turn to its "natural allies," the moderate Muslims. And several participants were at pains to say that the child killings in Beslan had nothing whatever to do with 9/11, Palestinian terrorism, or the insurgency in Iraq.

You would hardly have known that the event that occasioned this cool, academic discussion had been the largest hostage-taking in history, in which Muslim terrorists had gunned down over a hundred children. There was astonishingly little talk about actual murders or actual children. Obviously, these thin-blooded politicians did not want to face the depth of the evil they were up against. To continue to insist that the UN held the answers to such "problems," or that the perpetrators had been motivated by desperation and poverty, was obscene. Such acts are not a normal reaction to desperation and poverty. There are people in China and India and South America who are far poorer than most Islamist terrorists but who would never do such things. Atrocities on the scale of Beslan are the result of intense indoctrination in a life-despising ideology. After Beslan, it was pointless to discuss these matters with those who still refused to face this plain and simple truth.

Gratifyingly, the Beslan massacre did result in a measure of self-criticism on the part of some Muslims and Arabs. The general manager of Al-Arabiya TV admitted that while "not all Muslims are terrorists . . . almost all terrorists are Muslims." He called this "a pathetic record" and asked: "Does this tell us anything about ourselves, our societies and our culture?" * In the *Arab News*, Dr. Mohammed T. Al-Rasheed compared Islamist terrorists to vampires: "The madness of theological elitism has caught up with us, and what we silently nurtured over the decades has tasted blood and will not cease until you put a stake through its heart." Whether these were onetime maneuvers by people who felt that some expression of regret was tactically advisable, or genuine cries of frustration and shame, would presumably become clear in time.

An article in the British *New Statesman* ("Can Islam Change?") claimed that Beslan and 9/11 were "leading millions of Muslims to search their souls," that Muslim clerics were seeking "a more humanitarian interpretation of their faith," and that Muslim attitudes toward sharia law had undergone a "seismic shift." The only evidence for this was the fact that in India, the legislation that had previously permitted Muslim men to divorce their wives by repeating "I divorce you" three times (by telephone text message, if desired) had been overturned. *Time* magazine similarly sought out signs of hope, reporting that Morocco was leading the way with a new family law that brought an end to centuries of bias against women by providing equal divorce rights.

Despite these scattered reforms, however, there was little indication that Beslan had led to widespread reflection or regret in the Muslim

---

*The *New York Times*, which reported these remarks, also cited one anti-Beslan article apiece in newspapers in Kuwait, Jordan, Lebanon, Palestine, Egypt, and Saudi Arabia.

world. If a large majority of the planet's billion-plus Muslims were appalled by the murder of those children, why didn't they hold giant anti-terror demonstrations in every capital of Europe? In Oslo—where Muslims have turned out by the thousands for protests against America and Israel—about fifty Muslims rallied outside the parliament building to express their disapproval of the massacre. If a crime of this magnitude could not stir European Muslims to stand up and proclaim their shame and disgust, what would? *Time* had an answer: according to a "progressive scholar in Indonesia," the silence and ineffectuality of "moderate Muslims" was the fault of—who else?—America. "The moderates," said the scholar, "are finding it more difficult to discuss issues like human rights and democracy when photos of Americans torturing Iraqis keep appearing." As if "the moderates" had been busy discussing these issues before Abu Ghraib!* The head of France's Council of Muslim Democrats agreed: "America has created a situation where even modern, democratic and peace-loving Muslims have some ambivalent feelings."

When Omar Bakri Mohammed, "spiritual leader" of the banned Egyptian al-Muhajiroun sect (who had lived in Britain since 1985), said that it would be legitimate for an Iraqi to carry out a Beslan-type action in Britain in which women and children were "killed in the crossfire," a Labor MP called his remarks "an insult to most moderate Muslims, who are sick of people like this claiming to represent them." One hoped the MP was right. Yet it was hard not to wonder about these "moderate Muslims." Were they really sick of being spoken for by people like Bakri Mohammed? If so, what would it take to get them to say so themselves? Why did the *Sunday Telegraph* not quote one "moderate Muslim" condemning him? What did it mean that *no* Muslims at all were quoted?

IF THE NETHERLANDS gave Western Europe its martyred prophet of immigration and integration reform, it was Denmark that first introduced reforms aimed at addressing the problem. And just as Pim Fortuyn was the target of vicious attacks by the Dutch establishment, the Kingdom of Denmark found itself disparaged by politicians and journal-

---

*Thomas Friedman has noted: "The most oft-used phrase of Mideast moderates is 'We were just about to stand up to the bad guys when you stupid Americans did that stupid thing. Had you stupid Americans not done that stupid thing, we would have stood up, but now it's too late. It's all your fault for being so stupid.' "

ists across Western Europe—not to mention EU and UN bureaucrats. There was no little irony in this, for until its change of government in November 2001, Denmark had been the very model of what EU leaders and UN functionaries thought every country in the world should be: a civilized, orderly social-democratic state with an elaborate bureaucracy to collect all the money and send it back out again. Denmark is still all those things, but it has lately become something else as well: a country that's serious about overhauling immigration and integration. This has made the name of Denmark a byword, in elite circles throughout Western Europe, for—horrors!—populism.

Passing a newsstand in Copenhagen one day in July 2004, I noticed *Politiken*'s banner headline: "Council of Europe: Denmark Violates Human Rights." (Danish is easy to read if you know Norwegian.) Curious, I bought a copy—though I could guess what the Council of Europe was exercised about. Sure enough, the problem was Denmark's immigration policy. That policy has its roots in a unique study by Eyvind Vesselbo, a cultural sociologist. Vesselbo began by selecting a cohort of 145 Turkish men who, emigrating to Denmark as guest workers in 1969 and 1970, settled in the town of Ishøj, which has since become heavily Muslim. By the year 2000, when Vesselbo's study was completed, the importation of spouses and other family members, combined with a high fertility rate, had turned this group of 145 into a community of 2,813. Those who had married had all married Turkish women whom they brought over to Denmark under "family reunification." Some of these men were later divorced or widowed and then remarried, again to Turkish women. Three married yet a third time—and again, in each case, the wife was a Turkish import. The rate of "fetching marriages" among this group, then, was *over* 100 percent, while the average number of children per family was 6.4—several times the overall Danish average.

Until recently, European authorities took it for granted that immigrants' children would be more likely to marry natives than their parents were. Of the ninety-eight married sons and daughters of Vesselbo's original 145 immigrants, eighty-nine wed spouses imported from Turkey, seven married Turks already living in Denmark, and one married a Turk who lived in Sweden. Only one married a Dane with no Turkish background. There were ten second marriages—all to Turks. Among the third generation, there had already been sixty-two marriages by 2000—all but two of them fetching marriages. These findings caused a sensation, because they showed that the generation-to-generation saga of Turkish immigrants in Denmark added up to the opposite of an integration success story. If present rates persisted, ethnic Danes would be a minority in their own country within sixty years.

Then came 9/11. In Denmark, as elsewhere, Muslims took to the streets to celebrate. A few days later, a thousand Muslims gathered in Nørrebro for a protest against democracy; one speaker called for "holy war" against Danish society.

When parliamentary elections were held that November, immigration was the number-one issue. The vote proved historic: the Social Democrats, since 1920 Denmark's largest political party, fell from power, and Denmark got a new prime minister, Anders Fogh Rasmussen, who promised a policy under which immigration would be reduced and resources focused on a vastly improved integration program. This was desperately overdue. "Our integration has not gone well," a Danish teacher told *Aftenposten*. "I had a class in which nineteen of thirty-three children couldn't say anything in Danish, even though they were all born in Denmark. . . . It's a catastrophe for Denmark, what's happening." A young Copenhagen woman who had been a gung-ho multiculturalist said she now felt uncomfortable in her own country: "When someone like me thinks this way, it doesn't bode well for the society."

Fogh Rasmussen kept his promise. His new government made significant changes in immigration and integration policy—and was vilified every step of the way by the media, the UN, and the EU. Across Western Europe, Denmark became a symbol of racism for no other reason than that it had acknowledged the failure of its immigration and integration policies and made a serious effort at reform. Among the new measures was a rule prohibiting Danish citizens or residents from importing foreign spouses if either of the parties was under twenty-four years old. This so-called "twenty-four-year rule" grew out of the recognition that fetching marriages are almost invariably arranged, usually forced, and that most forced marriages involve young people in their teens or early twenties. The assumption behind the rule was that by the time a young person reaches age twenty-four, he or she is more capable of resisting parental pressure—and more likely to have met and fallen in love with someone in Denmark.

The twenty-four-year rule has proven highly popular among many young Danish Muslims, who want to get an education first and then marry, eventually, for love. Yet the rule does little or nothing to compel a change in the cultural practices that are the real problem. It also infringes upon the legitimate marriage rights of people under twenty-four who have chosen their own spouses. This is no minor drawback: Denmark is a small nation, and many young Danes study abroad. If they happen to fall in love while they're away, they can't bring their prospective spouses back with them if either is under twenty-four. Many ethnic Danes who've married foreigners have thus settled in Sweden, which is just across a bridge from Copenhagen, and which is glad to issue them residency permits. For many, then, Sweden is the hero of this story; yet its helpfulness in this regard is just one aspect of a reckless immigration policy that has burdened that country with one of the most formidable integration challenges in Western Europe.

The Danish government deserves great credit for its efforts, which have yielded an impressive reduction in fetching marriages. At the same time, Denmark continues to be guilty of the same kind of pusillanimity that afflicts its neighbors. When there were calls for a Muslim takeover of Nørrebro, the Danish government responded with silence; when the radical Muslim organization al-Muhajiroun established a Danish branch, the government did nothing to stop it. In Denmark, as throughout Western Europe, the establishment continued to take the view that it was less important to do what's right than to be politically correct in the eyes of the UN and EU.

Two rare exceptions to this rule were Helle Merete Brix and Lars Hedegaard, who in early 2004 became the center of national controversy. Nearly a year earlier, Brix, a freelance journalist and author, had proposed Hedegaard, a columnist for *Berlingske Tidende* and former editor of *Information*, for membership in the Danish chapter of PEN, the writers' organization dedicated to freedom of speech around the world. Given Hedegaard's résumé, one might have expected his PEN membership to be approved quickly. (I became a member of American PEN after having published one small-press book of literary criticism; the process seemed virtually automatic.) But months went by. Later in 2003, *In the House of War: Islam's Colonization of the West*, written by Brix and Hedegaard in collaboration with Torben Hansen, appeared. In January 2004, the board of PEN Denmark rejected Hedegaard's candidacy, citing the book's characterization of the growth of Islam in Europe as a "third jihad"—an attempt to extend Islam's influence through a "demographic overpowering of Europe's native peoples." This and similar passages, insisted the board, blatantly contradicted the PEN charter's support for "understanding and mutual respect between nations" and "the idea of one humanity in one peaceful world."

PEN's rejection of Hedegaard made headlines—and the Danish government admirably responded by withdrawing a 60,000-kroner subsidy. An award for colossal nerve should have gone to Knud Vilby, head of the Danish Writers Association, who argued that by withdrawing the subsidy (equivalent to about $10,000), the government was damaging PEN's participation in "the international struggle for freedom of expression"—this, after Vilby's organization had punished Hedegaard for exercising that very freedom!

Two things must be said about PEN's decision. First, it's grotesque for an organization dedicated to free speech to blackball an author for sounding the alarm about an ideology that's intensely opposed to free speech. Second, to compare even the strongest quotations about Islam from *In the House of War* to, for example, comments about democracy made at an April 2004 Muslim event in Copenhagen's Nørrebro district is to be reminded what is and is not hate speech.

That event, organized by the radical Islamic organization Hizb ut-Tahrir, was billed as a march "against capitalism and democracy." Thousands of participants waved black Islamic flags and pictures of Iraqi radical Moqtada al-Sadr while chanting the word "*takbir, takbir*" ("expansion" or "conquest") and shouting threats—some veiled, some not—"against all who collaborated with the United States and Israel." One sign read: "If the Danish people are worried about their security, they should put a stop to the crimes committed in their name." A speaker who outlined plans for a Muslim caliphate in Denmark, wrote Hedegaard (the only journalist to file a substantive report on the march), "made it clear that this caliphate would include Muslims as well as non-Muslims, who in their own interest should adapt themselves to the sharia-run unitary state." Among the rallying cries were the following: "Islam is the alternative to capitalism!" "Democracy is a big lie!" "There awaits great suffering for everyone who sets himself up against the caliphate." "Capitalism is . . . a pro-American activity that the Danes should put an end to, if they hold their lives dear." "We are a nation that prefers death over a life of servility."

The police had allowed Hizb ut-Tahrir to march down the main street of Nørrebro during rush hour, even though a couple of years earlier Jewish organizations had been denied the same privilege because police couldn't guarantee their security. With Hizb ut-Tahrir—which Denmark's public prosecutor had declined to outlaw, purportedly because he couldn't decide whether its plans for a caliphate were concrete or only theoretical—things were different. In this case, noted Hedegaard, "the police understand, correctly, that there is not the slightest risk that the march will be attacked." He concluded on a wistful note: "If neither the government, the judicial system, the municipality, nor the police are interested in the rise of Islamofascism, there must be others who are."

I flew to Copenhagen in September. That week, one of the top stories in Denmark concerned Shahid Mehdi, a mufti who'd said that women and girls who didn't wear headscarves (including non-Muslims) were undeserving of respect and were responsible if they were raped. Eva Kjer Hansen, Denmark's minister for gender equality (yes, there really is such a government post), was insisting on a straight answer from every imam in the country: did they agree with Mehdi or not? Strangely, she seemed to have been caught off guard by Mehdi's remark. Equally strange was her call for "an open debate." What was there to debate? The kinds of clothes that women will be allowed to wear if they want to be spared sexual assault?

Of the several imams who commented publicly on Mehdi's remark, only one, a Danish convert, flatly disagreed with him. One suggested that Mehdi had simply meant that "from an Islamic perspective, women who wear headscarves attain the greatest possible beauty"; another said that while all women should be respected as long as they respect themselves, "a woman can of course herself cause, or be to blame for, her own rape or assault"; and the third thought that perhaps Mehdi had been misunderstood owing to his difficulties with Danish.

I met Hedegaard and Brix for drinks at a café in downtown Copenhagen. Hedegaard, a distinguished-looking man with a neatly cropped white beard and a look of wry intelligence, told me that PEN had turned the controversy over his membership application to its advantage. "After the government withdrew its support," he said, "private donors came in to show their solidarity." PEN Denmark emerged richer by about 200,000 kroner. (Among the contributors was a foundation dedicated to "peace and understanding.") Hedegaard's career, however, would never be the same. By writing frankly about radical Islam, he'd destroyed many professional relationships. Nine out of ten Danish journalists, he said, were in agreement that he and Brix were "insane or criminals or both."

We talked about a recent mass meeting held by Hizb ut-Tahrir at Nørrebrohallen. The audience—which had been separated by gender, with female guards in full *chador* encircling the women's side of the hall to ensure that they behaved properly—had been treated to rants against secularism and democracy and angry calls for sharia law: "Sharia must not be our guide, or else we're extremists! The caliphate must not be our solution, or else we're fundamentalists! Jihad must not be mentioned as the solution in Iraq and Afghanistan, or else we're terrorists!" Organizers had barred *Berlingske Tidende*'s reporter, Claus L. Mikkelsen (who'd written forthrightly about them), leading other journalists to boycott the event, but people who attended posted accounts of it online. They made uneasy reading. "The atmosphere," one woman reported, had grown "more and more aggressive" as the meeting wore on. The level of rage at democracy had been through the roof. Especially worrying was the number of young Danish converts: several ethnic Danish girls had been in attendance, all in black *hijab*.

Over a thousand supporters had shown up that evening. "A thousand fascists with Oswald Mosley," Hedegaard said to me (referring to the British fascist leader of the 1930s), "would be a problem—but twelve hundred at a totalitarian rally for Hizb ut-Tahrir isn't seen as a problem!" Why? Because "it's *bad form* to be preoccupied with that!" In the view of the media elite, "we are giving away our low breeding and lack of culture when we talk about such things."

There's another factor at play here: '68-er nostalgia. Later, I would read an apologia for Hizb ut-Tahrir by Danish journalist Jacob Holdt, who had attended the rally at Nørrebrohallen and claimed to see in the radicals there "the same bewildered, fanatical, idealistic, justice-seeking, sympathetic, angry, and, especially, dreaming young people we ourselves once were." Holdt "felt immediately at home at HuT's meeting in Nørrebrohallen," he said, because it reminded him of old lefty gatherings about Vietnam and colonialism. Indeed, Hizb ut-Tahrir's "analyses and criticisms of capitalism and Western democracy" were precisely the same ones Marxists had made back in the good old days, and the young Muslims' cries of *"Allah Akbar!"* were thoroughly reminiscent of the old cries of "Red Front!"

Hedegaard was of the view, however, that the Danish establishment's benign neglect of Islamic extremism must have deeper causes than snobbism or hippie nostalgia. After all, he said, the Islamicization of the Nordic countries was "the most fundamental transformation" they'd experienced in a millennium. Something so monumental, in his opinion, could not be explained simply by a few people's foolishness or class snobbery. "Heavy consequences," he insisted, "must have heavy causes." The surrender of Denmark to Muslims had to be the result of some deep-seated compulsion.

Brix interjected that Danes, historically, "bargain with the enemy." They did it with the Nazis, and in earlier centuries they'd done it with one conquering army after another. Hedegaard agreed: "You try to accommodate an enemy that is so much stronger than you." But for him this Denmark-specific explanation, too, was insufficient. His theory was that Western Europe's ongoing surrender to radical Islam had its roots in the psychic devastation of the First World War. For while that conflict marked America's ascent to the rank of Great Power, Europeans took it as devastating proof, Hedegaard said, "that our culture was worthless. It was basically destroyed. And that prepared the way for two sorts of totalitarianism"—Nazism and Communism—and for "atrocities of a magnitude that is hard to imagine." Those atrocities, in turn, placed upon Europeans an unbearable burden of guilt. The Nazis, he said, "made Europe think it is doomed and sinful . . . *and deserves what it has coming.*"

"But the Danes have less to be ashamed of than any people in Europe," I protested. "They saved the Jews."

"Yes, they saved the Jews. But I doubt they would do it today. They've been reeducated." If, at some time in the not-too-distant future, fundamentalist Muslims began rounding up Jews, he said, "it would be racism to resist."

At first blush, it may sound preposterous—the idea that native Europeans, after enough daily doses of anti-Semitic and pro-Muslim propaganda, might reach a point at which they'd actually accept Muslims' right to execute Jews, or feel they had no right to stop it. But it's not a scenario that can be dismissed with a wave of the hand. Anyone who considers Hedegaard's scenario far-fetched need only recall the history of twentieth-century Europe. For Europeans to reach the point of accepting (again) the mass murder of Jews, what's required isn't a murderous anti-Semitism on their part, only that certain already well-developed attitudes—a reflexive inclination to appease, a readiness to "understand" suicide bombers, a susceptibility to victim rhetoric from aggressors, and a desperate eagerness to applaud "the good side" of terrorist organizations like Hamas and Hezbollah—continue to develop in the direction they're already moving.

There was another salient factor. Holdt found Hizb ut-Tahrir's young members "well educated and surprisingly well integrated," and Mikkelsen agreed. It seems counterintuitive, but many of Europe's most radical Muslims do indeed turn out to be among the best educated, highly fluent in the language of their country of residence as well as in English. Many have impressive technical, scientific, or computer skills; they enjoy much of what the West has to offer and are intelligent and gifted enough to make a real contribution to Western society. Perversely, however, they've embraced an ideology that's violently antagonistic to the modern world and dedicated to the establishment of a caliphate modeled after the medieval Arab empire. One such Muslim is Theo van Gogh's killer, Mohammed Bouyeri, whose would-be suicide letter was composed not just in proper Dutch but in the distinctive poetic form used by Dutch people in their traditional *Sinterklaas* letters. It was neither poverty nor ignorance nor cultural isolation, then, that drove Bouyeri to radicalism.

Hedegaard, Brix, and I repaired to a nearby Chinese restaurant. The pretty young Asian waitress spoke clear, confident Danish, and when I addressed her in Norwegian she replied in equally impressive English. At the next table, with their mixed-race little boy, sat a Danish man and a vivacious black Englishwoman, laughing together. Sitting there watching and listening to them, one might easily be lulled into believing that Denmark was a true melting pot, an immigration triumph.

Over dinner, in response to Hedegaard's dark view of Denmark's future, Brix was more hopeful. The media would eventually come around; crisis would be averted. "You have to be a little patient," she said. Not until the Eiffel Tower and the Tivoli in Copenhagen were blown up, she said, would the elite get it. Hedegaard agreed. But then again, he said, the destruction of those landmarks might have exactly the opposite result—the media might simply intensify its perverse cries of "Why do they hate us so much? What have we done to deserve this hatred?" The Western European attitude, he observed, is that "of a repentant criminal": too many Europeans are simply too willing to compromise their freedom. He mentioned a Danish firm with which he was familiar. It had recently taken on some new Muslim employees, and one of the longtime workers there had asked, in all seriousness: "When the Muslims start working here, can we still wear shorts in the summer?" Such readiness to adjust to Islamic norms—an attribute rooted in the fact that the reigning social ideal was not liberty but compromise—did not bode well for Denmark's future. "If there's any hope," Hedegaard suggested dryly, borrowing a line he knew I'd recognize from *1984*, "it lies in the proles." Yet we both knew that the "proles"—if they *did* take over the reins from the elite—might well lead Europe back down the road to fascism.

He did admit that he was glad to be living in Denmark and not elsewhere in Western Europe: "If there's any place where there's hope, it's got to be this country." But Hedegaard didn't hold out much hope even for Denmark. "Unless they build up a cadre of intellectuals in Europe who can think," he said, America "can kiss Europe good-bye." The Continent's future, he predicted, "is going to be vastly different than we imagine. . . . It's going to be war. Like Lebanon," with some enclaves dominated by Christians and others by Muslims. There will be "permanent strife," and no one will have the "power to mollify or mediate. . . . It will be more gruesome than we can imagine." When the horror comes, he warned, the journalists who helped bring it about will "wag their heads and flee—and leave it to those who can't flee to fight it out."

SINCE MOVING TO OSLO, I'd made an effort to keep abreast of political developments throughout Western Europe. But I paid special attention to news from the Netherlands. One reason was my lingering attachment to the country; another was my suspicion that it might just be the place where integration issues in Europe first came to a dramatic turning point. The very fact that the notoriously tolerant Dutch had gone so far in helping Muslims to build up segregated enclaves within their borders—subsidizing schools and mosques and neighborhood centers, while making virtually no demands on immigrants to work or learn the language—suggested it was there that radical Muslims might push too far and provoke a response.

The Dutch approach to immigration was summed up by Labor Party member Fatima Elati. "The attitude in Holland is: as long as you don't bother me, I don't mind that you're here. It's a kind of neglect." This has long been the Dutch way: mutual "neglect" kept the peace for generations among Catholics, Protestants, and secularists. ("The Dutchman," Dutch author Leon de Winter has observed, "is a tradition-conscious person, who knows exactly when he must turn his face away in order not to notice the strangeness of someone else.") What is clear now, however, is that adding fundamentalist Muslims to the mix was a bridge too far. Why? Because the principled libertarianism of the Dutch ("Do your own thing and let me do mine") conflicts dramatically with the very essence of fundamentalist Islam, which dictates in detail how people should live—and whose adherents are mightily uncomfortable living among people whose "thing" differs dramatically from their own. It's this Dutch dedication to individual liberty that Fortuyn was defending—which, of course, is why it's absurd to call him a reactionary.

In the days after Pim Fortuyn's murder, it had seemed that Dutch people were undergoing a major attitudinal shift. But would it last? How great a legacy would Fortuyn leave? As the weeks and months went by, the answer remained unclear. Sometimes it appeared that the rage in the

Netherlands over his murder had dissipated and that politics as usual had reasserted itself. By 2004, weakened by infighting, Lijst Pim Fortuyn had all but collapsed in disarray.

In January of that year, a Muslim teenager in The Hague shot a teacher dead in a school cafeteria. Media reports failed to clarify the motive, but when one read between the lines it seemed that the murderer, whose first name was Murat, felt his honor had been violated in some way. The most unsettling part of the story was that about thirty of Murat's fellow students held a demonstration in his support two days after the killing, banging on cars to signal their solidarity with him and holding up signs saying "Murat, we love you." How did Prime Minister Jan Peter Balkenende respond? Although, to his credit, he criticized the students for having "no feeling for a respectful society," he also blamed the murder—absurdly—on brutal images in the media and computer games, which "help violent acts become more acceptable in society." The fact that many young people in today's Netherlands grow up in a subculture in which violence against unbelievers is considered not only acceptable but obligatory went entirely unmentioned. So much for the legacy of Fortuyn.

Shortly after the school murder, a commission established by the Dutch parliament issued a report on the effectiveness of the nation's immigration and integration policy over three decades. Its conclusions were blunt and sobering: by 2017 at the latest, a majority of the residents of Dutch cities would be persons of non-Dutch ethnicity, most of whose families would perpetuate their segregation from mainstream society through a pattern of transnational marriages. "The Dutch have become one illusion poorer," commented the Danish journalist Jørgen V. Larsen. "In no other country in Europe has there been so strong a belief in multicultural society, in a community living in harmony, where natives and immigrants can each cultivate their own distinctive character while respecting certain basic shared norms and values." The report, of course, did not reveal anything that Pim Fortuyn had not already known—and said—several years earlier.

Yet there were promising developments, too—among them the rise to influence of a courageous young woman named Ayaan Hirsi Ali. Articulate and outspoken—and with striking looks that brought to mind her fellow Somalian, the fashion model Iman—Hirsi Ali was the daughter of Hirsi Magan Isse, an anti-Communist intellectual, politician, and leader of the pro-democratic guerrilla movement that sought to overthrow Somalia's Marxist government, installed in 1970. One of six children that her father had with four different women, Hirsi Ali sustained a permanent injury at age five when a teacher banged her head against a wall; at around the same time, without the knowledge or approval of her father—whose admiration for the American way of life had caused him to reject such customs—her grandmother had her ritually circumcised. When she was six, she and her family accompanied her father into exile, first to Saudi Arabia, then Ethiopia and Kenya. (She has said that "it was not until I got to Kenya that I found out that there were women who had not been abused in their childhood.") Along the way, she picked up five languages, including English.

She grew into a devout Muslim woman who wore full *hijab*. And as a devout Muslim woman should, she humbly submitted, at age twenty-two, to an arranged marriage to a Canadian cousin. During a brief stay in Germany en route to Toronto, however, she had a change of heart. Fleeing to the Netherlands by train, she secured political asylum and spent nearly a year at a refugee center, where, serving as a translator for other refugees, she heard horror story after horror story from Muslim women who'd been abused and rejected by their families. When she left the center—having in the meantime learned a sixth language, Dutch— she took a secretarial course, then went to Leiden University to study political science. "I wanted to understand why all we asylum seekers were coming here," she would later tell the *Guardian*, "and why everything worked in this country, and why you could walk undisturbed through the streets at night, and why there was no corruption, and why on the other side of the world there was so much corruption and so much conflict." *Naïve*

For Hirsi Ali, being in the Netherlands "was like being in paradise. . . . Imagine. Everybody is reasonable. Everybody is tolerant. Everybody is happy." Gradually, she turned away from Islam; 9/11 would be the decisive moment. ("I didn't believe in God anymore after the attacks," she told *L'Express* in a June 2005 interview.) Graduating shortly after 9/11, she was hired by a Labor Party think tank to research the lives of Dutch Muslim women and found herself, like Unni Wikan in Norway, coming up with policy proposals that scandalized party leaders: ditch *verzuiling*; close Muslim schools; curb immigration. She urged Labor leaders to take seriously the problems confronting women within the Muslim community; but, not wanting to be seen as allies of Fortuyn (whom they were busy demonizing), they refused.

Denied their support, Hirsi Ali began to speak out on her own, taking the Dutch government to task for its support of multicultural programs that perpetuated Muslim segregation. "I called it the paradox of the left," she told the *Guardian*. "On the one hand, they support ideals of equality and emancipation, but in this case they do nothing about it; they even facilitate the oppression." When she received threats from Muslims, the lame response of her party's leaders—whose first concern, it appeared, was not to offend even the most extreme Dutch Islamists—caused her to leave Labor in disgust. Social Democrats, Hirsi Ali later observed, "have traditionally protected the weak. But now the weak have become women and children in Muslim families, and the Social Democrats will not defend them, because it's not politically correct. So they abandoned them. They lost their moral authority in my eyes."

Joining the market-friendly Liberal Democrats in early 2002, Hirsi Ali kept up the pressure for reform. She became increasingly prominent; after Fortuyn's murder that spring, many viewed her as his natural successor. In November, the *New York Times*'s Marlise Simons compared her to Fortuyn—whom, curiously enough, Simons now appeared to celebrate: "He said out loud what had long been considered racist and politically incorrect—for example, that conservative Muslim clerics were undermining certain Dutch values like acceptance of homosexuality and the equality of men and women." *Sodom Gomorra*

At the time, Hirsi Ali was temporarily residing in the States after receiving death threats. Returning to the Netherlands in January, she took up a seat in the Dutch parliament, where her activism continued. "If the West wants to help modernize Islam," she argued, "it should invest in women because they educate the children." As Fortuyn had done, she recommended punishment for wife and child beating; she argued that the Netherlands should stop allowing immigrant-group children to take classes in their parents' tongues and stop funding the country's over seven hundred Muslim neighborhood clubs; and she opposed government plans to fund hundreds of new Islamic schools. Together with Labor members of Parliament—who by this point felt compelled to embrace at least some degree of reform—she sought legislation to protect Muslim girls from genital mutilation and to establish a database identifying the national origins of men who commit honor killings. (Labor had previously considered this discriminatory.) She also sought to close a mosque in Amsterdam where the congregation was reportedly encouraged to hate Jews, beat up women, and shun infidels. In addition to all this, she found time to write *Submission*, a short film about the plight of Muslim women, made in collaboration with Theo van Gogh.

Like Fortuyn, naturally, Hirsi Ali had enemies. Ali Eddaudi, a

Dutch-Moroccan "writer and cleric," accused her of "pander[ing] to the Dutch." Also like Fortuyn, she angered her party's leaders by speaking her mind instead of echoing the party line. A Moroccan immigrant rap group, DHC, recorded a song whose lyrics anticipated her murder and dismemberment ("I will slice you into small pieces and throw you in one of the seven seas"). And the ambassadors from Saudi Arabia, Pakistan, Malaysia, and Sudan insisted she be ejected from her party—to which the party chief replied by saying that Hirsi Ali was speaking only for herself. This reply, she commented afterward, only showed that he didn't "understand at all, at all, how radical Muslims think: they see it as a sign of weakness and as evidence that it pays to protest against my person."*

SUBMISSION AIRED ON Dutch television in August 2004. It was a short, simple film, consisting mostly of brief monologues by Muslim women who, looking plaintively into the camera, recounted their experiences with physical violence at the hands of Muslim men. At one point, words from the Koran were seen written on a woman's body—a reference to the harsh physical impact that Islamic doctrine had on some women's lives. Only weeks after the film was broadcast, its director lay butchered on an Amsterdam street.

Across Western Europe, the murder of Theo van Gogh led to anxious TV discussions, impassioned newspaper articles, and contentious public meetings. Muslim leaders and spokespeople were asked what they thought of the killing. Journalists and politicians who should have known better were stunned to learn that many of these community representatives could not bring themselves to denounce it or to stand up for freedom of expression—at least not without obvious hesitation or immediate qualification. Most Muslim groups in Europe refused point-blank to condemn the assassination. If for the majority of Europeans the lesson of the murder was the importance of protecting free speech, for many Muslims the lesson was the need for limitations on free speech. Statements and images offensive to Muslims should be forbidden; the Prophet and the Koran must be shielded from any criticism or mockery.

---

*In July 2004, remarks made by Progress Party leader Carl I. Hagen about Islamic fundamentalists resulted in a joint letter of complaint signed by the ambassadors to Norway from Egypt, Indonesia, Pakistan, and Morocco, plus the chargé d'affaires from Tunisia. They claimed he had "offended 1.3 billion Muslims," wrote Nina Berglund in *Aftenposten*. Hagen's reply: "Terror is being practiced in the name of Islam in large portions of the world, and where are the ambassadors then?"

Typical was Copenhagen imam Ahmed Abu Laban's comment that *Submission* had "crossed the limits of freedom of speech" and that Europeans must begin "an open debate on these limits. . . . Freedom of speech is not sacred." On German TV, a Muslim defended the van Gogh murder: "If you insult Islam, you have to pay!" Many politicians and journalists who hadn't previously grasped the nature of the challenge of fundamentalist Islam began to understand.

Yes, elite Europeans had known that according to Islam certain things were sacred and other things taboo. But only now did they begin to see that for many Muslims, freedom of speech was at best a silly, alien fetish and at worst a pernicious incitement to blasphemy. Christians in the West are used to the idea that their religion is open to criticism and ridicule; most of them accept this as the price of living in a free society, and even those who are deeply offended by criticism and ridicule aren't about to kill over it. But fundamentalist Islam, as many Western Europeans were suddenly realizing, is different. For all the reports over the years about honor killings, many Europeans had never really grasped the mentality behind these acts; they'd never perceived how dramatically the fundamentalist Muslim concepts of honor and respect differed from the Western concepts that went by the same names; they'd never quite appreciated the life-or-death seriousness with which fundamentalist Muslims viewed such matters; and they'd never faced the fact that all this was now, like it or not, their concern.

The death of van Gogh changed all that. Many Europeans saw that van Gogh's killer was neither a lone madman nor a representative of a tiny, far-out fringe but a man whom quite a number of Muslims viewed as having done a good thing. This new understanding was reflected in survey results announced on November 15. Asked by a Dutch TV station to name the greatest Dutchman of all time, viewers selected not Rembrandt, Vermeer, or Vincent van Gogh—or even the nation's revered founder, William of Orange—but Pim Fortuyn. The vote was, among much else, a stunning rebuke to the Dutch political and media establishment.

Van Gogh's murder had repercussions across northern Europe. In the Netherlands, Germany, Denmark, and elsewhere, politicians proposed that imams be required to preach in the language of the country. At a November 19 meeting chaired by Dutch immigration minister Rita Verdonk, the justice and interior ministers of EU member states agreed to require immigrants to learn the language of their new country and to adapt to "European values"—strong language indeed for the multiculturally oriented EU.

Not all Europeans reacted to the murder by standing up for "European values." Some echoed the Muslim argument that the main problem was not van Gogh's murder but van Gogh's film. In the Netherlands, a group of journalists, athletes, and performers concocted the daffy idea of selling orange wristbands to be worn as symbols of "respect" and "tolerance." The scheme, which drew the enthusiastic support of Prime Minister Balkenende, seemed an attempt to reinstate the very tolerance for intolerance whose folly the murders of Fortuyn and van Gogh had exposed.

Many blamed van Gogh for his own murder. On German TV, Middle East "expert" Ulrich Kienzie chastised the late filmmaker for breaking a "taboo." (Neither the moderator nor the other participants challenged him.) In Britain, the *Guardian*—describing Bouyeri, predictably, as "a lone Muslim extremist"—savaged van Gogh's and Hirsi Ali's "magnificent disregard for the feelings they might be offending." Dutch author Geert Mak, for his part, couldn't understand all the hullabaloo over the slaying: "we have only one murder, and everybody goes crazy."

Few European writers or filmmakers denounced their colleague's murder. Danish author Ebbe Kløvedal Reich explained his silence by saying that while the recently assassinated Anna Lindh "was from our neighboring country and was a charming and wise woman," the rude and abrasive van Gogh had been, well, something else. (Speaking about religion, Reich added, was always risky, "and we have to learn to live with that.") Dutch journalist Simon Kuper sought valiantly to hold the old establishment line—and demonstrated just how feeble that line now sounded. Posthumously slandering Fortuyn as the instigator of Dutch "Muslim-bashing" and "racist politics" and van Gogh as "a minor filmmaker on the make," Kuper played down his country's grave new problems ("a few Dutch Moroccans beat up gay men. . . . Some Muslim pupils wouldn't listen to lessons on the Holocaust") and dismissed Dutch concern about these matters as hypocritical: "The Netherlands had been inhabited for centuries by people who believed men and women were unequal, and that homosexuality was a sin, but it was now decided that Muslims holding such views were at odds with 'Dutch values.' " Presumably Kuper expected Dutch women and gay men to quietly accept the erosion of their liberties as the clock turned back—and not to the seventeenth century, either, but to the seventh.

Kuper, writing in the *Financial Times*, characterized criticism of fundamentalist Islam as "bashing"—a curious choice of words, given that literal bashing (of women, gays, Jews) was among the problems in question. He sneered at immigration minister Verdonk for wanting "to make all immigrants learn 'Dutchness,' though no one is clear what this is"—when in fact nobody who took a spin through Amsterdam's Oud West could fail to understand exactly what Verdonk meant. Kuper counseled that the Dutch should accept a level of street crime and a certain "risk of Islamic fundamentalist violence" (after all, "smoking still kills thousands of times more Dutch people than Islamic fundamentalism"); presumably he felt they should accept a certain level of gay-bashing, wife beating, and honor killing, too.

Meanwhile, social anthropologist Thomas Hylland Eriksen—Mr. Establishment Norway himself—was busy reassuring his countrymen about fundamentalist Islam by drawing ludicrous comparisons to Western culture. Worried about religious Muslims? Don't worry: they're just like members of Norway's Christian People's Party. Concerned about *hijab?* Don't be: the sexual fixation manifested in such garb is just like the "North Atlantic" sexual fixation manifested in "stripping and plastic surgery." Disturbed by Islamic authoritarianism? Better to worry about the West, where "nihilism and hedonism are just as acceptable as the other products of the lifestyle cafeteria."

One writer who wasn't looking for ways to praise Islam was Leon de Winter, who recounted a post–van Gogh conversation he'd had with other parents in his Dutch village when they were dropping their children off at school. One mother wondered "whether we shouldn't think about a guard"; someone else mentioned friends in Amsterdam who'd seen four Arab men photographing a school from a car. He and his fellow parents, wrote de Winter, "fear another Beslan."

I sensed a shift in attitudes toward America; it was as if a sudden wave of reflection in some circles had caused a tempering of reflexive anti-Americanism. Some European leftists, noted British journalist Charles Bremner, were now actually looking to their antagonist across the Atlantic as a model. Similarly, Fredrik Engelstad, head of Norway's not exactly conservative Institute for Social Research, told the Communist newspaper *Klassekampen:* "I'm often struck by how liberal the U.S. is when it comes to people's personal beliefs. There are a number of cultural features of American society that I hope we'll experience in this country in the future."

The most welcome surprise was the respectful hearing CNN gave to outspoken politician Geert Wilders, who, though under death threats, did not pull his punches. "Why isn't the Dutch government doing something about this?" he asked in a surprisingly frank hour-long report about the Dutch predicament, and answered the question himself: "Because they are incompetent." Twenty-five Dutch mosques had terrorist connections, and their imams preached monstrous things about gays, women, and democracy—yet the government dared not close them down. Echoing Fortuyn, he said: "We will lose our country. It's as simple as that." The Dutch people, he said, "have been too long too tolerant to the intolerant."

In Norway, physician Zahid Mukhtar, the longtime leader of the nation's Muslim Council, was asked on TV2's *Holmgang* how he felt about the van Gogh murder. He said combatively that he had "understanding" for the killer. He added that, as a Muslim, he could not accept the subordination of sharia law to Norwegian law. And though he accused van Gogh and others of stigmatizing Muslims, his own conduct toward his fellow guests on the program was insulting, even bullying. Addressing Progress Party leader Carl I. Hagen and Hege Storhaug, both critics of fundamentalist Islam, Mukhtar said aggressively that people like them "should be stopped." At the beginning of every episode of *Holmgang*, viewers are invited to phone in during the program and answer a question relevant to the evening's topic. That night the question was: "Are Muslims a threat to Western values?" By a whopping ninety-seven to three margin, callers voted "yes."

In an "open letter" to TV2's managing director, Kåre Valebrook, a Muslim lawyer named Abid Q. Raja savaged TV2 for even daring to raise the question of whether Islam was a threat. Simply to ask this, he raged, was stigmatizing, an example of "raw . . . populism." (He had clearly learned the lingo of political correctness.) Raja offered nothing in the way of a rational argument, only hectoring and assertion: his manner was that of a street thug seeking to intimidate—shouting too loud, standing too close, and repeatedly poking a finger in his interlocutor's chest. In capital letters that seemed intended to convey exasperation over even having to say such a thing, he maintained that "MUSLIMS REJECT THE MURDER OF THE FILMMAKER VAN GOGH!" But of course all Muslims did not reject it. Several had been involved in it; many others had celebrated it; some had openly defended it.

Norway's Muslims, who'd demonstrated many times against the war on terror, had never been moved to congregate in opposition to terror itself. Two weeks later, plans for such a protest were announced. The organizer, NRK reporter Noman Mubashir, explained that he'd "hoped for the longest time that a Muslim organization, a Muslim spokesman, or the Muslim Council would take the initiative of organizing such an event. But since no one is doing so, I'm speaking out." Mubashir, an attractive young man who covers whimsical, offbeat stories with an ever-playful smile and boyish charm, hardly seemed to belong in the same category as the likes of Mukhtar and Raja, with their macho bluster and ire. Indeed, it soon emerged that in the eyes of many Muslims in Norway, Mubashir didn't even count as a Muslim: his family belonged to the Ahmadi sect, founded in 1889, which describes itself as encouraging "interfaith dialogue," advocating "peace, tolerance, love and understanding among followers of different faiths," and "strongly reject[ing] violence and terrorism in any form and for any reason." Ahmadis, whom a 1974 amendment to Pakistan's Constitution declared to be non-Muslims, are the only self-identified Muslim group that the Saudi Arabian government bars from Mecca. In 2004, in Bangladesh (where Ahmadi books are outlawed), a gang of young Islamists murdered Ahmadi author and women's rights supporter Humayun Azad; in Pakistan, massacres of Ahmadi Muslims take place regularly.

On the evening of November 4, I made my way to the plaza facing Oslo's main train station, where participants had been asked to gather. From there, everyone would proceed up the city's main street, Karl Johans Gate, to the parliament. Several journalists predicted a huge turnout; *Klassekampen* said that the protest could prove to be "a massive interreligious demonstration for freedom of expression and liberal values." It was clear that the Norwegian establishment wanted—and fully expected—a convincing display of Muslim solidarity with Norway.

My own expectations were quite different. But even I was surprised by the meagerness of the crowd at the train station. Barely two hundred people had come, most of them non-Muslims. A surprising number were famous faces—among them leaders of the major political parties, government ministers, at least one former prime minister, and the current prime minister, Kjell Magne Bondevik. Not to mention Unni Wikan. But Muslims? There were no more than fifty of them—fifty!—out of a total Norwegian Muslim population of around seventy thousand (most of whom live in Oslo). Given the size of Muslim families, it was not inconceivable that every last one of those in attendance was a relative of Mubashir.

Despite the disastrous turnout, the organizers plunged ahead. Four or five politicians delivered speeches. They said little about freedom of speech or Islamist violence and murder—Theo van Gogh was hardly mentioned—but focused instead on that familiar bogeyman, Norwegian racism. Never mind that four out of five immigrants interviewed in a recent survey had said they'd never experienced racism; the politicians talked as if Norway's Muslims were brutally oppressed. The low, dishonest language flowed fast and furious; much of the speechifying consisted of little more than the usual laundry list of buzzwords: "inclusion . . . multicultural . . . diversity . . . stigmatization . . . respect."

But the politicians were outdone by Abid Q. Raja, who, having been invited by Mubashir (presumably in a gesture of unity) to co-chair the demo, let loose a violent harangue, furiously rejecting the demonstration's entire premise and ranting belligerently about the disgraceful treatment to which Muslims were subjected in Norway. A foreign listener would never imagine how much money the average Norwegian Muslim family collects in government largesse; would never guess that the rate of Muslim-on-Norwegian crime is alarmingly high and the rate of Norwegian-on-Muslim crime essentially zero; would never guess that despite their supposedly terrible treatment, Muslims in Norway do everything they can to get their relatives in, too. Raja insisted that Norway's Muslims had yet to receive their full rights as residents of a democratic nation—yet he said not a word about Muslims' respecting the democratic rights of non-Muslims, including their right of free speech, which was supposed to be the point of the gathering.

When the speeches were over, torches were lit and we all walked the half mile or so to the parliament building. We passed more Muslims along the way than there were in the march.

The next day the Norwegian media were full of reports about the demonstration's spectacular failure. The same newspapers that had predicted a big turnout—and assured their readers that this would prove once and for all that the nation's Muslims loved Norway, cherished democracy, and hated terrorism—now contained articles vigorously maintaining that the low turnout didn't prove anything.

Only a few months earlier, twelve hundred Muslims had shown up for Hizb ut-Tahrir's antidemocracy rally in Copenhagen. On countless occasions in recent years, Muslims had filled the streets of major European cities to rail against America, Israel, the West, democracy, homosexuality, and a wide variety of perceived slights and insults. In early 2004, hundreds of Muslim women had participated in an Oslo march protesting the proposed French ban on head coverings. But though Muslims had gathered time and again to condemn the invasion of Iraq, they'd never gotten together to criticize Saddam; though they'd marched repeatedly against Israel, they'd never organized a protest against Hamas or Hezbollah. Before the murder of van Gogh, the only large-scale public reactions by European Muslims to terrorist acts had taken the form of cheering and celebration. On 9/11, young Muslims across Europe had applauded Al Qaeda in the streets; when Madrid was struck, there were more festivities; after the murder of van Gogh, still more.

Now, if I were a seriously religious Muslim who truly despised terrorism, who was genuinely revolted at the sight of my co-religionists giving it a merry thumbs-up, and who considered such responses profoundly at odds with the tenets of my faith, I like to think I would have welcomed the chance to show the world that there were Muslims who believed as I did. By doing so, I would've been able in one fell swoop to help rescue my beloved religion from distortion, to contribute to greater social harmony, and to provide young Muslims with an alternative faith model. Norway's Muslims were given precisely that chance; but more than 99.9 percent of them turned their backs on it. It was tantamount to spitting in the Norwegian establishment's face. They made the prime minister and other government leaders look like naive, credulous fools (which, come to think of it, is not all bad).

One could forgive an observer for viewing this as an unambiguous expression of disrespect for the country, its government, and its values— and a clear indication that many immigrants felt absolutely invulnerable. They'd long since taken the measure of the Norwegian state, and they knew that no matter what they did, Norway would never expel them, punish them, or cut off their financial support. Mukhtar said that by not showing up for the demonstration, "we [Norwegian Muslims] have shown that we have backbone. . . . We refused to bend our neck and walk with our heads down." Or was it truer to say that Norwegian Muslims were bending their necks to the likes of Mukhtar? Could it be that even for moderate Muslims, simply to dissociate oneself openly from Islamist violence and murder was to engage in an unacceptable act of self-humiliation? An observation made by Hans Rustad in another context seemed relevant here: "Muslims are used to being the majority. They're not that in Europe. Therefore they feel like victims who are being discriminated against. This is, in my view, a disguised desire for dominance." Certainly this was the impression given by the Danish Muslim leader who, in 2004, called secularism "a disgusting form of oppression." By this logic, the only way *not* to oppress Muslims is to hand all power over to them and allow them to oppress *you*.

IN THE WEEKS after Theo van Gogh's murder, some individuals and governments were facing up to these sobering facts, and choosing at last to stand up for liberty; at the same time, others were redoubling their efforts to appease illiberalism. The latter tendency was particularly noticeable during the Christmas season of 2004. As the holiday approached, many Europeans made unprecedented efforts to avoid offending Muslims with Christian images or references. In Britain, the Red Cross banned Christmas trees and nativity scenes from its charity shops; in Italy, a school in Treviso replaced its traditional nativity play with a skit about Little Red Riding Hood and a school near Milan substituted the name of Jesus in a hymn with the word "virtue."

Certainly accommodation appeared to be the order of the day in Britain. In December 2004, the National Audit Office ordered inheritance tax rules overhauled because they unfairly penalized Muslims with multiple wives. In January, it was reported that after Muslim pressure had persuaded the Advertising Standards Authority to ban an underwear-ad billboard near a mosque, Muslims were increasingly defacing ads they found offensive. (An organization called Muslims Against Advertising had even set up a Web site with instructions in vandalism.) The approach of an election in May 2005 caused British politicians to reach new heights of sycophancy. ("Many Labor MPs," noted Nick Cohen in the *Observer*, "will do anything to win back the Muslim vote.") In a March speech, Chancellor of the Exchequer Gordon Brown celebrated Islam's moral teachings, hailed "the contribution of British Muslims to British life," and called Muslims "our modern heroes." In a piece for *Muslim Weekly* that columnist Melanie Philips quite aptly described as a "groveling plea" for votes, Labor minister Mike O'Brien wrote: "Ask yourself what will [Tory leader] Michael Howard do for British Muslims? Will his foreign policy aim to help Palestine? Will he promote legislation to protect you from religious hatred and discrimination? Will he give you the choice of sending your children to a faith school? Will he stand up for the right of Muslim women to wear the *hijab*? Will he really fight for Turkey, a Muslim country, to join the EU?"

Then there was the latest chapter in the saga of the king of all grovelers, George Galloway, reportedly the recipient of hundreds of thousands of dollars in payoffs from Saddam Hussein (to whom he'd once said: "Sir, I salute your courage, your strength, your indefatigability"). After being ejected from Labor, Galloway founded a party called Respect and ran for Parliament in the heavily Muslim constituency of Bethnal

Green and Bow, telling voters repeatedly, according to Johann Hari, that Prime Minister Blair was "waging a war on Muslims . . . at home and abroad." But though Galloway had (as Val MacQueen put it) "adopted almost every conservative Islamic position on almost everything," he was nearly lynched one day during his campaign by a group of Muslim fanatics who called elections "un-Islamic" and condemned Galloway as a "false prophet." ("The police saved my life," he admitted.) Yet in the end the voters of Bethnal Green and Bow elected him to the House of Commons.*

Meanwhile, there were some rather surprising signs of resolve in France. The government banned Hezbollah's Arabic-language TV channel and began deporting imams who preached wife beating; the stoning to death of a young Tunisian-born woman in Marseille inspired a large demonstration by a Muslim women's group called Neither Whores nor Submissive; and British journalist Charles Bremner observed that France's "left wing, which long shunned criticism of Islam as the stock-in-trade of Jean-Marie Le Pen," was now finally denouncing "the 'totalitarian,' anti-feminist, antisemitic doctrines of the fundamentalists." *Sacre bleu!* Even Dominique de Villepin was calling it "unacceptable" that most French imams were not French citizens, and that a third didn't speak French. Yet despite these welcome developments, social division in France continued to rise; the nation's Muslim Council, established to advance religious moderation, was instead reportedly "coming increasingly under the effective control of radicals."

In the Netherlands, Integration Minister Rita Verdonk told imams at a November 2004 meeting that radical Muslims must be "isolated and eliminated." While making the requisite comments about the desirability of dialogue, she expressed the hope that at their next encounter, the imams—most of whom had required a translator—would be able to carry on that dialogue in Dutch. (*Touché!*) In February, Verdonk announced that non-Western applicants for Dutch residency would now

---

*Galloway later made an appearance in Washington. Called before a Senate committee investigating the expropriation of billions in UN Oil-for-Food lucre, he showed no contrition regarding his ties to Saddam and other thugs; instead, he acted like a demagogue, openly insulting the committee members in an audacious—but characteristic—display of boorish arrogance. On both sides of the Atlantic, many on the left cheered him for "speaking truth to power." Appearing on Syrian TV after the 2005 London bombings, Galloway called Bush and Blair terrorists and lionized the Iraqi "resistance" for "defending all the people of the world from American hegemony." The transformation of this despicable character into a hero of the left reflected a naked partisanship emptied of everything decent, moral, and human.

Rejecting this abomination, Muslims are right

be required to take an examination assessing their understanding of Dutch language and culture—*before* entering the country—and would be sent a videotape that explained Dutch life and culture (and that included explicit depictions of nude sunbathing and a gay wedding). The Dutch had also learned from Denmark's experiences: henceforth, imported spouses would have to be over twenty-one, and the spouse already residing in the Netherlands would have to fulfill an income requirement.

In the chaotic days after the van Gogh murder, the Dutch people waited for some response from their beloved queen. Would she speak stirringly of the Dutch heritage of liberty? Would she praise Hirsi Ali, a model immigrant who'd courageously reminded the Dutch people of their deepest values? Would she honor the memory of the martyred van Gogh? Days went by. Then, in a crushingly disappointing—but classically multicultural—gesture, Queen Beatrix emerged from her palace and was driven to . . . a Moroccan youth center, where she made friendly chitchat with the regulars. Beatrix never said a single word in public about van Gogh's murder. (It later emerged that van Gogh's family had received a letter stating that the royal family wouldn't be able to fit his funeral into their schedules.) And she refused to meet with Hirsi Ali—a duly elected member of her own parliament. *Beatrix a coward*

In April a Rotterdam court acquitted a teenaged terror suspect in whose home the authorities had found maps of various government buildings, the Amsterdam airport, and a nuclear power plant, notes on how to get to these buildings and circumvent security, a silencer and clip holders for automatic weapons, a bulletproof vest, and various chemicals. He'd also collected documents on jihad martyrdom and taken notes on the topic. But the judge acquitted him, ruling that he "apparently was . . . interested in religious extremism." Following the Amsterdam gay-bashing of U.S. journalist Chris Crain in May 2005 by a group of Muslim youths, Rene Soeren, head of the Netherlands' leading gay rights group, admitted that tolerance in that city was "slipping away like sand through the fingers" and that "gays and lesbians are less willing to walk hand-in-hand because they might be beaten up." Visiting his homeland in August, Dutch expatriate Pieter Dorsman noted that his fellow countrymen were more outspoken in private conversation about immigrant tensions, but also lamented that "a sense of resignation is omnipresent . . . the Dutch are confused about where to go next."

In Germany, several states had prohibited teachers from wearing headscarves; forced marriage had finally been outlawed; new immigration rules stipulated six hundred hours of German language courses plus thirty hours of instruction about German society; and a government venture called "Operation Sweep-Out" was deporting hundreds of radical Islamists. But even Turkey's ambassador to Germany found these efforts inadequate: "We have warned German authorities against fundamentalist tendencies," he said. "But our offer to help was not given sufficient attention."

The closest thing to a bright spot in Western Europe was Denmark, where Fogh Rasmussen's reforms were showing results. Though the number of incoming foreigners remained about the same (owing to an influx of American and Chinese students and job seekers from Eastern Europe), family reunification figures had declined significantly and the number of asylum seekers had been cut by 80 percent. Ordinary Danes were happy: in February 2005, they voted to retain Fogh's government— the first time in their country's history that a nonsocialist government had been returned to power. And there were new rules, too—among them one preventing young people who'd attended Koran schools abroad from importing spouses.

Yet the Danish establishment remained, well, the Danish establishment. After the Iraqi elections in January 2005, in effect a stunning endorsement of the American invasion by the people of Iraq themselves, a thousand people showed up for a demonstration "arranged by 344 artists and university people" to protest Denmark's involvement there. The same establishment continued to hold Fogh's policies in contempt. Likening Fogh's policy changes to the "Bush revolution"—which was not meant as a compliment—Norwegian journalist Simen Sætre went on at length about the damage Fogh had supposedly done to Denmark's international reputation and about the purported rise in Danish "nationalism." Nowhere in a very long article did Sætre even mention the actual problems that had necessitated Fogh Rasmussen's initiatives.

If Beatrix, queen of the Netherlands, responded to the van Gogh murder by cravenly avoiding his funeral and visiting a Moroccan youth center, Denmark's queen, Margrethe, proved tougher. A tall, gregarious, down-to-earth chain-smoker who during her reign has also been a professional costume designer, translator, and artist (she illustrated the Danish edition of *Lord of the Rings*), Margrethe asserted in an official 2005 biography that the West must take the challenge of fundamentalist Islam seriously and that "there are certain things of which one should not be too tolerant." Recalling her 1984 New Year's address, in which she criticized her people for a lack of hospitality toward their new countrymen, she confessed to having been naive: "Once in a while one must run the risk of having a less than flattering label placed on oneself. Quite clearly, we've let things go for altogether too long. Because we're tolerant—and kind of lazy." Among Europe's crowned heads, she was the only one who could conceivably be considered part of the liberal resistance.

While Denmark was making a serious effort to tackle its immigration and integration problems, Sweden was doing nothing—and going to hell in a handbasket. Crime figures were making major jumps *every year.* The number of ghettos was rising at a dizzying speed. Sweden now had a murder rate twice that of the United States. Yet politicians and journalists continued to pretend there was no problem. Instead, the establishment was persecuting people for belonging to the Swedish Democratic Party—the one party that acknowledged the problems and wanted to put them on the national agenda. In a blonder version of Mao's Cultural Revolution, Swedish Democrats were being driven from their jobs as a result of staged "people's protests" organized by the youth divisions of other parties.* Since 2002, left-wing activists had broken up Swedish Democratic meetings more than once, issued death threats, and committed acts of violence against party members, including severe beatings and at least one attempted murder. On the country's National Day in June 2005, Stockholm was rife with radical-left unrest: a thousand protesters marched in masks; several extremists burned the Swedish flag while calling for their country's downfall; and members of the far left and right clashed brutally in a subway station.

The hub of Sweden's integration crisis was Malmö, the country's third-largest city, now nearly 40 percent non-Swedish. In Malmö, the incidence of rape was five or six times higher than in nearby Copenhagen; child rapes had doubled in a decade; during the autumn of 2004 alone, the number of robberies had gone up by 50 percent. Teenagers were torching schools, laughing at the firemen who came to put out the fires, and then torching them again. Anti-Semitic harassment was now routine; so were honor killings. Things were so bad that even the Swedish media couldn't entirely ignore them. ("Do you have control over the situation in Malmö?" a reporter for *Aftonbladet* asked a police investigator. "No, I can't say we do," he replied.) Swedes were leaving the city in droves. The only ethnic Swedish children left in some schools, said one observer, were "the children of welfare cases and drug addicts."

---

*The difference between Denmark and Sweden these days is summed up in one illuminating statistic: while Michael Moore's *Stupid White Men* sold over 100,000 copies in Sweden, it sold fewer than 5,000 in Denmark.

In late May, Sweden's government released a report blaming the failure on the racism of Swedes, who wrongly thought of integration in terms of "two hierarchically ordered categories, a 'we' who shall integrate and a 'they' who shall be integrated." The report, which essentially asked Swedes to sacrifice democracy on the altar of multiculturalism, was the work of Iranian-born Masoud Kamali, whose appointment to run the research project was protested by the several dozen researchers involved, who said his appointment politicized their work. On the day the report was released, an Iraqi immigrant, in an apparent honor killing, murdered his ex-wife in a Stockholm suburb.

Meanwhile, Norway hovered uncertainly between Sweden's mindless, self-destructive multiculturalism and Denmark's energetic new spirit of reform. Some *snillister* seemed at last to be changing their tune: Petter Skauen of Norwegian Church Aid, a longtime pillar of leftist dogoodism, recommended a "time out" on immigration. But most of the Old Reliables were still at it. Condemning Denmark's reforms, Labor Youth leader Gry Larsen claimed (in defiance of all evidence) that "the Swedish policy leads to tolerance and integration." Religion researcher Berit Thorbjørnsrud, while grudgingly admitting that Islamic law limits women's rights, stressed that native Europeans also had gender-related problems. And Thomas Hylland Eriksen fretted about the direction of Norway's Islam debate—namely, the fact that the truth was finally starting to emerge and the problems to be addressed. For him it was too much: "It's stupid-making to talk about Islam as either woman-hating or woman-friendly," he said. "If we just thump Muslims [he meant Muslim men] in the head with the charge that they're woman-hating, we take the risk that Muslim women will pull themselves out of the debate and feel degraded." (Of course, many European Muslim women, far from being in the debate, weren't even in mainstream society; they were sequestered in their homes, where they were literally, not figuratively, being thumped in the head on a regular basis.) In late February 2005, Ulf Erik Knudsen, a member of the Norwegian Parliament, appeared with a bodyguard at a debate on Islam in the immigrant-rich city of Drammen. Knudsen explained that he and others in his "populist" Progress Party had been receiving an increasing number of death threats. Lise Christoffersen, a member of Parliament for the Labor Party, charged angrily that Knudsen's use of a bodyguard was a "disgusting PR stunt" and added that Knudsen, who could have remained sitting, chose to "make his remarks while standing," thereby rendering himself more vulnerable. "Who would do that if he were threatened?" Christoffersen seemed to take it for granted that reasonable people give in to intimidation. The idea that Knudsen might consider it a matter of principle *not* to be cowed by threats was apparently beyond her comprehension.

Renewed attempts were also being made to deport Mullah Krekar—unleashing, predictably, a new wave of media efforts to whip up sympathy. "The man that Norwegian politicians have branded one of the world's most powerful terror leaders . . . cannot afford to go to the dentist," blubbered Morten Øverbye and Kadafi Zaman in *VG*. "He lives on his wife's salary, and . . . the Krekar family receives slightly over 2,000 kroner [$300 a week] in supplemental assistance from the social-security office." The temptation to write the poor mullah a check was tempered by news of taped conversations in which Krekar had said he'd "blow himself up gladly" in a suicide bombing, that the U.S. embassy in Oslo would be "a good target," and that children might make better suicide bombers than adults. In response to all this, Norwegian authorities told *Aftenposten* that he might be expelled from the country "as soon as conditions in Iraq are safe for Krekar."

One day over drinks at an Oslo sidewalk café, Hege Storhaug and her associate Rita Karlsen recalled their founding of Human Rights Service (HRS) five years earlier. Storhaug had been a journalist specializing in the rights of Muslim women and girls; Karlsen had a background as a researcher. One day they found out that a young neighbor of theirs in an involuntary transcontinental marriage was being raped regularly by her "husband"—and that nobody was lifting a finger to help. They soon discovered that this was a not uncommon pattern among "new Norwegians"—and that the Norwegian populace and authorities knew next to nothing about it. Even more shocking was the realization that in the whole elaborate support apparatus of the Norwegian welfare state—in which they believed passionately—there was nobody whose job it was to help her. They began collecting anecdotes and statistics to give the government an idea of what was going on in Norway's immigrant communities—and began going on TV to make their case. Their blunt truthfulness ruffled feathers, but also won them broad respect and support. In the years since HRS's founding, they have been responsible for major changes in Norwegian law, worked closely on reform issues with the Danish government, and met with Ayaan Hirsi Ali in the Netherlands. Only days before our meeting, Norway had seen its first forced-marriage trial.

But the *snillister* habit was hard to break. Norway was at a point, Storhaug maintained, "where if we don't take the right steps soon, in five or ten years we'll have such big problems that even trying to address them will strain the system in a way we've never seen before." Failed integration was already burdening the national budgets of Denmark and Sweden to the tune of billions of kroner every year. The failure of job integration in Germany, it was reported, was already costing between twenty and forty billion euros annually. Huge numbers of young Muslims were now approaching adolescence; HRS predicted "an explosion in fetching marriages."

IN CONCERT WITH these trends, evidence of increasing alienation and violence among the Continent's young Muslims seemed particularly frightening. In March 2005, a young Berlin woman became posthumously famous—not because of her brutal murder by her brothers, but because of the teenage boys who, during a classroom discussion of the homicide, said that "she only had herself to blame" and "deserved what she got." Why? Because "the whore lived like a German." In Denmark, Hans Peter Bak wrote that in his largely Muslim neighborhood, people on the street—including small children—regularly called him "Danish pig" or "Christian pig." Graffiti near the doorway of his apartment building read "The police fuck" and "Fuck the Danish." Bak himself had been a victim of three assaults—and the police, he said, had done nothing. Recalling a child of ten who'd called him "stupid Danish pig" and said, "We're coming and killing you and your family and burning your house down," Bak commented: "They obviously learn from childhood to have no respect for Danes and Christians." Bak's fiancée, a Syrian Christian, was walking with a Muslim classmate from her Danish language class one day when the woman's five-year-old child said: "Mommy, why are you talking with that Christian pig?" Bak said he knew not all Muslims were like these, but that those who are should be taken much more seriously.

Across Western Europe, schools were becoming increasingly segregated, with increasingly vocal—and successful—demands for separate lessons and facilities. In February 2005, it was reported that British secondary-school students in religious education courses would now be compelled, every time they wrote the name of Muhammed, to follow it with the letters *PBUH*—short for "peace be upon him." May marked the kickoff of a nationwide project to teach Islam in British primary schools, using instructional materials furnished by the Muslim Council of Britain. Statistics released in August showed that some Danish schools were segregating rapidly—within a year, one had gone from 80 to 96 percent non-Danish, another from 64 to 75 percent. In Amsterdam, the city council issued a report in March 2005 confirming that while segregation of that city's neighborhoods was on the rise, "in education, segregation is more or less complete." Soon afterward came the news that children at a school in The Hague idolized van Gogh's murderer, Mohammed Bouyeri, so much that they had pictures of him on their schoolbags. A teacher said that a decade earlier, ten-year-olds were saying, "We Moroccans are going to take over the Netherlands"; now five-year-olds who could hardly write were scrawling "Fuck you Netherlands" on scraps of paper.

In March, a sensational report written by Jean-Pierre Obin of the French Ministry of Education—but not officially released—was leaked on the Internet. The product of an investigation of sixty-one schools, it noted the powerful influence on pupils of young Muslim intellectuals whom they look up to as "big brothers" and who teach them to think of themselves solely as Muslims, not French. The report was in large part a catalog of refusals: increasingly, Muslim students were refusing to sing, dance, participate in sports, draw a face, or play an instrument (all of which have been permitted by Islam in the past, but not by the fundamentalists now dominant in Europe). They refused to eat school cafeteria food that isn't halal (that is, prepared according to sharia law) and refused to draw a right angle in math class because it looks like part of the Christian cross. They refused to swim because they didn't want to be polluted by "infidels' water." They refused to read Enlightenment authors such as Voltaire and Rousseau because they're antireligion, *Cyrano de Bergerac* because it's too racy, *Madame Bovary* because it promotes women's rights, and *Chrétien de Troyes* because it's, well, *chrétien*. They refused to accept basic facts of Christian and Jewish history and they rejected outright the existence of pre-Islamic religions in Egypt. Many refused to learn English because it's "the vehicle of imperialism" (an opinion one can imagine many of their teachers sharing). Less experienced teachers practiced self-censorship, steering around "sensitive" subjects; but such capitulation only encouraged students to raise the pressure.

Anti-Semitism was ubiquitous and justifications of Hitler, Nazism, and the Holocaust routine. Some Jewish children tried to keep their Jewishness secret, "but the family names of pupils don't always allow this." New pupils—and new teachers, as well—were often confronted by Muslim students demanding to know their religious affiliation. The result,

Obin concluded, was that Jewish children "can now no longer be given an education anywhere" in France. Then there was "the decline in the circumstances of females." Muslim girls were increasingly under rigorous surveillance by boys, often their younger brothers. They dressed more and more conservatively and were steadily dropping out of social and athletic activities. Muslim girls who resisted being reined in were pressured and threatened by classmates. So were all Muslim youngsters, male or female, who'd prefer to be French. Often Muslim parents didn't even know that their children were turning down *haram* (non-halal) food in the cafeteria until they were told so by teachers. In one primary school, pupils had reserved one toilet for "Muslims," another for "Frenchmen"; another school had been ordered by a local Muslim leader to institute separate gym dressing rooms because "the circumcised should not have to undress alongside the impure." Given all these signs of intensifying social division, banning headscarves seemed a minor gesture—much too little, much too late.

In Sweden, after students damaged a school building in Malmö, destroying equipment and throwing dangerous chemicals around, the school's principal and a couple of teachers discussed the incident on TV without ever mentioning that the students were immigrants, as if determined to leave the impression that this sort of thing was a problem with Swedish youth generally. In June it was reported that a secondary-school teacher in Malmö had entered a computer classroom where a dozen or so Arab boys were huddled excitedly around a computer, cheering as they watched a DVD of American and Jewish hostages being decapitated in Iraq. When the teacher protested their enthusiasm over the murder of innocent people, they didn't understand; and when she told the principal what had happened, he chided her, saying she'd intruded upon "the students' private business." When she insisted it was her job to teach democratic values, he accused her of exaggerating the problem. And when she persisted in taking the matter seriously, he sardonically suggested she take a job elsewhere, in a school "with well-behaved Swedish students!"

A particularly ominous event took place in Paris on March 8, 2005. It began ordinarily enough: an army of privileged *lycée* students marched through the streets of the French capital to register their objection to various educational reforms. Such peaceful, inconsequential protests are a regular part of life in France, as typically Gallic as a glass of chardonnay or a wedge of brie. But this time was different. A thousand or so immigrant-group youths—most of them from Seine-Saint-Denis and neighborhoods north of Paris—attacked the marchers, beat many of them up, stole wallets and MP3 players, and smashed cell phones, all the while spouting racist epithets. The police were all but useless; arrests were mimimal.

Later, some of the young gangsters told interviewers that they'd done it partly for the money, partly for the pleasure of hitting people, and partly out of a desire for revenge against whites, "the little Frenchmen with *têtes de victimes.*" People who'd been worried about anti-Semitic violence had been told frequently by bien-pensant types that things would eventually calm down; instead, the aggression had now spread. Jews were no longer the only victims: all "little French people" were potential targets—and easy ones, too, because they "can't fight and don't go around in gangs."

Other violent incidents included a series of November 2004 attacks on Berlin Jews by Muslim youths that were said to have "sharply raised concerns" (not about the attacks themselves, but about the possibility of an anti-Muslim reaction); a June 2005 mass mugging by five hundred Muslim teenagers of beachgoers on a strand near Lisbon; a June 2005 brawl in Drammen, Norway, involving Somali and Turkish youths wielding "knives, iron rods and bats"; and a pattern of rampaging by Muslim boys in Stockholm, who terrorized schools, chased non-Muslims away from public pools, and attacked firemen and ambulance crews who came into their own neighborhoods to help. In the spring of 2005, after a Muslim nightclub bouncer shot a co-religionist to death in Nørrebro, Denmark, an imam proposed that the murderer's family, to avoid a revenge killing, pay 200,000 kroner in "blood money" to the victim's family, a practice common in Muslim societies. Integration Minister Rikke Hvilshøj quite reasonably rejected the offer as incompatible with democracy, adding that in Denmark "we don't trade camels, either." Frighteningly, *Politiken* liked the imam's proposal; so did a law professor, who said that "there are a number of things in the Islamic way of tackling a conflict that we can learn from."

Early on the morning of June 8, Hvilshøj's car was set on fire outside her home as a protest against her goverment's "racist refugee policy." The fire spread to the house, where the minister, her husband, and their two young children were sleeping. The media snapped to attention—cautioning against overreaction and expressing sympathy for the attackers. A sociologist from Alborg University described the crime as "a spectacular symbolic act" and said, "It is important not to demonize the activists." Politician Kamal Qureshi said that the action was a result of immigrants being "beaten down, killed, and stabbed" by natives—the opposite of the actual situation. "If it hadn't been for the smoke alarm, Denmark would have had its own Fortuyn assassination," noted *Weekendavisen*. While *Politiken* was hopeless, both *Berlingske Tidende* and *Jyllands-Posten* appeared to have developed spines; the latter editorialized: "There is only one answer to violence, threats, revenge killings, taking the law into one's own hands, blackmail, private justice, blood feuds, camel economics and imams who have not understood what society and what century they live in: NO!"

IN MOST OF WESTERN EUROPE, however, the multicultural elite was, almost without exception, allied with the Islamic right on all these fronts—explaining away delinquency, suppressing reports of violence, standing up for *hijab*, and so forth. The most visible sign of this alliance was the establishment's astonishing assault on free expression—the real purpose of which was to protect its Islamic allies by preventing open debate or acknowledgment of Muslim-related problems. In Britain, for example, Home Secretary David Blunkett, in hopes of winning Muslim votes for the Labor Party, proposed a law that would make it a crime to insult someone else's religion in a way that might "stir up religious hatred." Since this prohibition would apply to publications, plays, films, and broadcasts alike—and would have outlawed a film like *Submission*—one might have expected the entire British literary, theatrical, film, and television community to rise up against it. Nope. Only one prominent artist in the entire country spoke out. It was, of all people, Rowan Atkinson, the comic actor who plays Mr. Bean and Blackadder. In a letter to the *Times* of London, he wrote: "For telling a good and incisive religious joke, you should be praised. For telling a bad one, you should be ridiculed and reviled. The idea that you could be prosecuted for the telling of either is quite fantastic."

Some journalists protested, to their credit. Among them was *Daily Mail* columnist Melanie Phillips, who on January 13, 2005, attended a public meeting sponsored by several organizations supporting Blunkett's proposal, including "the Commission for Racial Equality, the Association of Chief Police Officers (ACPO), Justice, the British Humanist Association and the Muslim Council of Britain (MCB)." Phillips asked Iqbal Sacranie, the MCB's general secretary, "whether he thought that any public statements about Islamic terrorism, or any speculation about the number of Muslims in Britain who might support Islamic terrorism, would constitute incitement to religious hatred. He said: 'There is no such thing as an Islamic terrorist. This is deeply offensive. Saying Muslims are terrorists would be covered by this provision.' So now we know what the MBC wants to prosecute under this proposed new law." *Daily Telegraph* columnist Charles Moore created a firestorm simply by affirming that Britons should have a right to say whatever they liked about other people's religions. The Muslim Association of Britain demanded his dismissal, complaining that "almost fifteen years on from the infamous Salman Rushdie affair, one would have thought that the likes of the *Daily Telegraph* and its editors would have known better than to allow such filth and drivel to adorn their pages." What did the Muslim Association mean by this? That the British press should have learned from the Rushdie case that the limits of free speech in the West were now for imams to determine? Sacranie, too, brought up Rushdie, saying that "We seem to be revisiting the arguments that came to the fore during the *Satanic Verses* affair. Is freedom of expression without bounds? Muslims are not alone in saying 'No' and in calling for safeguards against vilification of dearly cherished beliefs."

A few weeks later it emerged that a bill to protect Muslims and gays from discrimination had been altered. "Downing Street," explained journalist David Cracknell, "fears that Muslims . . . might feel offended if they were 'lumped together' with homosexuals." So gays had been dropped from the bill. Given that Britain's Muslim voters were thought to number about 1.3 million and gay voters around 3 million, one could only imagine what would happen when the rapidly increasing number of the former came to outnumber the latter. Already, politicians like London mayor Ken Livingstone—who a few years earlier had eagerly courted gay votes—were happily trampling on gay rights to curry favor with fundamentalist Muslims. In Norway, Christian and Muslim leaders were beginning to work together to defeat gay rights. It was beginning to look as if gay rights in Europe might turn out to have been a brief blip on history's radar screen, an instant of freedom framed by long eras of oppression.

Supporters of Britain's proposed new legal protections for Muslims defended them on the grounds that British Muslims suffered from widespread and brutal Islamophobia. But did they? Interviewing dozens of Muslims, Kenan Malik discovered that "everyone believed that police harassment was common, although no one had been stopped and searched. Everyone insisted that physical attacks were rife, though few had been attacked or knew anyone who had."*

In December 2004, several members of the British National Party, including its leader, were arrested for calling Islam "wicked" and "vicious." The BNP is an explicitly racist group that, in addition to several defensible positions (it calls for expulsion of illegal immigrants, an end to affirmative action, withdrawal of Britain from the EU, and reinstatement of the death penalty and of compulsive military service), also opposes mixed-race marriages, has had associations with neo-Nazi groups, and requires members to be of British (or "closely kindred") stock. Not a pretty picture. Yet to see *anyone* arrested in Britain for criticizing a religion was unsettling. This wasn't how democracies were supposed to work.

Free speech in Britain wasn't being attacked only in the name of Islam. On December 18, 2004, over a thousand Sikhs protested a performance at the Birmingham Repertory Theatre of a play that depicted murder and rape in a Sikh temple. The protestors, who broke windows and threw eggs, managed to bring the production to a halt after twenty minutes, injuring three police officers in the process. The playwright received death threats and went into hiding. But Home Office Minister Fiona Mactaggart refused to criticize the violence, which she actually tried to spin as an admirable exercise of free speech: "it is a great thing that people care enough about a performance to protest." Reprehensibly, the Catholic archbishop of Birmingham supported the protesters, proclaiming through a spokesman that "with freedom of speech and artistic license must come responsibility." A Sikh organization agreed: "We are not against freedom of speech, but there's no right to offend."

Nor was it only in Britain that some officials sought to resolve cultural frictions by restricting freedom of expression. In November 2004, Dutch justice minister Piet Hein Donner suggested enforcing a long-

---

*Addressing the claim that under Britain's post-9/11 terror law, police were targeting "the whole Muslim community" for stops and searches, Malik noted that only about 1,500 of Britain's 1.6 million Muslims had been stopped and that two-thirds of those searched were white. Yet Sacranie, in an interview with Malik, "insisted that '95–98 percent of those stopped and searched under the anti-terror laws are Muslim.' The real figure is 14 percent (for Muslims). However many times I showed him the true statistics, he refused to budge. His figures appear to have been simply plucked out of the sky. . . . All these figures are in the public domain. Yet not one reputable journalist challenged the claim that Asians were being disproportionately stopped and searched. So pervasive is the acceptance of Islamophobia that no one even bothers to check if it is true."

dormant blasphemy law to protect Islam from insults. (The proposal roused such indignation that Donner quickly withdrew it.) In December, Minister of Economic Affairs Laurens-Jan Brinkhorst opined that Hirsi Ali "should not have made *Submission.*" And in January, two schoolboys in Ijsselstein, Patrick Balk and Mark de Mooij, were ordered to remove Dutch flag patches from their backpacks because Moroccan students might consider them "provocative." It turned out that this ban on flags was in effect at many, if not all, Dutch schools.*

When Hirsi Ali revealed in February that she was living at a marine complex for protection and that her parliamentary colleague Geert Wilders was spending his nights in a prison cell, many Parliament members—instead of being outraged that their colleagues had to live in such circumstances—blamed them for their plight, arguing that if they hadn't been so outspoken, everything would be fine; several journalists and MPs even suggested, shamefully, that the two should resign. Meanwhile Hirsi Ali was being sued by an Islamic foundation that considered her comments on Islam illegal and sought a court order forbidding further blasphemies. (The judge found her innocent, but advised circumspection.)

In May 2005 came news of what might prove to be the most high-profile court case of its kind: an Italian magistrate ordered Oriana Fallaci to stand trial for "vilification" of Islam. Responding to a charge leveled by Adel Smith, president of the Muslim Union of Italy, Judge Armando Grasso ruled that a passage in Fallaci's 2004 book *The Force of Reason* was "without doubt offensive to Islam and to those who practice that religious faith." This wasn't the first time Fallaci—who was dying of cancer and living under the shadow of death threats—had been forced to stand trial for this crime: in 2003, eleven young Muslims from Lyon had hauled her into a French court over an earlier book, *The Rage and the Pride.* (She won.) Fallaci was admittedly no master of tact: imbued with her passions (for freedom and for the glories of Western civilization) as well as her prejudices (she despises gays nearly as much as she does Muslims), both of the books for which she's been sued are rife with outrageous, over-the-top characterizations of groups and individuals. It's hard to imagine someone who wouldn't be offended by something or other in them. But in a free country, it should be Fallaci's right to say what she thinks. The very fact that she could be put on trial in two Western

---

*The same thing was happening in Sweden, where a headmaster loath to offend Muslims sent two schoolgirls home "for wearing sweaters showing a tiny Swedish flag."

European nations for writing books only confirmed those books' main point: that Europe, by appeasing a totalitarian ideology, was imperiling its liberty.

In April 2005, after virtually no public debate, the Norwegian parliament passed a sweeping law that made it punishable by fine or imprisonment to say anything "discriminatory" or "hateful" about anybody else's skin color, ethnicity, religion, or sexual orientation. The burden of proof was placed on the accused: unless you could prove you hadn't done or said something offensive, you'd be presumed guilty. Only the "populist" Progress Party had opposed this legislation. Hege Storhaug told me she looked forward to being the first Norwegian to go to jail under the new law.

ACROSS WESTERN EUROPE, then, authorities were cracking down on free speech—or trying to. Meanwhile, many artists, writers, and "culture workers" were practicing pragmatic self-censorship—taking down "offensive" artworks, canceling screenings of "offensive" movies, thinking "offensive" thoughts but not daring to voice them. For example, Dutch film director Albert Ter Heerdt, who'd been planning a sequel to his "multicultural comedy" *Shouf Shouf Habibi!*, was "warned by Muslim friends to postpone" it and was leaning toward taking this advice. ("I don't want a knife in my chest," he said.) In February 2005, a scheduled screening of *Submission* at the Rotterdam International Film Festival was canceled by its producer, Gijs van de Westelaken. ("Does this mean I'm yielding to terror?" he said. "Yes. But I'm not a politician or an antiterrorist police officer; I'm a film producer.") The festival's theme, ironically, was "censored films"; in place of *Submission*, the festival audience saw two movies sympathetic to suicide bombers.

Amsterdam's Cobra Museum faced a similar challenge when an exhibition by a Moroccan-Dutch painter, Rachid Ben Ali, who favored gay themes and satirized Islamist violence, drew threats. Admirably, the museum stood firm, though Marlise Simons noted that some Dutch people "have quietly asked if self-censorship might be acceptable to keep the social peace." Threats did work on the World Culture Museum in Gothenberg, Sweden, which took down a painting, *Scène d'Amour*, that the artist, Louzla Darabi, described as a "response to Muslim hypocrisy about sexuality, above all women's sexuality." (An e-mail to the museum had warned that "you and your disgusting work are going to set the Muslims in Sweden on fire. Learn from Holland! The world's greatest superpower cannot protect you, so the question is how you will protect yourself.") Museum director Jette Sandahl told Reuters that "the painting was removed to prevent public attention shifting from the exhibition's main message about AIDS and globalization." "Provocative" art was all right, in short, so long as it didn't actually provoke anybody.

Indeed, in the post–Theo van Gogh era, many European artists, rather than being "provocative," appeared to be aiming for new heights of meekness. In March 2005, NRK profiled Norwegian singer-songwriter Åge Aleksandersen, who had a new album out, *Two Steps Forward*. "This time he wants to build bridges between Islam and Christianity," reported Arne Kristian Gansmo, who quoted the lyrics of "I Want to Be Your Friend"—described by the performer as "a song about unbounded love":

> *You stone your mothers*
> *Whip your sisters*
> *Mutilate your daughters*
> *Behind the veil*
> *But I want to be your friend*

Hard though it was to believe, Aleksandersen wasn't being sarcastic.

In April 2005, Pope John Paul II died after a lingering illness. Though I found many aspects of his legacy deeply troubling, his strong and consistent leadership in the struggle against Communism was unquestionably heroic. His death, coming so soon after Reagan's, seemed to silence the last great thundering voice of anti-Communism, leaving behind almost nothing but Lilliputian pipsqueaks. To many, John Paul's replacement by his right-hand man, Cardinal Joseph Ratzinger, seemed above all a vote for continuity: both men were not only strong enemies of Communism but also firm opponents of liberal theological reform. (Coincidentally, Ratzinger had had his first encounter with academic European Marxism at the same place I did—the University of Tübingen, where he'd taught theology in the late sixties.) But after Benedict XVI's installation came signals of a likely shift in emphasis. John Paul had sought rapprochement with Islam, which he appeared to view as a strategic ally in the struggle for "family values" and against post-Enlightenment thinking; during his pontificate, the Vatican had teamed up with Islamic governments at international human rights conferences to thwart European proposals for Third World birth control and other modernist evils.

The new pope, however, seemed more inclined to view Islam as a

Destroying the civilized West by Thirdworlders is not evil?

rival. During his years as prefect for the Congregation of the Doctrine of the Faith, he'd bemoaned the contrast between Islam's vigorous rise and Christian Europe's tired decline, complained about the failure of the EU's proposed constitution to acknowledge Europe's Christian roots, and protested that a godless Europe was inviting extinction. As recently as 2004, in an essay arrestingly entitled "If Europe Hates Itself," he'd written that "Europe, precisely in this its hour of maximum success, seems to have become empty inside. . . . There is a strange lack of desire for a future." Though I was, to say the least, displeased by the enthusiasm he expressed in the essay for outlawing homosexuality and prohibiting criticism of religion, I couldn't argue with his assertion that Europe was suffering from "a hatred of itself, which . . . can only be considered pathological."

It appeared likely, then, that Pope Benedict would do everything he could to reverse the secularization of Europe's Christians and to halt its colonization by Islam. Robert Spencer, an Islam expert, didn't mince words: "The Catholic Church has cast a vote for the survival of Europe and the West."* Yet Benedict's project was problematic. For one thing, his posture was essentially undemocratic: he didn't despise the suppression of individual rights in the Islamic world—he envied it. For another thing, any attempt to lure Europeans back to religion—especially a religion defined by Benedict's severe traditionalism—seemed doomed to failure. As far as I was concerned, the answer to the narrow strictures of fundamentalist Islam lay not in the narrow strictures of Ratzinger's brand of Catholicism but in democratic liberalism, pluralism, and tolerance—the liberty that had made America prosperous and powerful and that had drawn people from around the world to its shores.

If the European self-contempt to which Ratzinger referred had a ground zero, it was surely Sweden. In 2004, Minister of Integration Mona Sahlin spoke at a Kurdish mosque. Wearing a head covering, she told her Muslim audience that many Swedes were jealous of them, because they had a unifying culture and Swedes had only silly things like Midsummer's Night. Karen Jespersen, Denmark's former minister of integration, commented with obvious disgust that "it's hard for cultural self-denial to be more monstrous and horrifying than this." At an April 2005 conference, with Sahlin's comments in mind, Hege Storhaug asked Swedish integration official Lise Bergh: "Is Swedish culture worth pre-

---

*Or would Benedict continue the policy of his predecessor after all? In July 2005, the Vatican canceled a concert in memory of the victims of terrorism because it didn't want to do anything that might be interpreted as "a public statement" about terrorism.

serving?" Bergh replied: "Well, what is Swedish culture? I think I've answered the question." Storhaug noted that Bergh didn't even try "to disguise the cultural self-contempt with either word or expression. . . . In Sweden, the leadership seems to display Europe's most comprehensive cultural self-denial . . . quite simply, a deep self-contempt that many believe is the recipe for driving a peaceful nation-state into the ditch. . . . In gloomy moments," concluded Storhaug, "I wonder if it is just a question of time before Sweden cracks."

ONLY A FEW MONTHS after 9/11, media around the world had begun reporting rumors that systematic torture and abuse were taking place at the U.S. base at Guantánamo Bay in Cuba, where terror suspects were being detained. The Western European media gradually built up an image of Guantánamo as the equivalent of a Nazi death camp or Soviet gulag. In the spring of 2004, the first photographs documenting prisoner abuse by American guards at Abu Ghraib in Baghdad were released. I was appalled; European journalists seemed barely able to conceal their glee. Daily, the same photos were reprinted and rebroadcast across Europe. The inexcusable conduct depicted therein was treated as representative not just of the American military but of Americans generally. Abu Ghraib was nothing less than America's dark soul, bared at last. Norwegian journalists who soft-pedaled the offenses of Mullah Krekar self-righteously denounced the evil at the heart of America's war effort. To them, Iraqi freedom didn't matter—nobody's did.

If many members of the Western European elite didn't understand or appreciate their freedom, people elsewhere seemed to. In the early months of 2005, the new wave of democracy that had begun with Georgia's 2003 "rose revolution" and continued with Ukraine's 2004 "orange revolution" appeared to peak: the Iraq elections marked a "purple revolution" of ink-stained fingers; the Lebanese, in a "cedar revolution," booted out Syrian troops; elsewhere in the Muslim world, too, oppressed populations were growing more restive. These developments could be seen as validating the Bush administration's widely ridiculed theory that the liberation of Iraq would awaken a hunger for democracy throughout the region. Some, indeed, thought this might be Europe's only hope— that democratic revolutions unleashed by the Iraq War would defeat radical Islam at home and ultimately temper it in Europe. But if a new democratic spring was in fact under way, the Western European establishment was indifferent, if not openly hostile, to it. The idea that American military action might actually spur the rise of democracy challenged the European elite's precept that war never yields positive results—and many, instead of reevaluating that precept, preferred to turn away from reality or accentuate the negative. Some seized on rumors of CIA involvement in these fledgling democratic movements: for many media outlets, the difference between democracy and dictatorship was apparently a trivial detail compared to the question of whether America had been involved (in which case, of course, no revolution was welcome or legitimate). For the most part, however, European journalists preferred to pursue other angles on the war on terror, filing stories on anti-American protests, American soldiers defecting to Canada, and the like. The governments of France and Germany weren't exactly busy celebrating democracy's spread either: they were too preoccupied with strengthening economic and cultural ties to Communist China, Putin's increasingly autocratic regime in Russia, and various Arab tyrannies. Meanwhile, EU foreign ministers were initiating dialogue with Islamist opposition groups in the Middle East.

Certainly, there were plenty of aspects of Bush's conduct of the war on terror that deserved criticism—for example, his maddening inability to admit any error whatsoever and his disturbing friendship with the oppressive rulers of terrorist-producing Saudi Arabia, who (among much else) fund radical mosques in Europe. But the European media's standard line continued to be that Bush's policy in Afghanistan and Iraq had nothing to recommend it, period. Positive developments, or stories that reflected well on the United States, were either ignored or mentioned briefly and then dropped down the memory hole. America's image in Europe was now worse than ever: I grew weary of the idle, superior sneers from Norwegians who'd been pummeled by their media into seeing my country as a heartless, bloodthirsty imperial power, barely indistinguishable from Nazi Germany and certainly worse than the Soviet Union. In June 2005, Donald Rumsfeld made a brief visit to a NATO base in Stavanger, Norway. In addition to the expected protestors, a group of Kurdish refugees presented him with flowers as a token of gratitude for the liberation of Iraq. In both Norway and Sweden, journalists reporting on this detail made it clear they found it hilarious.

At times the European establishment seemed at least half in love with tyranny. Records of a secret meeting between Hamas leaders and EU official Alastair Crooke indicated that the latter had praised Hamas, rejected the designation "terrorist" in favor of "freedom fighter," and let pass a comment blaming Israel for 9/11. In a similar spirit, EU commissioner

Louis Michel, on a Cuba visit, scolded pro-democracy dissidents for provoking Castro. Not long before this scolding, the EU had publicly promised Castro that EU embassies in Havana would thenceforth "craft their guest lists in accordance with the Cuban government's wishes"—meaning that dissidents would not be invited.* The promise motivated Václav Havel to do some scolding of his own, rightly accusing the EU of "dancing to Fidel Castro's tune." "I can hardly think of a better way for the EU to dishonor the noble ideals of freedom, equality and human rights," wrote Havel, who'd been a dissident in Soviet-controlled Czechoslovakia and later president of the free Czech Republic. Havel expressed the hope that new EU members in Eastern Europe would "not forget their experience of totalitarianism" and that these memories would strengthen "the common spiritual, moral and political foundations of a united Europe."

But what future was there for "a united Europe"? In May, the French, by a comfortable margin, and the Dutch, by a huge one, gave a proposed European constitution a definitive thumbs-down in nationwide plebiscites. Remarkably, it was the first time the Dutch had ever voted on any aspect of their country's participation in the EU: as was the case with many other EU members, every previous decision along the way had been made by a political establishment that, along with the media, had been united in its support of the EU. Though the "*non*" and "*nee*" votes had been predicted, Europe's elites appeared to be stunned. So accustomed were they to running the show from their Parnassian perch that many of them seemed unable to process the fact that the peasants had rejected their finely crafted handiwork. Even before the French vote, EU president Jean-Claude Juncker had told Belgium's *Le Soir* that "if at the end of the ratification process we haven't managed to solve the problems, the countries that said 'No' will have to ask themselves the question again." In other words, keep voting until you give us the right answer. After the French and Dutch plebiscites, politicians and bureaucrats across Europe echoed this sentiment: yes, the people had spoken, but they'd made a mistake, and somehow must be persuaded to correct it. Bizarrely, Jacques Chirac's response to the French "*non*" was to elevate to the office of prime minister the ultimate Euro-elite popinjay,

*It was Prime Minister Zapatero of Spain who stood behind both these despicable pro-Castro EU initiatives. When in July 2005 Spain became the third European country (after the Netherlands and Belgium) to institute gay marriage, Zapatero hailed it as an advance for "liberty and tolerance"; no one asked him how he reconciled his enthusiasm for gay rights with his aggressive support for Castro, who punishes homosexuality with imprisonment.

Dominque de Villepin, aptly described by British author Paul Johnson as "a frivolous playboy who has never been elected to anything and is best known for his view that Napoleon should have won the Battle of Waterloo and continued to rule Europe." Johnson added, not unfairly: "What is notoriously evident among the EU elite is not just a lack of intellectual power but an obstinacy and blindness bordering on imbecility." Elite reactions to the constitution's demise only suggested that the Continent's rulers had long since forgotten the meaning of the words "representative democracy." *

There were, to be sure, a variety of reasons for the French and Dutch votes on the constitution: the French feared increasing market liberalism; voters in both countries opposed EU membership for Turkey; and both the "yes" and "no" camps in both countries had appealed to voters' anti-Americanism. But the overriding, remarkable fact was that in two founding members of the EU, a constitution supported by virtually the entire political, academic, and media establishment had gone down to defeat. Could it be that the era of unresponsive government by Western Europe's elites was approaching its end? Were ordinary citizens on the verge of taking back their countries? If so, what would they do with them? An ascendant populism didn't necessarily mean fascism—it might signal the advent of a more democratic polity that placed liberty above multiculturalism. But given the Continent's history, and given the ongoing rise of neo-Nazism in Germany, Sweden, and elsewhere, it wasn't unreasonable to worry that many Europeans, if given the chance, would respond to the looming Islamist fascism in their midst with a fascism of their own.

Indeed, to the EU establishment, the very fact that Europe's populist parties were attracting more and more votes meant that fascism was on the rise. Yet most of the support for these parties clearly didn't come from neo-Nazis or other far-right elements. They came from ordinary citizens tired of being governed by elites who for decades had mocked their national pride, taxed them heavily to support an inefficient welfare state, and endangered their national security through reckless immigration policies. Most voters weren't drawn to these parties by hate rhetoric but by commonsensical views on immigration, the EU, and the

---

*Even after the constitution was rejected, the EU commission continued to throw its weight around in the usual inane ways: in July 2005 it threatened legal action against member states that hadn't adopted EU noise-pollution standards; in August came a stern new set of regulations designed to protect outdoor workers from sunburn.

Atlantic alliance. Yet though many of these parties were decidedly *not* far-right, racist, or xenophobic, a legitimate fear remained that, as Europe's crisis deepened, they might easily move in that direction.

ON JULY 7, 2005, suicide bombs in London ripped through three underground trains and a double-decker bus, killing fifty-six. Londoners handled the chaos with admirable composure, recalling the city's legendary stoicism during the Blitz. When it turned out that the perpetrators had been born and bred in Britain, had been regarded as well integrated (one, a primary-school teaching assistant, had mentored immigrant children), and had been converted to radicalism at a government-funded youth center in Leeds, astonishment reigned. How could British lads do this? It was as if the Madrid attacks (carried out by Spanish Muslims) and the murder of Theo van Gogh (committed by a Dutch Muslim) had never taken place.

Watching the BBC that day, I was pleasantly surprised to notice that reporters were eschewing the usual euphemisms and actually using the words "terrorist" and "terrorism." Might this signal a change in establishment attitudes? Alas, BBC news chief Helen Boaden soon put an end to this, ordering reporters to speak of "bombers," not "terrorists." Even the BBC's 7/7 reportage, archived online, was retrospectively cleansed of the offensive words. Recalling that the Ministry of Truth in Orwell's *1984* had been based on the BBC, Gerald Baker remarked in the *Times* of London that "I can't think of a better recent example of pure Orwell than this painstaking effort at rewriting the verbal record to fit in with linguistic orthodoxy."

Indeed, establishment orthodoxy was quick to reestablish itself. The chief victims of the attacks, we were told again and again, were the country's Muslims—since they were now under even greater suspicion than before. Journalists fretted so much about the possibility of a backlash that at times these imaginary acts of vengeance took on greater dimensions than the terrorist atrocities that had actually happened. Though polls taken shortly after the attacks suggested that they had made the British more supportive of the U.S. alliance, polls taken days later showed that a majority now blamed the attacks, in whole or in part, on Blair's collaboration with Bush. Unsurprisingly, dhimmitude was alive and well in the media: Richard Ingrams suggested in the *Observer* that non-Muslim Britons had "an obligation of sorts to change their ways . . . to secure the respect of Muslims."

Unequivocal condemnations of the terrorists were soon replaced by sympathetic accounts of their supposed motives. Interviewed in the *New York Times*, friends of one of the terrorists recited the usual formula: "I don't approve of what he did, but I understand it." They shared their late friend's fury at Britain, which they attributed to British racism, oppression, economic inequality, and involvement in the Iraq War. (Oddly enough, the *Times* reporter, after citing these supposed motives, admitted that the rage of young European Muslims like these is rooted in an antipathy for democratic pluralism and tolerance and a desire to institute a caliphate.) In the *Guardian*, "trainee journalist" and self-identified "Yorkshire lad" Dilpazier Aslam also oozed sympathy for the terrorists, arguing that their crimes were ultimately the West's fault: Britain had Iraqi blood on its hands, and young British-born Muslims like himself and the terrorists were angry. Compared to their immigrant parents, Aslam said, "we're much sassier with our opinions." Exactly what those opinions were became clear when it emerged that Aslam belonged to Hizb ut-Tahrir and had published an article advocating a caliphate and declaring that his loyalty lay with "the Ummah" (worldwide Islam) and not with "any nation-state." Confronted with these facts about its "trainee journalist," the *Guardian* issued a statement noting that Hizb ut-Tahrir was a legal organization in Britain.

Indeed, young British Muslims interviewed in the aftermath of 7/7 routinely attributed the atrocities to Britain's foreign policy. British soldiers, they complained, were killing Muslims; Blair didn't value Muslim lives as much as he did Christian ones; Britain supported dictatorial regimes in the Muslim world. Huh? Britain had just helped *overthrow* two dictatorial regimes in the Muslim world. It had *liberated* Muslims. British soldiers were risking their lives to help Afghanis and Iraqis put their countries back together so they could live in freedom and build prosperity. It was Islamist "insurgents" in those countries who were trying to ruin it all, murdering Muslim men, women, and children in almost daily suicide attacks. Why weren't young British Muslims angry at *them*?

On 7/7, British Muslim leaders condemned the terrorists without qualification—or at least with less qualification than usual. Britain's four Muslim MPs agreed that Muslim extremists must be dealt with, and Britain's Sunni Council issued a fatwa condemning the perpetrators' "perverted ideology." Yet as the days and weeks went by, more and more Muslim leaders qualified their condemnation, calling for "understanding" of the terrorists' rage at the West. Discussing the terrorists' motives, Tariq Ramadan told CNN: "This [British] government is helping the

Iraqi people to be killed." And Azzam Tamimi of the Muslim Association of Britain told a rally: "My heart bleeds, I condemn it, yes, but I did not make those boys angry. I did not send those bombs to Iraq. I do not keep people locked in Guantánamo Bay and I do not have anything to do with Abu Ghraib, except to denounce it. Politicians, see what you have done to this world." It was as if jihad had not existed before the invasion of Iraq.

The contrast between American and European responses to terror was embodied in the difference between Rudolph Giuliani and London mayor Ken Livingstone. On 7/7, Livingstone condemned the terrorists in tough, stirring language that many compared to that of Giuliani on 9/11. But a couple of weeks later, when Jewish and gay groups protested the granting of a visa to an extreme imam from Qatar, Livingstone brusquely defended him. And by July 20, he was fully back in form, blaming the bombings on "eighty years of Western intervention into predominantly Arab lands because of the Western need for oil."

As America's leading ally in the war on terror, Britain had seemed in an important way to resist the general Western European decline into appeasement. Yet 7/7 underscored Britain's role as the Continent's jihad headquarters. Islamists, using London as a base, bragged about their unwritten "covenant of security" with the authorities: you leave us alone, and we'll leave you alone. Denmark's *Weekendavisen* reported that so many Islamists were based in London that in France the city was known as "the antechamber of Afghanistan"; the *New York Times* cited the nicknames "Londonistan" and "Beirut-on-Thames." Islamists could actually seek asylum in Britain on the grounds that their extremist beliefs were unwelcome in their native lands. Moreover, instead of being placed in asylum centers, as elsewhere in Europe, they could reside where they wanted—and collect welfare. Most Islamist leaders in Britain were living on support payments from the nation they'd vowed to destroy.

It was hard to believe, but when it came to such things, France was far ahead of the UK. As Daniel Pipes noted, Chirac had ordered French intelligence after 9/11 to share all terrorism data with *les américains*. "The British may have a 'special relationship' with Washington on Iraq," Pipes said, "but the French have one with it in the war on terror." If France had banned the *hijab* in schools, in Britain the test case on pupils in *hijab* had been decided the other way—and the Muslim girl who'd brought the case had been represented in court by none other than the prime minister's wife, Cherie Blair. In the wake of 7/7, the French government reinstated border controls and vowed to crack down on radical preachers; the House of Commons, to its disgrace, went ahead and passed the noxious

Racial and Religious Hatred Bill—which sought to pacify Britain by making it a crime to criticize the very radicalism that had just taken fifty-six lives. (Ironically, it took a nondemocratic body, the House of Lords, to uphold democracy by rejecting the bill.) In August, Tony Blair named Tariq Ramadan (banned from the United States and France) and Inayat Bunglawala (who'd called Osama bin Laden a "freedom fighter") to a task force responsible for tackling Muslim extremism.

The attacks did lead to tougher measures. On July 20, plans were announced to prohibit the training of terrorists in Britain (yes, until then it had been legal), to deny visas to foreign radicals, and to deport radicals who'd settled in Britain. Among the latter were Jordanian Abu Qatada, a convicted terrorist who'd entered the UK with a forged passport in 1993, and Saudi refugee Mohammed al-Massari, who'd published a terror manual online. In themselves, these new measures seemed painfully inadequate; the authorities freely acknowledged that potential deportees could stay for years while mounting legal challenges to their expulsion. In many official quarters, inane political correctness still reigned supreme. The chief constable in Nottinghamshire gave his four thousand officers green ribbons to wear as a sign of solidarity with Muslims. The Bedfordshire police put out orders that when raiding Muslim homes, officers should remove their shoes, not disrupt prayer, look away from uncovered women, and not use dogs (who would "desecrat[e] the premises"). Channel 4 canceled a documentary examining abuse of girls by immigrant-group men because the police worried it would "increase community tension." *

The attacks did seem to awaken Britons to the dimension of the problem they faced—and to the need for dramatic action. Many insisted—some with exasperation—that it was past time for moderate Muslims to do something. "I understand and accept that there are many moderates among British Muslims," griped Charles Moore, "but I want to know why Britain gets so pitifully little to show for their moderation." Arguing that Britain had "reached a turning point in the relations between the Muslim community and the rest of us," Tory MP and *Spectator* editor Boris John-

---

*While Britain was dusting itself off after 7/7, Mohammed Bouyeri was being tried in the Netherlands for murdering van Gogh. "I acted purely in the name of my religion," he told the court. "Someday, if I should be set free, I would do exactly the same thing." Addressing van Gogh's mother, he said: "I cannot feel for you . . . because I believe you are an infidel." Even as his trial was under way, a neighborhood council in Amsterdam forbade the erection of a memorial at the murder site on the grounds that it would be divisive; only a stirring protest by van Gogh's mother, who called the council members cowards, caused them to reverse their decision.

son called on moderate Muslims "to show real leadership." Complaining that "we have blindly allowed our country to be a haven for fanatics" and that "euphemistically named 'centers' " like the al-Magreze Center for Historical Studies—whose director had called the attacks legitimate—served as "jihadist recruiting stations," Niall Ferguson said that Britain's future lay in the hands of "law-abiding European Muslims" who "must now take a much closer look at what is being preached in the name of their religion." Rejecting French interior minister Nicolas Sarkozy's proposal for surveillance of all mosques in the EU, British home secretary Charles Clarke proclaimed his faith in the eagerness of the "mainstream Muslim community" to work with the authorities to defeat Islamism.

Yet where *were* the moderate Muslims? Most British Muslims seemed sincerely to deplore the London attacks. But though hundreds of thousands of them had marched in protest against the invasions of Afghanistan and Iraq, 7/7 occasioned no sizable Muslim demonstration against Islamist terror. That a silent majority of European Muslims believed in democracy and despised terror was by now a truism. Observers found themselves thinking, however, that if that silent majority existed at all, it had to be one of the most silent majorities ever. It had remained silent after 9/11, Madrid, Beslan, and van Gogh's murder. Each time, European journalists and politicians had repeated the mantra that extremists were not representative of most European Muslims, who were peace loving and rejected violence. Yet why were these declarations always being made by non-Muslims and almost never by Muslims themselves? What did it mean to claim that European Muslims were overwhelmingly moderate when, as Kevin Myers noted in the *Telegraph*, "11 percent of Britain's two million Muslims approved of the attacks of 9/11, and 40 percent support Osama Bin Ladin"? Was one seriously supposed to consider these people "moderates"?

A post-7/7 poll of British Muslims for the *Telegraph* was described by Anthony King, who reported the results, as "at once reassuring and disturbing." In fact it was simply disturbing. Six percent of those surveyed said they considered the terrorist attacks on London justified. An additional 24 percent admitted to sympathizing with the terrorists' motives and feelings; 56 percent said that they could understand why someone might commit such acts; 26 percent rejected Tony Blair's description of the terrorists' ideas as "perverted and poisonous"; 18 percent said they felt little or no loyalty to Britain; 32 percent agreed that "Western society is decadent and immoral and that Muslims should seek to bring it to an end." Only 73 percent said they would inform the police if they knew of plans for a terrorist attack; only 47 percent said they would report an imam preaching anti-Western hatred. These were terrifying numbers.

For many Europeans, the question of moderate Muslims had been a source of increasing frustration. Now, after the London bombings, political leaders and journalists were finally urging moderate Muslims to take sides—and take action. But would they? After van Gogh's murder, British author David Pryce-Jones had argued that many Muslims did indeed "look with horror upon what is being done in their name" but "few of them have the courage to speak out." Charles Moore had agreed, suggesting that moderate Muslims "cannot find the courage and the words to get to grips with the huge problem that confronts Islam in the modern world. This is: how does a belief system founded, in part, on conquest, and preaching a virtual identity between religious and political power, live at ease in plural, free, secular societies? Instead of answering this question, they tend to attack the people who ask it, and ask for special laws to silence them."

One "moderate" Muslim after another turned out not to be so moderate at all. Salman Rushdie noted wryly that Sir Iqbal Sacranie—who'd been knighted by Blair the previous June largely to give "moderate Islam" a high-profile public face—had responded to the 1989 fatwa against Rushdie by saying that "death is perhaps too easy" for the author. ("If Sir Iqbal Sacranie is the best Mr. Blair can offer in the way of a good Muslim," wrote Rushdie, "we have a problem.") When another supposed moderate, Mohammed Naseem of Birmingham's central mosque, was invited to a police press conference "to help calm fears of racial or religious tension" after the arrest of a terror suspect, he called Blair a liar and questioned Muslim involvement in 7/7. And an *Observer* investigation in August 2005 revealed that the Muslim Council of Britain, "officially the moderate face of Islam" in Britain, in fact "had its origins in the extreme orthodox politics in Pakistan."

For many, the term "moderate Muslim" seemed inexact. Hege Storhaug suggested replacing the term "moderate Muslim" with "secular Muslim," defined as "a believer who wishes to maintain a clear division between politics and religion"—as opposed to a "political Muslim," who disdains democracy but works within it with the goal of transforming it, or a "politically violent Muslim," who doesn't bother undermining democracy from within but simply gets a gun or knife or bomb. Others spoke of "practicing" and "non-practicing" Muslims. In the aftermath of the van Gogh murder, some journalists claimed that only a small percentage of European Muslims were actually "practicing" (meaning they visited a mosque at least once a week). The figure for France was said to be around 10 percent; fewer than fifty of that country's 1,685 mosques, moreover, were believed to have radical connections. A *Washington Post* report stated that about half of Italy's Muslims didn't attend mosque regularly, with an even larger proportion (70 percent) calling themselves "non-practicing." However valid these figures might be, to view them in combination with other statistics was to recognize their limited reliability as indicators of individuals' alienation from mainstream society.

In 2005, according to German interior minister Otto Schily, 1 percent of his country's Muslims were Islamist radicals; Kamal Nawash of Free Muslims against Terrorism suggested that "as many as 50 percent of Muslims around the world support the goals of the extremists"; pollster Daniel Yankelovich estimated that about 10 percent of all Muslims are fundamentalists, with the number varying widely from country to country. Daniel Pipes put the total figure at between 10 and 15 percent— which would mean that between 85 and 90 percent are moderates.

Many European Muslims may themselves be moderates, yet may have a concept of religious identity that makes it difficult for them to side with infidels against even the most violent of their fellow Muslims. If this is far less of a problem with American than with European Muslims, it's because America's melting-pot ethos enables and encourages immigrants to think of themselves as Americans while Europe's multicultural-mosaic model discourages newcomers from seeing themselves as British, Dutch, French, or whatever. This decadent model must be scrapped; Europe must do everything it can to help Muslims identify with the country in which they live. Most important, their children must be raised on a strong concept of national identity based on the democratic values of tolerance, pluralism, and equal rights. It must become impossible for children growing up in Western Europe to be raised to see their religious affiliation as the be-all and end-all of their identity.

Then there's the problem of intimidation. Many European Muslims are moderates, but dare not speak up against their more radical coreligionists for fear of exclusion from the community—or worse. Unless something changes, they never *will* speak up and, in the end, will meekly follow those radicals into a Europe ruled by sharia law. If that happens, what's in their hearts hardly matters: practically speaking, they're the radicals' allies. In order to prevent this, European governments must do everything they can to break the power of Islamist radicals within Muslim communities—and must match the pressure of the radicals with a pressure of their own.

The bottom line is this. One has no trouble believing that a majority of European Muslims privately despise terrorism and feel that it gives Islam a bad name. But this silence cannot endure, for U.S. and allied military forces can't win the war on Islamist terror on their own—let alone the even greater struggle against the gradual, day-to-day erosion of pluralist democracy in Europe. Only moderate Muslims can do so—by deciding to fight extremism actively within their communities. If they don't vigilantly oppose the bullies among them—and stand up for their own right to live free lives in Western countries—the alternatives for Western Europe will be stark and unappealing: total surrender or mass expulsion. Ultimately, in short, Western Europe's fate lies in the hands not of European liberals but of moderate Muslims—for only they can defeat extremism by disavowing and discrediting it as an expression of Islam. *No "OR"; this should be done!*

SO IT STOOD. Western Europe was a runaway train, racing at an ever-increasing speed toward a harrowing precipice. Its engineer was irrationally oblivious, refusing to acknowledge that anything was wrong; of its passengers, long accustomed to passivity, only some were aware of the problem, and among them, only a handful were up out of their seats, shouting, attempting to alert others to their impending doom. Would the passengers listen, and act wisely, in time to avert catastrophe? Would they take over the controls only to send the cars hurtling down another track, toward a different disaster? Or would they do nothing, and race to their calamitous end with docile fatalism?

Given Europe's long record of extraordinary condescension toward its savior and protector across the sea, it would be perfectly understandable for Americans to respond to Europe's present predicament with a sense of satisfaction ("serves 'em right"). But for Americans to settle into a posture of schadenfreude toward Europe's deepening crisis would serve neither the obligations of charity nor, frankly, America's own self-interest. Though Western Europe's governing elites have treated us worse than shabbily, Europe remains our largest trading partner. Elite attitudes notwithstanding, hundreds of millions of its inhabitants share our values and our culture.* The European establishment's anti-Americanism, it

---

*One hopeful sign was the rise, in October 2005, of pro-American, reform-minded Angela Merkel to the office of German chancellor; another was the growing support in France for the similarly disposed Nicolas Sarkozy.

must be remembered, is not the thoughtfully considered philosophy of a morally sensitive international power but the pathetic posturing of a tired, ailing civilization's insecure and envious leaders—bureaucratic souls who are frightened of the future and desperate for an easy scapegoat. Europe, to America, is rather like a thankless, cantankerous old mother with whom we may be exasperated but on whom we can hardly turn our back. Besides, in an age when freedom is threatened by Islamism, when Americans constitute barely 5 percent of the world's population, and when an economically expanding but still unfree China seems destined to challenge America's global supremacy in the not-too-distant future, America needs all the allies it can get. And it may well be, as Havel hopes, that new EU members in Eastern Europe will balance out—and perhaps even exert a positive influence upon—Western European attitudes toward freedom and tyranny, America and Islamism.

This would certainly be a step in the right direction for Western Europe, for if Islamists are out to destroy America, they're equally determined to subdue and colonize Europe. For them, it's no mere historical fact that most of Iberia and large swaths of Eastern Europe were once integral parts of the Islamic empire. Now, nearly the whole of Western Europe is practically within their grasp. Western Europeans, having already abandoned their religion and scorned their national identities, have little that matters to rally around. The backbone of America is its people's determination to honor and build upon their heritage of freedom; by contrast, Western Europeans—whose '68-er elites have sought to make them feel ashamed of their heritage, contemptuous of their freedom, and willing and eager to settle for any kind of "peace" at any cost—have been encouraged, and permitted, to take pride only in the supreme achievements of their social-democratic systems: multiculturalism, the welfare state, and the "European project." It's as if Europe, after all the horrors it inflicted on itself in the twentieth century in the name of God and country and *Volk*, were determined to yank up all its roots, pull down all its flags, and base its sense of identity on safely superficial things. Yet as current events are proving, a civilization with so prosaic a self-understanding is a house of cards, easily toppled by a foreign people possessed of a fierce, all-subsuming sense of who they are and what they believe.

Do the EU votes in France and Germany mark the beginning of a reversal of all this? Are grassroots Europeans beginning to turn against the colorless paper-pushers and practitioners of dialogue? Are they rebelling at last against the European identity that's been foisted on them and recovering their national consciousness? If so, this isn't necessarily a fearful development. On the contrary, if there's any hope for Western Europe, it has to begin with a new pride by the people in their sovereign democracies—and a determination to defend them from all enemies, foreign and domestic. If I sometimes feel more hopeful for Norway than for some of its neighbors, one reason is that patriotism has never been as *déclassé* here as it is elsewhere on the Continent. Not only did Norwegians vote twice against EU membership; they're also—amazingly—unashamed of their flag. At Christmastime they decorate their trees with strings of tiny flags; on National Day, May 17, children march by the thousands up to the royal palace in Oslo, each waving a flag. In Britain, by contrast, the Union Jack is identified by many not with the Battle of Britain but with BNP-style xenophobia; Germans, because of their Nazi past, are much more comfortable flying the EU flag than their own. Almost everywhere in Western Europe, flying the flag is seen as unsophisticated—it's something Americans do. But it's the absence of a patriotism as powerful as America's—the absence, that is, of a life-or-death belief by individuals in their country's essential goodness and in their people's future—that's helping Western Europe to slip toward its doom. *Read Ezekiel 38 - 39*

Every American must hope that a change is afoot—that the French and Dutch rejection of the EU constitution reflects a rising sense of national consciousness and a determination to stand up to an unrepresentative, multicultural-minded establishment in the name of liberal democracy. But even if many Western Europeans are rejecting the EU and rediscovering their national identities, it seems very possible, given their continent's history, that this development will lead them in undemocratic directions. In the 1930s, the ascent in Europe of a totalitarianism of the left—Communism—fed the rise of a totalitarianism of the right. Might the spread of Islamism in Europe today give rise to an opposing but equally inhuman neo-fascism? The signs are not good. Over a decade, support for the National Front in France has rocketed from 1 to 16 percent. In the Netherlands, the murder of Theo van Gogh ushered in a period of Nazi-style hooliganism directed at Muslim schools and mosques. In July 2005, Italian authorities broke up an anti-Islamist vigilante group that had been formed after the bombings in Madrid. When Europe finally awakens fully and responds to the rise of Islamism in its midst, is this the form its response will take—or will it stand up for liberal values? In either case, alas, the picture Lars Hedegaard painted over dinner in Copenhagen seems all too grimly plausible: a long twilight of Balkanization, with Europe divided into warring pockets of Mus-

[handwritten: Yes, probably, until God intervenes for his people.]

lims and non-Muslims, the latter of whom may be either democrats or fascists, or both. Alternatively, Europe may simply persist in its passive ways, tamely resigning itself to a gradual transition to absolute sharia law and utter dhimmitude. *[handwritten: Yes, yea]*

Either of these prospects should boil the blood of any freedom-loving Westerner. For either prospect would mark the end of the West as we know it—and perhaps the beginning of the end of freedom, too. *[handwritten: —I and end of the world]*

At the close of World War I, a humbled Germany was compelled to change its form of government. Kaiser Wilhelm was forced to abdicate, the German Empire disappeared into history, and Germans were given their first democracy. The Weimar Republic, as it later came to be known (because its constitution was drafted in the city of Weimar), lasted for fourteen mostly shaky years. Like Western Europe today, it was run by a social-democratic elite and derived much of its support from that elite's labor-union allies. But drastic economic problems did it in. Skyrocketing inflation and unemployment sent Germans' standard of living spiraling downward. Voters grew frustrated, disgusted, enraged—and, in larger and larger numbers, drifted away from their blandly well-meaning centrist government and toward the upstarts at both extremes of the political spectrum—the Communists on the left, the Nazis on the right.

Now, once again, Europe is at a Weimar moment. Poised between the aggressive reality of Islamism and the danger of an incipient native neo-fascism, it is governed by an elite, many of whose members, even now, remain determined not to face reality. The spectacular failure of integration has brought some nations to the verge of social chaos and is leading others steadily in that direction; and European leaders, unwilling to shake off their faith in multiculturalism and the welfare state, are spending ever-increasing sums to subsidize and deepen that failure, thus leading their nations inexorably toward economic ruin as well.*

[handwritten right margin: who ever thought it would prove a prodig—table]

In the end, Europe's enemy is not Islam, or even radical Islam. Europe's enemy is itself—its self-destructive passivity, its softness toward tyranny, its reflexive inclination to appease, and its uncomprehending distaste for America's pride, courage, and resolve in the face of a deadly foe.

On one crucial question there remains profound uncertainty and

*In August 2005, Anthony Browne noted in the London *Times* that curbs on international marriages were still "barely on the radar" in Britain; even after the van Gogh murder, Paul Scheffer dismissed as extreme Geert Wilders' proposal to expel two hundred to three hundred radicals from the Netherlands, saying it "would lead to further estrangement of the Muslim community."

disagreement: Is Islam compatible with democracy? Many insist that it isn't, and point to the traditional demand that Muslims seek to establish sharia law wherever they live. But religions can change, dramatically, for both good and ill. The Old Testament is full of cruel tribal laws from which even today's Orthodox Jews dissociate themselves. Christianity, whose founder preached a radical love for one's neighbor and a simple faith that transcended dogma and tribe, has been burdened over the generations with thousands of doctrines that he never taught and that diverge dramatically from the spirit of the early church. Most evangelical Christians today adhere to a theology (dispensationalism) that was invented out of whole cloth in the 1830s. Naivite

The American invasions of Afghanistan and Iraq were predicated on the assumption that Islam is compatible with democracy; some cite Turkey as proof that at least some varieties of Islam can coexist with a kind of democracy. The crucial fact here is that a religion is whatever its individual believers understand it to be. If Islam is to coexist with democracy—whether in the Middle East, South Asia, Europe, or America—Muslims, like millions of Jews and Christians before them, must discover more liberal ways of understanding their faith. They won't

Two-thirds of a century ago, with most of Western Europe either crushed by Hitler or on the verge of capitulation, the British found themselves virtually alone in their defiance. In late May of 1940, the heroic evacuation from Dunkirk made clear to everyone in Britain the dimensions of the threat facing them from across the Channel. On June 4, Winston Churchill made a famous speech to the House of Commons:

> We shall go on to the end, we shall fight in France, we shall fight on the seas and oceans, we shall fight with growing confidence and growing strength in the air, we shall defend our Island, whatever the cost may be, we shall fight on the beaches, we shall fight on the landing grounds, we shall fight in the fields and in the streets, we shall fight in the hills; we shall never surrender, and even if, which I do not for a moment believe, this Island or a large part of it were subjugated and starving, then our Empire beyond the seas, armed and guarded by the British Fleet, would carry on the struggle, until, in God's good time, the New World, with all its power and might, steps forth to the rescue and the liberation of the old.

Churchill's eloquent defiance, which has no equivalent in Western Europe today, not only galvanized his people's determination to resist but also—as he had hoped—helped win American sympathy for Britain's cause, which would be critical to the success of the joint war effort after Pearl Harbor. What, today, can Americans do to help a Europe once again in peril? When a *Wall Street Journal* reporter asked Oriana Fallaci in June 2005 what might be done to prevent Europe's collapse, she exploded: "How do you dare to ask me for a solution? It's like asking Seneca for a solution. You remember what he did? . . . He committed suicide!" Alas, Fallaci may be right: it's hard to imagine that Americans could do much to rescue Europe from its present fate, short of launching another D-Day. But a couple of suggestions may be in order. When visiting Europe, many Americans, to avoid discomfort and court easy praise, take every opportunity to put down their country in terms designed to gratify European sensibilities and reinforce European stereotypes. Those who do this are traitors—not to America, but to the truth, to themselves, and to their interlocutors—and should cut it out. All their lives, Europeans have been fed a severely distorted image of America that has poisoned their minds against the very values that might save them; every conversation between an American and a European is a precious opportunity to challenge that image and give Europeans something to think about, believe in, and act on.

It strikes me as perverse that current U.S. immigration policy penalizes Western Europeans. I know plenty of America-friendly Europeans who'd move to America in a heartbeat. The United States should let them in. Educated, law-abiding, ambitious, fluent in English, and gung-ho about American values, they'd be a terrific asset to their new nation. And the spectacle of Europe's best and brightest once again forsaking their homelands and pouring through the Golden Door would give their countrymen something to think about—and perhaps even act on. Similarly, the American government, as well as Americans in business, the media, and other institutions, should forge ties with, and lend support to, those intrepid men and women who are bucking the European establishment in the name of liberal values—*American* values. Embattled heroes like Ayaan Hirsi Ali and Hege Storhaug need all the help they can get—as do the millions of Europeans who look up to them as courageous torchbearers and truth-tellers. It's deplorable that in a special October 2005 issue celebrating "European heroes," *Time* magazine honored Amsterdam's *dhimmi* mayor Job Cohen (a hero only to Dutch-establishment types who revere pragmatic compromise above all else) instead of Hirsi Ali, whom the Dutch people recognize as a champion of freedom.

I've long felt that the best thing that could be done to strengthen the unity and democracy of the West would be to radically expand secondary-school exchange programs between America and Europe. Jean-François Revel has written vividly about how his negative attitude toward America, shaped by decades of exposure to the systematic false-hoods of the European media, was flipped 180 degrees by a visit. If every young European could spend a year living with an American family and attending an American school, all the journalists and politicians in the world wouldn't be able to twist their awareness of the reality of America—and of American liberal democracy—into an ugly cartoon. And the more America-friendly Europeans are, the more inclined they'll be to behave like Americans in the ways that count—that is, to eschew appeasement and stand up for freedom. But it may already be too late for such remedies. Europe is steadily committing suicide, and perhaps all we can do is look on in horror. *Armaggedon*

For in the end, Europe's future lies in Europe's hands. To read Churchill's wartime speeches is to experience an attitude and a rhetoric that, in today's Europe, seem alien or antique. All that talk of fighting—how uncivilized! Reading Churchill's speeches, one can imagine Johan Galtung's reaction to such language—one can see him sneer and hear him speak in smooth, soothing tones about peace, understanding, ac-commodation, and the need to refrain from demonizing one's opponent. In the contrast between these two stout, white-haired, well-tailored men—Churchill then, Galtung now—is encapsulated the stark differ-ence between the unwavering moral conviction that led to Allied victory in World War II and the unprincipled spirit of compromise and capitu-lation that is guiding today's Europe, step by step, to the gallows.

I FIRST TRAVELED to the Netherlands in 1997 and thought I'd found the closest thing to heaven on earth. What sentient being, I won-dered, wouldn't want to live there?

On March 24, 2005, my partner and I flew to Amsterdam for the weekend. Walking into our hotel room shortly past 8:30 P.M., I turned on the TV. The news had just started on the Dutch channel AT5. Mus-lim intolerance of homosexuality, said the anchorperson, was making life more dangerous for gays in Amsterdam.

Survey results released in April showed that every third Dutchman wanted to leave the country. In February, our old *vriendje* Marlise Simons had reported that since the van Gogh murder, the number of people emigrating from the Netherlands—most headed for "large

English-speaking nations like Australia, New Zealand and Canada"—had risen dramatically. The main reason? Fear of radical Islam. The article made poignant reading.

In May 2005, Norwegian TV ran a long report on the many Dutch families moving to rural Norway. Why were they leaving home? The reporter cited crime and population density—not immigrant problems. The only hint of the truth came at the end, when a Dutchman said Norway was "twenty years behind the Netherlands in its social situation" and that by the time it caught up, he'd be old and past caring. The reporter chose not to explain what he meant by "social situation."

As we walked around Amsterdam that March weekend, I thought about those Dutchmen emigrating to Canada, Australia, and New Zealand. Unlike Muslims in Europe, they'd integrate quickly—they'd find work, contribute to society, fit in. They already spoke English. Yet what, years from now, would their children think? Their grandchildren? What, for that matter, would they themselves think when they lay in bed at night, far from home, their minds flooding with images of the small, lovingly tended land of their birth, with its meticulously laid-out roads and walks and bicycle lanes, its painstakingly preserved old houses, its elaborate, brilliantly designed systems of dikes and canals?

The irony was tragic: having protected themselves with nothing short of genius from the violence of the sea, having instituted a welfare system meant to safeguard every last one of them from so much as a moment's financial insecurity, and having built up a culture of extraordinary freedom and tolerance that promised each of them a life of absolute dignity and perfect equality, postwar Dutch men and women had raised up their children into tall, strapping, healthy, multilingual young adults—veritable masters of the world for whom (they were confident) life would be safe, pleasant, and abundant in its rewards. They seemed to have brought Western civilization to its utmost pinnacle in terms of freedom and the pursuit of happiness, and the road ahead, very much like the actual roads in the Netherlands, seemed to stretch to the horizon, straight, flat, smooth, and with nary a bump.

And yet they'd turned a blind eye to the very peril that would destroy them.

[handwritten margin note, right side:] was'nt Pd to say that?

[handwritten note at bottom:] It seems that Dutchmen preferred the "behindness" of Norway to the progressive Dutch "social situation" even at the painful price of abandoning their home.

Afterword to the Paperback Edition

SINCE THIS BOOK FIRST appeared, European freedoms have faced a series of aggressive challenges by radical Muslims—challenges that have been met mostly with appeasement and apologies, censorship and self-censorship. During this time efforts have intensified across Europe to ban "Islamophobia"—a word that has been employed with increasing frequency in attempts to silence criticism of anything whatsoever relating to Islam.

I had already handed in what I thought was the final draft of *While Europe Slept* when the London bombings occurred on July 7, 2005. Fortunately there was time to insert a few pages about that atrocity. A few weeks later, however, when Paris suburbs were being terrorized nightly by Muslim rioters—and the media, ignoring (with few exceptions) the cries of "Allahu akbar!", chose to portray the mayhem as a desperate response to poverty and oppression—it was too late to make further additions to the text. Instead, in an op-ed that appeared in the *Christian Science Monitor* on November 17, 2005, I noted that Muslims in many European cities had already claimed jurisdiction over their neighborhoods and that the riots should be recognized, in this context, as "early battles in a continent-wide turf war." (Indeed, in the wake of the riots, French police have effectively ceded control of hundreds of neighborhoods to Muslim residents.)

When the book came out in February 2006, yet another crisis was under way. When Flemming Rose, culture editor of Denmark's largest newspaper, *Jyllands-Posten*, learned that Danish artists were too fearful of reprisals to illustrate a forthcoming biography of Muhammad, he decided to make a statement about free speech. He invited illustrators to submit drawings of Muhammad, and on September 30, 2005, he printed twelve of them. Most were innocuous. Nonetheless, Muslims went ballistic. Protesters filled Copenhagen's streets. Death threats were issued. On October 12, ambassadors from ten Muslim countries demanded a meeting with Prime Minister Anders Fogh Rasmussen. He refused. "It is so self-evidently clear what principles Danish society is based upon," he admirably explained, "that there is nothing to have a meeting about."

His reward was a torrent of international criticism. In December, Louise Arbour, UN High Commissioner for Human Rights, promised that "action" on the cartoons would be forthcoming. (Apparently free speech was not on her list of human rights.) The Committee of Ministers of the Council of Europe condemned the Danish media's "intolerance." On February 9, Franco Frattini, EU Commissioner of Justice, Freedom, and Security, urged the media to "self-regulate" to avoid giving offense; three days later Kofi Annan told Danish TV, "You don't joke about other people's religion, and you must respect what is holy for other people." It was now, apparently, the job of the EU and UN to tell free people what to respect.

Meanwhile Danish Muslims were stepping up pressure. A group of Muslims associated with Denmark's Islamic Society traveled to the Middle East, where they stoked fury at their adopted country by showing incendiary drawings that had never appeared in any Danish publication. In late January, Saudi Arabia pushed for a boycott of Danish goods. Hacker attacks closed down Danish blogs and newspaper Web sites. Terrorists ordered Scandinavians out of Gaza. Palestinians burned Danish flags. Mobs torched the Danish embassies in Damascus and Beirut. Every day, it seemed things couldn't get worse—and they kept getting worse. In the end, over 100 murders in the Muslim world were attributed to anger over the drawings.

For many, the *Jyllands-Posten* cartoons represented the powerful mocking the faith of the weak. No: what was happening was that a gang of bullies—led by a country, Saudi Arabia, where Bibles are forbidden, Christians tortured, women oppressed, Jews labeled "apes and pigs" in the state-controlled media, and apostasy from Islam punished by death—was trying to compel a tiny democracy to follow theocratic rules.

To succumb to this pressure would simply be to invite further pressure, and would lead to further concessions—not just by Denmark but by the entire West. The list of democratic phenomena that offend the sensibilities of many Muslims is, after all, a long one—ranging from religious liberty, sexual equality, and tolerance of gay people to music, alcohol, dogs, and pork. After a few cartoons, what would be next?

This was, in short, no isolated incident. It was one step in a long-term effort to erode liberty. Encouragingly, most Danes rejected surrender: in January, 79 percent said Fogh Rasmussen owed no apologies.* Yet even after the Madrid and London bombings and Paris riots, many European leaders continued to deny reality; others, as eager as Neville Chamberlain at Munich to "keep the peace," had already opted for a policy of gradual capitulation, accompanied by flurries of sycophantic praise for Islam and apology for Western freedom. And they were supported by millions of Europeans who, never having learned to appreciate their freedom in the first place, were quickly internalizing Islamic taboos. For them, Muslim rage—and its expression in violence and death threats—had already become an accepted part of life; the fault for any unrest lay with those who provoked it by failing to toe the line. "There is something wrong with a democracy," read a viewer's text message sent to a Norwegian discussion program, "where an editor can put the whole country in danger!" EU Trade Commissioner Peter Mandelson was one of many officials who spoke of outraged Muslims as if they were a force of nature: every re-publication of the cartoons, he complained, was "adding fuel to the flames."

To be sure, many European editors—including some whom I'd written off as shameless *dhimmis*—did in fact reprint the cartoons in a show of support for *Jyllands-Posten* and free speech. Even *Le Monde* ran its own wittily apposite Muhammad drawing. But most of the politicians and journalists who'd distanced themselves from van Gogh after his murder now distanced themselves as well from *Jyllands-Posten*'s editors and cartoonists. Having called van Gogh vulgar and insensitive, they now used

---

*Still, as the months went by, efforts by the Danish media and Fogh Rasmussen's political opponents to weaken Danes' resolve had an inevitable, and deplorable, impact. In a November 2006 talk in Copenhagen, I praised the Danish government's defense of free speech, and was astonished when several Danes told me how important it was for them and their countrymen to receive this affirmation from a foreigner. They explained that many Danes, having been told repeatedly that Fogh Rasmussen's stance had damaged their country's image abroad, had come to doubt his actions and to feel ashamed of their country.

the same words to describe the cartoons. And their American counterparts were no better. Most of the politicians who commented on the cartoons echoed the verdicts of Bill Clinton ("totally outrageous") and the State Department ("offensive").* "After this act of betrayal," Danish journalist Lars Hedegaard e-mailed me, "one might well ask why we should keep our troops in Iraq and increase our presence in Afghanistan." Indeed. Almost no major U.S. newspapers reprinted the cartoons; *60 Minutes'* contribution was an egregious report depicting Danish Muslims as frightened, innocent victims of a viciously racist majority.

In Norway, the cartoons were reprinted in several major newspapers, but attention, curiously, became focused on a tiny Christian periodical, *Magazinet*, which ran them on January 10, 2006. When Norway's embassy in Syria was burned by protesters, Prime Minister Jens Stoltenberg said *Magazinet* deserved part of the blame; Norway's Foreign Ministry sent embassies a statement expressing regret for *Magazinet*'s actions. Though *Magazinet*'s editor, Vebjørn Selbekk, was inundated with death threats and received (at best) tepid support from his fellow journalists, he stood firm for free speech in a series of TV interviews and debates with pusillanimous public officials.

Then, on February 10—the day before a planned demonstration against the cartoons—Norway's Minister of Labor and Social Inclusion, Bjarne Håkon Hanssen, hastily called a press conference. There, in the presence of cabinet ministers and the largest assemblage of imams in Norwegian history, Selbekk issued an abject apology to Mohammed Hamdan, head of Norway's Islamic Council (and brother of a Hamas member of the Palestinian parliament), who, accepting Selbekk's apology on behalf of forty-six Muslim organizations, asked that all threats against the editor and his family now be withdrawn. It was a scene right out of a sharia courtroom, with the contrite *dhimmi* being pardoned by the Muslim leader and placed under his protection. It was as if Hamdan, not the Norwegian police and military, held in his hands the security of Norway's citizens.†

---

*Later, in an interview with *Jyllands-Posten*, Assistant Secretary of State Daniel Fried insisted that the U.S.'s posture was one of "unconditional solidarity" with Denmark.

†On September 29, 2006, some months after the cartoon crisis had ebbed, Norway's minister of culture and church affairs, Trond Giske, met publicly with Hamdan to announce a jump in annual state support for the Islamic Council from 60,000 to 500,000 kroner. This highly suspicious bonanza occasioned virtually no comment in the mainstream media.

Norwegian authorities hailed this national humiliation as an act of "reconciliation." Jonas Gahr Støre, the Villepinesque foreign minister who had assailed Selbekk on live TV for resisting intimidation by thugs, called the editor's capitulation an act of "integrity and courage." The imams who had witnessed the apology agreed that it gave Norway "a higher status than before." *Aftenposten* cheered Selbekk's surrender. Days later, as if Norway hadn't already been disgraced enough, an official Norwegian delegation met in Qatar with imam Yusuf al-Qaradawi (a defender of suicide bombers and the murder of Jewish women and children) and implored him to forgive Selbekk. He did. "To meet Yusuf al-Qaradawi under the present circumstances," observed the Norwegian-Iraqi writer Walid al-Kubaisi, "is tantamount to granting extreme Islamists and defenders of terror a right of joint consultation regarding how Norway should be governed."

Sweden's conduct was, if possible, even more despicable than Norway's. On February 9, 2006, Swedish foreign minister Laila Freivalds closed down the right-wing Swedish Democratic Party's Web site because it had published a Muhammad cartoon. "It is frightful," she sniffed, "that a small group of Swedish extremists can expose Swedes to a clear danger"—as if it were the Swedish Democrats who were threatening violence. And if Kofi Annan's comments hadn't already made the UN's position clear, it was spelled out, months later, on October 16, 2006, at a cartoonists' roundtable at UN Headquarters. At the end of the panel discussion, Under-Secretary-General Shashi Tharoor, in a "summary" of the participants' comments, said that they had called for self-censorship and had insisted that "a proper balance . . . must be found" between freedom and cultural sensitivity. Balderdash. The cartoonists had, on the contrary, stressed the importance of free speech and criticized the absence of press freedom in several countries, especially in the Muslim world. What Tharoor served up was not a "summary" but the UN line. It was chilling to imagine what the UN might do with Western freedoms if it had the power.

NOT ONLY DENMARK was under siege for defending freedom. So was Ayaan Hirsi Ali. First, in an incident that recalled some of the more cowardly episodes of Dutch wartime collaboration, a group of her neighbors in The Hague turned on her. Anxious about living near a terrorist target—never mind that she was a target precisely because she was risking her life to defend their freedoms—they won a court battle to evict her on the grounds that her presence in their midst endangered their safety. Then Dutch immigration minister Rita Verdonk did essentially the same thing on a national scale. Citing incorrect details on Hirsi Ali's applications for asylum in 1992 and citizenship in 1997 (which Hirsi Ali had explained years earlier), Verdonk sought to rescind her Dutch citizenship and deport her.

During the embattled days that ensued, I spoke to Hirsi Ali several times by telephone and was awed by her moral courage and sheer graciousness under extraordinary stress. In the end she retained her citizenship—and the Dutch government fell. Yet she did resign from Parliament and, in September, moved to Washington, D.C., to work at the American Enterprise Institute. I felt happy for her but sorry for Europe, a continent perversely determined to shelter its enemies and drive away its heroes.

The pope, too, came under attack. On September 12, 2006, in a scholarly lecture at Regensburg University, he quoted a fourteenth-century Byzantine emperor's criticism of Islam. The Muslim world erupted. So did the Western academic, media, and political elite. "What the pope did was very unwise and unnecessary," griped a member of the European Parliament. And the *New York Times* accused Benedict of having "sowed pain" and "encouraged dissension between Christians and Muslims. . . . He must offer a deep and convincing apology and thereby prove that words also can heal." Implicit throughout was the belief that it's foolish and immoral *not* to let yourself be silenced by the possibility of violence.

Among the few prominent defenses of the pontiff was an op-ed by philosophy teacher Robert Redeker that appeared in the French newspaper *Le Figaro* on September 19. Redeker's piece, in which he spoke up for Enlightenment values and aired some relevant truths about Islam (including the plain fact that many of its adherents "seek to compel Europe to yield to its vision of man"), led to death threats that forced him and his family into hiding. Though France's education minister, Gilles de Robien, declared "solidarity" with Redeker, he advised that "a public employee must display prudence and moderation"; Pierre Rousselin, editor of *Le Figaro*, while also pledging "solidarity," later apologized on al-Jazeera. As for Prime Minister de Villepin, he called the threats "unacceptable," but added that "everyone has the right to express his views freely—as long as they respect others, of course." This was quickly becoming the rule in Western Europe: that one has to respect others. The lesson of the Redeker affair, said Villepin, was "how vigilant we must be to ensure that people fully respect one another"—not a word about ensuring free speech. Of course, what Villepin meant was that one must respect Muslims—one is free to revile the president of the United States, the pope, and other infidels. In any case, such "respect" really isn't respect at all, because respect is freely given and must be earned; when Villepin said "respect," he meant "submission"—the Arabic word for which, needless to say, is "Islam."

If the pope's and Redeker's comments caused such ire, it's because they defied a growing tendency toward self-censorship—not only in the news media but among writers and publishers, filmmakers and theatrical producers, artists and museums. And, of course, academics. In October 2006 an intelligence expert wrote that when he had warned British educational authorities about terrorist groups' efforts to recruit Muslim students at universities, they had responded by hurling abuse, threatening legal action, and trying to silence him. In Europe, as in the United States, institutions of higher learning have used free speech as an excuse to provide Islamists with a forum (as if free speech meant the right to a platform) while denying a voice to critics of Islam (on the grounds that the university is supposed to be a "safe zone" for minorities). For example, terrorist-group members were invited to Dublin's Trinity College to debate terrorism in October 2006 with Muslims who opposed it. There were, the arranger explained, "two valid sides" to the issue. Naturally he hadn't invited anyone who viewed Islam itself as a problem—thereby indicating that while supporting terror was "valid," criticizing Islam was not.

In an October 4, 2006, editorial, the British newspaper the *Independent* celebrated the new wave of European self-censorship, praising it as a "new sensitivity . . . developing in many quarters," and condemned Redeker's *Figaro* op-ed as "disgusting" and "needlessly offensive." According to the *Independent*, then, it's wrong to acknowledge disturbing truths about Islam, but acceptable to insult someone who's acknowledged those truths. When such thinking prevails, can one doubt that European history books will sooner or later be cleansed of "offensive" facts, just like their counterparts in the Islamic world?

In the same editorial, the *Independent* maintained that tensions over such phenomena as the pope's speech and Redeker's op-ed had nothing to do with free speech but represented "a clash between religious and secular fundamentalists." This is a major recent trend: pinning labels such as "fundamentalist" and "extremist" on defenders of freedom. In Norway, politicians lumped Selbekk, the *Magazinet* editor, in with those who threatened to kill him, calling both parties "extremists." Similarly, both Anglo-Dutch professor Ian Buruma and Europe "expert" Timothy Garton Ash have described Hirsi Ali as an "Enlightenment fundamentalist"—thereby equating a brave fighter for human rights with patriarchs who think rape victims should be slaughtered.* For some, the words "fundamentalist" and "extremist" have proven insufficient. The *Independent*'s editors, for example, insisted that to exalt free speech above all other rights is to be a "single-issue fanatic." One might expect the word "fanatic" to be reserved for the kind of people who blow up embassies; but no, the very media elite that refuses to call terrorists by their rightful name doesn't hesitate to label defenders of freedom "fanatics." Hence Somerset Maugham was a "single-issue fanatic" when he wrote that "a nation that values anything more than its freedom will lose it"; and George Orwell was a "single-issue fanatic" when he wrote that "if freedom means anything at all, it means the right to tell people what they don't want to hear."

Free speech is not only coming under increasing criticism in Europe; it's being outlawed and prosecuted. In Norway, offensive statements about religion became punishable in 2006 by fine and imprisonment. (Under the new act, which received almost no media coverage, the accused is guilty until proven innocent.) In Belgium, which has a similar law, a blogger was forced in 2006 to remove a supposedly racist text from his Web site. In Britain, among the many grotesque cases of government action against free expression have been those of a fourteen-year-old Manchester girl, Codie Scott, who was arrested and jailed in October 2006 on suspicion of racism after complaining that she was unable to communicate with Pakistani classmates who couldn't speak English, and thirteen-year-old Samantha Devine of Gillingham, who in January 2007 was ordered by her teachers not to wear a crucifix necklace because it violated "health and safety" regulations (which, of course, Muslim and Sikh pupils' tokens of faith did not).

France's justice system experienced one of its darkest days in decades. Back in 2000, the TV station France 2 had broadcast a staged videotape purportedly showing the killing of a Palestinian boy, Muhammed al-Dura, by Israeli soldiers. When journalist Philippe Karsenty exposed the

---

*To call a free-speech advocate a "fundamentalist" is, of course, to utterly misuse the word: a fundamentalist, by definition, claims to have found the ultimate truth in some system of thought (whether literalist Christianity or Islam, Marxism, or Nazism); to such a person, free speech threatens the perfect truth of which he's in possession.

deception, France 2 slapped him with a libel suit; and on October 19, 2006, in a decision every bit as shameful as the 1894 Dreyfus verdict, he was found guilty. The message was clear: "good" lies were permitted; "bad" truths would be punished. Nor did the rest of the French media cover themselves in glory: though the trial went all but unreported while it was in progress—obviously because journalists didn't want to draw attention to the accusations leveled at their colleagues—the verdict was announced in huge front-page headlines.*

The most consistently abusive language in Europe today is the rhetoric heard in mosques about Jews, gays, and others—but this kind of speech goes unprosecuted. In 2006 Stockholm's Grand Mosque was charged with "racial incitement" for a lecture in which Jews were called "the brothers of apes and pigs"—but the Swedish chancellor of justice dropped the charges, explaining that such language was "permissible" since it's part of a conflict in which insults are "everyday . . . rhetoric."

SINCE *While Europe Slept* first came out, I've seen numerous claims that Europe is (as it were) no longer asleep. On October 11, 2006, the *New York Times* reported that an increasing number of mainstream European politicians were now "arguing that Islam cannot be reconciled with European values." If there's some truth in this, it's because European leaders have felt increasingly compelled by developments to address Muslim issues; but while a few have indeed ventured tame criticisms of Islam, far more have gotten into the habit of responding to every such tame criticism with harsh condemnations of so-called Islamophobia. (The EU, for its part, seeks to ban the term "Islamic terrorism.")

In fact, only one Western European head of government is definitely wide awake—Anders Fogh Rasmussen, the prime minister of Denmark. To be sure, Angela Merkel, who became German chancellor on November 22, 2005, has been impressive: after a 2006 Berlin staging of the Mozart opera *Idomeneo* was canceled because it included a prop meant to be Muhammad's head, she insisted that the production go forward. More typical of Europe's political elite, however, is Dutch Minister of Justice Piet Hein Donner, who said in 2006 that if two-thirds of all Dutch voters wanted to introduce sharia law in the Netherlands—a country where Muslims will soon be a majority in the larger cities—he would have to

*The best English-language reporting on this case was provided not by a major newspaper or TV network but by Nidra Poller, writing on the Pajamas Media Web site.

accept it, because "it would be a disgrace to say: 'This is not permitted!'"
In much the same spirit, Dutch Socialist Party leader Jan Marijnissen
compared Muslim terrorists, in July 2006, to the World War II resistance. Tony Blair, meanwhile, has sent mixed signals, one minute calling
for Muslims to modernize and the next praising the Koran as "progressive . . . a reforming book."

A few journalists are awake. Responsible reporting on these issues
can be found regularly in the *Times*, *Telegraph*, and *Daily Mail* in Britain,
De Volkskrant in the Netherlands, and *Jyllands-Posten* in Denmark.* On
October 2, 2006, Norway's TV2 broadcast a stunningly honest documentary, "Threatened into Silence," about how Norwegian politicians
and journalists betrayed free speech during the cartoon crisis; on January
15, 2007, Britain's Channel 4 aired "Dispatches: Undercover Mosque,"
a surprisingly frank exposé of supposedly moderate, "interfaith" British
mosques at which imams call for the murder of gays and Jews and for the
imposition of sharia law in the West.†

Most coverage of Islam, immigration, and integration, however,
either airbrushes the ugly parts or blames them on the West. Five days
after "Undercover Mosque," CNN aired its own heavily promoted documentary, "The War Within," in which Christiane Amanpour inanely
attributed Islamic supremacism in Britain to George W. Bush's war in
Iraq (a subject that none of the jihadist imams on Channel 4's documentary even mentioned). On October 23, 2006, a Reuters article actually
suggested that an open discussion of integration problems "risks further
isolating these minorities instead of integrating them"—in other words,
one damages integration by admitting it's been a fiasco.

The autumn of 2006 saw a renewed wave of anarchy in France,
where every day, on average, over 100 cars were burned and over fourteen police officers assaulted; but I had been following this "civil war" (as
a French police union called it) on blogs for several weeks before the
mainstream media outside France began issuing brief, sanitized bulletins
about it. The BBC shocked many when it admitted in October 2006 that
its news broadcasts were one-sided, especially in regard to Islam—yet
despite this *mea culpa*, the BBC was at the same time trying to suppress

---

*Meanwhile, I've been increasingly dismayed by the apparent refusal of some of Amer-
ica's most respected newspapers to face the uncomfortable facts reported in this and
other recent books on Islam and the West.

†Unsurprisingly, nobody in the British government publicly addressed the revelations
in "Dispatches: Undercover Mosque."

a report criticizing its distorted Middle East coverage. And when Manchester's top imam was quoted in October 2006 as supporting the execution of gays, the BBC, true to form, spun the report as an attempt to smear Islam—entirely suppressing the fact that Islam does, indeed, prescribe capital punishment for homosexuality.

Some Europeans get it. A 2006 survey found that 53 percent of Britons were concerned about the impact of Islam, up from 32 percent in 2001. Yet many in Europe still focus their fears on the United States. In an April 2006 poll, 45 percent of Germans called the United States a greater danger to world peace than Iran; only 28 percent put Iran ahead. Though a January 2007 report by the Dutch government warned that ethnic tensions in the Netherlands were "seriously underestimated" and that the nation faced the prospect of France-like riots, Dutch voters in the November 2006 elections rejected the one party whose leader had promised to take on integration problems. "Attempts to regulate and control expression, stifle debate, and cleanse history," lamented Dutch-Canadian blogger Pieter Dorsman before the elections, had only intensified in the Netherlands since van Gogh's murder. This is true of Western Europe generally.

There have, to be sure, been isolated crumbs of good news—a radical imam deported here, an extremist group banned there—and the occasional unexpected bit of anti-dhimmitude (both Romano Prodi and Jack Straw have criticized veils). But on the whole, dhimmitude is on the march. European imams still get away with preaching jihad; European governments still subsidize mosques and Muslim schools (indeed, in January 2007 it was reported that the Dutch government was considering financing a Koran school in Afghanistan, and that the Norwegian minister of education wanted to discontinue German, French, and Spanish as obligatory third languages in high schools and instead introduce Urdu, Turkish, and Arabic); and Muslim "councils" and "associations" with terrorist links are still treated respectfully by governments and media (and funded by taxpayers). In several countries, parallel systems of sharia law (praised as "legal pluralism" by Dr. Prakash Shah of Queen Mary University) are being introduced. It's impossible to keep track of every new absurdity: in Britain alone, in recent months, burka-style hospital gowns were introduced; an outspokenly anti-Christian Muslim became Birmingham's head school inspector; a Muslim cop was excused from protecting the Israeli embassy in London; police agreed to "consult a panel of Muslim leaders before mounting counter-terrorist raids"; police officers received "diversity training" at a terrorist-connected Muslim school;

an Immigration and Nationality Directorate official turned out to belong to the radical group Hizb-ut-Tahrir; British Police Commissioner Sir Ian Blair arranged to share intelligence about potential terrorists with Muslim community leaders; it was decided to teach British children "race relations and multiculturalism with every subject they study—from Spanish to science"; British prison toilets were rebuilt so that inmates would not have to face Mecca while using them; and the head of Britain's Islamic Medical Association told Muslims that vaccinating their children against measles, mumps, and rubella was "un-Islamic." When Ken Livingstone met Daniel Pipes before an audience of thousands in a major January 2007 debate about "the clash of civilizations," the mainstream British media almost entirely ignored it; in the same month, there was a rash of arrests in connection with a plot to behead a British Muslim soldier.

Crime has continued to rise. Riots have occurred in cities ranging from Windsor to Brussels. In April 2006, it was reported that parts of Berlin were "lurching out of control" and that teachers at one school "had lost all authority and were now so afraid" of immigrant students that they brought mobile phones to class "so they could call for help." In April 2006, Oslo's city court said that "criminal youth" were "destroying the environment in Oslo for young people," and that summer the city experienced a wave of gay-bashings by young Muslims; yet Oslo police said they were "reluctant to crack down on gangs out of fear for their own safety." In November 2006, a survey of ninth-grade boys in the predominantly Muslim Stockholm suburb of Rinkeby found that in the last year 17 percent had forced someone to have sex, 31 percent had hurt someone so badly as to require medical care, and 24 percent had committed break-ins. While staggering numbers of terror plots (dozens in Britain alone) and terror suspects (over 1,600 in the UK) have been identified, European Muslim leaders have reacted by accusing officials of "demonization" and "state terrorism."* Repudiating Tony Blair's call for Muslims to help fight terror, for example, Muhammed Abdul Bari of the Muslim Council of Britain said: "We know what happened in Nazi Germany, and we have to be on guard against entire communities being demonised." Veiled threats have become commonplace: routinely, European Muslim leaders suggest that even the mildest antiterror efforts will turn peace-loving Muslims into jihadists. Yet at the same time many of

---

*It was reported in November 2006 that at Charles de Gaulle Airport alone, seventy-two airport employees lost their security clearance because of terrorist connections.

them deny wholesale the very reality of Islamic terrorism: in September 2006, the major Muslim figures in Norway refused to acknowledge that Muslims were responsible for 9/11—the real culprit, they said, was either the United States or Israel. When asked in January 2007 about the proper response to a Dutch comic, Ewout Jansen, who tells Muslim jokes, the spokesman for an Amsterdam mosque said it was perfectly appropriate to "finish him off."

Polls taken in 2006 left little doubt as to where European Muslim sympathies lie. In Britain, over 40 percent of Muslims said they want to see that country under sharia law; at least one in four openly approved of the 7/7 attacks; 70 percent refused to condemn suicide bombers; two-thirds rejected free speech. Of young Dutch-Moroccans, 40 percent reject democracy. Yet European delusions endure. In August 2006, the Associated Press reported that Germans were "stunned" by news of a planned train bombing because they thought their "opposition to the Iraq war would insulate" them from terrorism. That same month, following the arrest of "English lads" who had planned to blow up London-to-U.S. flights, Britain's communities secretary, Ruth Kelly, promised to consider a Muslim proposal to pacify would-be terrorists by introducing sharia law in immigrant areas.

Throughout Europe, open anti-Semitism continues to mount. In December 2006, *Der Spiegel* provided ample evidence that "right-wing adolescents and young Muslims are displaying levels of anti-Semitism that were long considered unthinkable in Germany." Three developments in Norway paint a clear picture. In January 2006, Finn Graff, the country's leading cartoonist, who has depicted Israelis as Nazis, announced that he wouldn't draw Muhammad. "I set the limit for my cartoons at death threats," he explained. "You've got to draw a line someplace." Equating Jews with Nazis is safe, in short, precisely because Jews *aren't* Nazis—so why not do it? By contrast, criticizing Islam is *not* safe, for reasons we all know, so better not go there: such is the ethical calculus found at the highest levels of the European media today.*

On August 5, 2006, Norway's most famous living writer, Jostein Gaarder (*Sophie's World*), published in *Aftenposten* a poisonous piece of Jew-hatred entitled "God's Chosen People," which would never have been accepted by any mainstream U.S. daily (though it would have fit nicely into the Nazi paper *Der Stürmer*). Comparing Israel to Taliban-

---

*Three months after making this announcement, Graff won the first annual Humanist Culture Award from the Norwegian Humanist Association.

run Afghanistan, Gaarder wrote throughout as if it were Israeli Jews, and not millions of Muslims in the countries surrounding and threatening their tiny democracy, who were still living by the barbaric codes enshrined in ancient scriptures. Though Gaarder drew some criticism, he won strong support from leading intellectuals and Norwegians generally. People were still talking about the piece on September 17 when shots were fired at Norway's only synagogue by four young men who, it emerged, had also plotted to blow up the U.S. and Israeli embassies.

To walk the streets of Oslo today is to recall that this is a city where, within human memory, Jews were rounded up and shipped off to their deaths while their neighbors sat in their kitchens placidly consuming *kjøttkaker* and boiled potatoes. There can be little doubt that Europeans' still largely suppressed guilt over the Holocaust, and over their enduring, irrational Jew-hatred, are significant factors in Europe's ongoing self-destruction.

It is true that in the last year or two, more and more Europeans seem to recognize that Europe *is* self-destructing. Some have spoken up. But not enough. The process continues. And the atmosphere is increasingly ominous. I've grown used to seeing the truth turned on its head—the vicious aggressors depicted as innocent victims, the defenders of freedom represented as hateful and inflammatory. I've long argued that if we don't cherish our liberties as passionately as the jihadists treasure their faith, we'll lose. Benjamin Franklin's words seem more apropos than ever: "Those who would give up essential Liberty, to purchase a little temporary Safety, deserve neither Liberty nor Safety." Alas, in Europe today millions have been brought up to prize safety and appear never to have learned what liberty means.

Index

About the Author

BRUCE BAWER is the author of *A Place at the Table*, one of the most influential books ever written about homosexuality, and *Stealing Jesus*, described by *Publishers Weekly* as "a must-read book for anyone concerned with the relationship of Christianity to contemporary American culture." He has also published several volumes of literary criticism, including *Diminishing Fictions*, *The Aspect of Eternity*, and *Prophets and Professors*. Praised by *Kirkus Reviews* as "an essayist for the ages," he has written for the *New York Times Magazine*, the *New Republic*, the *Hudson Review*, the *Wilson Quarterly*, and many other publications. A native New Yorker, he now lives in Norway.

prophetic view of the perspective
    consequences of mass "bar-
baric" [term from reader] invasion of Europe (p. 51)
White self-race hatred, suggest-
    ing to let Europes white
    race to be extinguished and
    be replaced by inferior races.
God, Almighty how long tole-
        rate this?
Is the prophecy of Ezekiel
    (chapters 38-39) in the making?
It looks very much like
it is.
P. 201 "Illiberalism"; dogoodism
        (= hypocritical leftist
radical liberalism)